D1714668

Causal Powers

Causal Powers

EDITED BY
Jonathan D. Jacobs

OXFORD
UNIVERSITY PRESS

OXFORD
UNIVERSITY PRESS

Great Clarendon Street, Oxford, OX2 6DP,
United Kingdom

Oxford University Press is a department of the University of Oxford.
It furthers the University's objective of excellence in research, scholarship,
and education by publishing worldwide. Oxford is a registered trade mark of
Oxford University Press in the UK and in certain other countries

© the several contributors 2017

The moral rights of the authors have been asserted

First Edition published in 2017
Impression: 1

Published in the United States of America by Oxford University Press
198 Madison Avenue, New York, NY 10016, United States of America

British Library Cataloguing in Publication Data
Data available

Library of Congress Control Number: 2016954719

ISBN 978-0-19-879657-2

Printed and bound by
CPI Group (UK) Ltd, Croydon, CR0 4YY

Links to third party websites are provided by Oxford in good faith and
for information only. Oxford disclaims any responsibility for the materials
contained in any third party website referenced in this work.

Contents

Part IV. Mind

Acknowledgments

This book would not have been possible but for the help and support of many. First and foremost, I am grateful to all the contributors, for their amazing work and patience. Second, I am grateful to many philosophers for help in thinking through the topics addressed here: Scott Berman, Alexander Bird, Jeffrey Brower, Gabriele Contessa, the graduate students in my causal powers seminar, Ruth Groff, John Heil, Timothy O'Connor, and Timothy Pawl, to name just a few. Third, several graduate students helped with this project, including Joshua Anderson, Audra Goodnight, Bob Hartman, and Andrew Jones. Fourth, my family is due thanks for their support and patience. Fifth, the participants in the conference on causal powers at Saint Louis University helped improve the papers greatly. And, sixth, the referees for Oxford University Press were amazingly helpful. All of these are due many thanks. Thank you! My work on this project was partly supported by the John Templeton Foundation, for which I am grateful. (The views expressed herein are those of the authors and not of the John Templeton Foundation.)

List of Figures

List of Contributors

RANI LILL ANJUM, Norwegian University of Life Sciences

LAUREN ASHWELL, Bates College

ALEXANDER BIRD, University of Bristol

NANCY CARTWRIGHT, Durham University and University of California San Diego

ANJAN CHAKRAVARTTY, University of Notre Dame

HEATHER DEMAREST, University of Colorado Boulder

JOHN HEIL, Washington University in St. Louis

JONATHAN D. JACOBS, Saint Louis University

MAX KISTLER, Université Panthéon Sorbonne and IHPST, Paris

ROBERT C. KOONS, University of Texas at Austin

ANNA MARMODORO, University of Oxford

STEPHEN MUMFORD, Durham University and Norwegian University of Life Sciences

TIMOTHY PAWL, University of St. Thomas, St. Paul, MN

ALEXANDER PRUSS, Baylor University

DAVID ROBB, Davidson College

NEIL E. WILLIAMS, University at Buffalo

1

Introduction

Jonathan D. Jacobs

Causal powers are ubiquitous. Electrons are negatively charged; they have the power to repel other electrons. Water is a solvent; it has the power to dissolve salt. Rocks are hard; they have the power to break windows. We use concepts of causal powers and their relatives—dispositions, capacities, abilities, and so on—to describe the world around us, both in everyday life and in scientific practice. But what is it about the world that makes such descriptions apt?

While most philosophers agree it is appropriate to use causal power concepts to describe the world, there is substantive disagreement about what it is that makes it appropriate. Philosophers divide into roughly two camps. One is the 'neo-Humeans.' According to the neo-Humean metaphysic, defended most prominently by David Lewis (1986, 1994), the world is simply a vast collection of particular, local matters of fact—it's just one thing and then another. Necessary connections between distinct existences are, on this view, anathema. "[A]nything can coexist with anything else. . . . Likewise, anything can fail to coexist with anything else" (1986, 87–8). The world is but a mosaic of facts, not unlike a pointillism painting, and the connections between the facts—causal, nomic, modal connections—supervene on the patterns or regularities in that mosaic. There is nothing intrinsic about, say, negative charge, that makes its bearers have the power to repel other negatively charged particles. Rather, matters extrinsic to negative charge fix the powers its bearers have. Causal powers understood as intrinsically powerful, bringing with them their own causal, nomic, and modal nature independent of extrinsic patterns and regularities—even fixing those regularities—are inconsistent with neo-Humeanism.

For much of the twentieth century, the neo-Humean picture was the dominant one. Anti-Humeans were scarce and often occupied with defensive, rearguard action. Causal powers, understood in an anti-Humean way, were *suspect*. But thanks in large part to pioneering work by Rom Harré (e.g. 1970 and with Madden 1975), Roy Bhaskar (1978), Nancy Cartwright (1983, 1989), C. B. Martin (1984, 1993a, 1994), Brian Ellis (2001, 2002, and with Lierse 1994), Stephen Mumford (1998, 2004), John Heil (2003, 2005, and with Martin 1999), and Alexander Bird (2007a), among others, an alternative, anti-Humean picture began to take shape. Unlike the neo-Humeans, this second camp has no eponymous standard-bearer. It would be no less historically accurate to claim Aristotle as the standard-bearer than it would for the neo-Humeans to claim David Hume, but I shall resist. On this *anti-Humean* view, causal powers in some way bring with them their own, intrinsic causal, nomic, and modal nature, independent of (and indeed in some sense fixing) the extrinsic patterns and regularities in which they are embedded.

But it is not enough to give a negative characterization of causal powers (as *not* neo-Humean). A positive account of causal powers and their connections to a wide variety of topics within metaphysics and philosophy of science, both broadly construed, is needed. This collection is, in that sense, programmatic. The papers contribute to the ongoing development of a research program, from a broadly anti-Humean perspective, by fleshing out the connections between causal powers and other phenomena within metaphysics and philosophy of science.

To be sure, the contributors do not all agree on the nature of causal powers; nor do they all agree on the scope of the relevant research program. (There are deep and important disagreements among neo-Humeans as well.) Some, following Mumford and Bird, think of causal powers as *relational*. Others, following Martin and Heil, think of causal powers as *powerful qualities*. Some think the application of causal powers is limited to understanding the metaphysics of laws of nature and causation. Others think a systematic and far-reaching metaphysics of causal powers, including applications beyond metaphysics and philosophy of science, is attractive. So in this sense, the chapters stand on their own as important contributions to the literature on the specific topics they each address.

Taken as a whole, however, the collection enables two important tasks. First, it enables us to think with much greater detail and clarity about the positive nature of causal powers. For one way to uncover their nature is to see what they would have to be like given the theoretical work they are given; by putting powers to work, we can indirectly address what their nature would have to be like in order for them to do that work. But second, and perhaps more importantly, they enable us to assess the research program as a whole. To the extent that you agree with the contributors that accepting an anti-Humean account of causal powers allows us to give a successful account of a wide variety of phenomena, you will likely also find the research program worthwhile and the resultant, anti-Humean picture of the world plausible.

1. The Chapters

In Part I, Nancy Cartwright, Anjan Chakravartty, and Heather Demarest address issues connecting causal powers to scientific practice and laws of nature. In Chapter 2, Cartwright argues that you need both causal powers and the overall results that happen when they act, but you also need a third kind of item intermediate between the two: the exercising of the power, or what she calls its contribution. On her view, both powers and their contributions have full citizenship in the world that science presents to us. But, she argues, the neo-Humean account of laws cannot accommodate contributions. Of course the overall result that occurs when powers act is in the neo-Humean mosaic, but the contributions are not. That's problematic because the power of gravity, for example, or the power of Coulomb repulsion and attraction, and their separate contributions to overall acceleration are not part of the neo-Humean mosaic. But if that's right, then the laws that govern them do not state facts that are in the neo-Humean mosaic. Yet we use those laws to get results. Our account of laws, on her view, should admit as laws enough to make sense of why the practices that work so well can do so. To do that, you need a non-Humean mosaic.

Chakravartty argues in Chapter 3, in contrast, that realism about causal powers is not *entailed* by taking scientific practice seriously. At most, we can establish the necessity of a linguistic acceptance of dispositional predicates. But it is consistent with scientific practice to think these linguistic practices have no ontological significance. Still there is, according to Chakravartty, a different route from science to realism about causal powers. What exactly are the properties of scientific interest? What is it that makes electric charge the property that it is? On Chakravartty's view, it is the powers it confers on the things that have it.

On the alternative, neo-Humean picture, negative charge is something that is ultimately unknowable. There is, he argues, a kind of pragmatic incoherence on the part of the antirealist about causal powers in the context of the sciences: the natures of properties investigated by the sciences are entirely unempirical. Hence, non-Humean causal powers can do some valuable work in saving the scientific phenomena. If we accept them we can have a coherent view of the sciences as our best hopes for learning what we can about the natural world.

Heather Demarest, in Chapter 4, argues that the best package is anti-Humean in its ontology, but Humean in its account of laws. She presents the traditional, neo-Humean best systems account of the laws of nature championed by Lewis, and raises three objections to it. But, according to Demarest, one can solve these problems without jettisoning the best system account of laws. One needs only to reject that the mosaic is a neo-Humean one. If we accept *potencies*, which can be thought of as dispositional versions of Lewis's perfectly natural properties, then the result is a science-friendly ontology.

In Part II, Anna Marmodoro, Stephen Mumford and Rani Anjum, John Heil, and Timothy Pawl address causation and modality. Marmodoro, in Chapter 5, develops an Aristotelian account of causation built around the fundamental idea that causation is the exercise of causal powers. All powers, on her account, have mutual power-partners, and each power depends on its partners both for their manifestation and, indeed, for their existence.

When there is mutual and simultaneous manifestation, there is causal interaction, which is one event but two different types of activities. On such a view, all of reality is, at bottom, a network of causal powers that are dependent on each other for their existence and manifestation. The network of such powers is not made up of polyadic relations, but monadic relatives, which are the powers, the ontological foundation of reality.

In Chapter 6, Mumford and Anjum investigate how powers stand to their manifestations, and in particular, C. B. Martin's "mutual manifestation" model. On the contrasting "stimulus" model, powers do nothing unless they are stimulated. But on Martin's model, powers are as active as their partners and work together to produce something that neither could have produced on its own.

In contrast to accounts of causation as a relation between two events, Mumford and Anjum "understand causation as involving continuous processes that are extended through time involving changes of properties." They argue for nonlinearity of mutual manifestation where the partners change as a result of their partnership. Martin's model, they argue, shows us something that is more like mereology than like causation. Instead, they think of the mutual manifestation as being caused by the component powers working together, which allow that powers produce something that may be novel, and which may result in a transformation of its causes into something else.

In Chapter 7, Heil offers reasons for thinking that an ontology of causal powers provides the resources for truthmakers for modal truths, truths about possibility and necessity. Rather than accepting a worldview according to which objects are obedient subjects in a realm of laws, according to Heil, we ought to return powers to the objects themselves. This will require a new understanding of the prevailing conception of causation, a conception that had been tailored to a picture of a universe made up of passive objects governed by laws. In particular, rather than explicating dispositionality by reference to necessitation, we should think that claims about possibility and necessity, modal claims, are made true by the dispositional structure of the universe.

In Chapter 8, Pawl discusses in detail what such an account of modality might look like. He considers nine objections to a causal powers account of possibility, which claims that possibility claims are true because of the causal power of actual things, and responds to each of them. He argues that a moderate causal powers account of possibility should be combined with an Iteration principle, according to which we needn't have actually existing objects with powers to bring about a putatively possible state of affairs, but rather some actually existing object with the power to initiate a *chain* of states of affairs resulting in the putatively possible state of affairs. The result, according to Pawl, is a causal powers account of possibility that can answer the nine objections.

In Part III, Alexander Bird and Neil Williams discuss the relatively underexplored (at least within the anti-Humean camp) topics of space, time, and persistence. In Chapter 9, Bird considers the objection to dispositional essentialism that, since space and time are inert, spatial and temporal relations cannot be causal powers. He argues that we have reason to reject the understanding of space and time on which the objection depends. In particular, we might think of space and time as noncausal because we think of them as *metaphysical background*. But, according to Bird, general relativity does not conceive of space and time as background. Hence, we are entitled to treat them as fundamental natural features of the world, and so amenable to a causal powers account.

In Chapter 10, Williams argues that persistence is open to a causal powers account. In particular, powers can give an account of the link between temporal parts needed by a perdurantist account of persistence. According to perdurantism, objects persist by having temporal parts, but perdurantism needs an account of the glue that holds object stages together. If immanent causal connections will do the job, then we can give an account of the glue in terms of powers: temporal parts of a perduring object are linked by powers instantiated by the temporal parts, whose manifestations are the later temporal parts of that same object. Such a view will require, among other things, that powers can have manifestations that are type-identical with the powers that produce them, and that the manifestation of some powers are produced unilaterally, needing no reciprocal partners.

In Part IV, Lauren Ashwell, Max Kistler, Robert Koons and Alexander Pruss, and David Robb use causal powers to give accounts of phenomena in the metaphysics of mind and mental states. In Chapter 11, Ashwell investigates the connection between desires and dispositions. It seems that often conflicting desires do not bring with them conflicting dispositions. We feel pulled in different directions without being disposed to act in two different ways. If that's right, then we can't give an account of having a desire that P as being disposed to act in ways that would tend to bring it about that P in a world in which one's beliefs were true. On Ashwell's view, the dispositions that we have in virtue of particular desires do not depend on the totality of our mental states. Instead, when we have conflicting desires, we also have conflicting behavioral dispositions. We are, in such cases, disposed toward conflicting actions.

Kistler argues, in Chapter 12, that thinking of colors and appearances as powers helps to solve a paradox resulting from our finite discriminatory capacities. Suppose there are three colors that appear differently, but when compared to each other in different viewing conditions end up being indiscriminable by us. The first color might appear identical to the second, and the second might appear identical to the third, but the first appears different than the third. Kistler suggests that we construe colors as objective powers of the surfaces of objects. Such powers ground, not a single disposition to manifest itself in one way, but a whole set of dispositions whose manifestation depends on the context. And this explains why we can have the seemingly paradoxical combinations of judgments. They are different manifestations of the same causal power.

In Chapter 13, Koons and Pruss argue that the only way to give an account of functionalism in the philosophy of mind is in terms of causal powers. For a functionalist account of mind to be properly naturalist, an account of normativity is needed. But, they argue, only an Aristotelian metaphysics of causal powers can give an account of normal behavior. Hence, if you want to be a functionalist, you must accept non-Humean causal powers.

Finally, in Chapter 14 Robb argues that a powers ontology can rescue identity theory in the philosophy of mind from the problem of mental causation. The identity theory, according to which mental properties *are* physical properties, faces the objection that it is only in virtue of being physical that a mental property is causally efficacious. Robb argues that a causal powers ontology gives a simple answer: a mental property is its mental nature and its physical nature. For a mental property's physical nature to be causally engaged just is for its mental nature to be engaged.

PART I

Science and Laws of Nature

2

Causal Powers

Why Humeans Can't Even Be Instrumentalists

Nancy Cartwright

1. What This Chapter Aims to Do

What makes a powers ontology, a *powers* ontology? Many answers are possible. One that matters to thinking about science—at least any science where the analytic method is employed—is that a powers ontology allows not just for powers and the overall results that happen when they act, but for a third kind of item as well, intermediate between these two: the exercising of the power, or what I have called its *contribution*. Hume urged that there is no difference between the obtaining of a power and its exercise; others, that there is no difference between its exercise and the overall result that occurs. This chapter will rehearse the reasons, based in the success of the analytic method in a variety of sciences (and often in daily life), for taking exercisings to be real and separate from both the obtaining (along perhaps with triggering if needed) of a power and the overall result.

But the central aim is not to defend this view. Rather I aim here to show how the need for exercisings makes problems for the Mill–Ramsey–Lewis (MRL) view of laws, which is deeply rooted in the assumption that nature is devoid of powers, causings, necessities, potentialities, and anything else we might try to refer to using modal concepts. If exercisings are real, I shall argue, then the MRL view of laws is in trouble, at least if laws are going to cover much of what happens, since exercisings of powers surely should not be admissible into any ontology the view allows. One might hope to rescue the MRL account by retaining its central demand that laws cover as much as possible as simply as possible but give up the requirement that they be true. In that case laws could involve exercisings but not as true features of the world, rather as part of an instrument for deriving the kinds of facts that the view lets into its ontology.

This chapter adumbrates this proposal and argues that it will not work. If laws are to cover much of what we think they do, we will have to have exercisings in our ontology and, the chapter argues (contrary to a proposal floated by Richard Corry), we need both exercisings and powers. So we had best accept that powers and their contributions have full citizenship in the world that science presents to us.

I begin by explaining the role of exercisings in the analytic method which is typical of many sciences, especially much of modern physics and economics. The analytic method is two-stage. First, identify how powers exercise when they operate 'on their own' (in my vocabulary, this is to identify their canonical *contribution*). Second, derive what the overall results will be in a given situation by the use of some rule for calculating what happens when the powers that operate in that situation are exercised together. Then I shall turn to the MRL account of laws.

2. Contributions: Why We Need Them

Let us begin by considering the paradigm where contributions have been seen to enter since at least J. S. Mill onwards: mechanics and its force functions. I am going to take a caricature of mechanics for illustration, supposing that there are only two kinds of powers that affect accelerations: gravitational and Coulomb. As I shall describe more fully in the next section, the MRL view is concerned with what is called the 'Humean mosaic' (HM), which consists of all the facts that are in some special category taken to be unproblematic by contrast with facts involving powers, causes, necessities, and possibilities. Here are the principles of my caricature theory (CT):

LoG ('law' of gravity):   An object located at a distance r from a system of mass M experiences a contribution to its acceleration $a_G = GM/r^2$.

CL (Coulomb's 'law'):   An object of charge q_1 and mass m located at a distance r from a system of charge q_2 experiences a contribution to its acceleration $a_C = \varepsilon q_1 q_2 / r^2 m$.

LoC ('law' of composition):   The total acceleration an object undergoes = vector sum of all the contributions to its acceleration.

I maintain that LoG and CL are not descriptions of regularities in the HM because component accelerations should not be in the HM. Component accelerations are rather the contributions that result when the causal powers associated with mass M and charge q_2 are successfully exercised. There are thus (at least) three kinds of items in the ontology of this theory: causal powers, the contribution they make when successfully exercised, and the overall result, which we may assume to be a feature in the HM—here the total acceleration. This, recall, is one of the chief objections Hume had to causal powers. He thought contributions were not legitimate. There is no distinction between the presence of a power and its exercise.

There has been a lot of discussion about whether component accelerations or component forces can be admitted into the Humean mosaic along with total accelerations and total forces. So perhaps it is a tactical error to use this example. I do so because it is such a familiar one. But it is far from special. Science is rife with contributions. They appear wherever we employ the analytic method. Here for instance is just one of a great many equations from economics I could cite, this from a paper by Nobel Prize-winning labor market expert Christopher Pissarides. Let V denote the value of a vacancy; J, the value of an occupied job; A, the product per worker; κA, the cost of holding a vacancy; q, the transition rate of a typical vacancy; r, a discount factor; and b, the income of the unemployed worker.

Pissarides (2006) tells us: "The Bellman equations giving their values are,

$$rV = -\kappa A + q(J - V) + \dot{V}$$
$$rJ = A - w - \lambda J + \dot{J}."$$

He also tells us: "The wage rate is assumed to be a weighted average of the unemployed worker's income and the output per person:

$$w = (1 - \beta')b + \beta'A, \beta \in (0, 1)."$$

In this case no one would think that the value of a vacancy has three distinct pieces, each there in the same way that the value of the vacancy is. Nor that there are two proper pieces of wage rate that belong in the HM along with the actual wage rate.

Kevin Hoover in his extended study *Causality in Macroeconomics* backs up this point, illustrating with a mechanical example:

A gear that forms a part of the differential in a car transmission may have the capacity to translate rotary motion from one axis to another perpendicular to it. . . . The capacity of the differential to transmit the rotation of the engine to the rotation of the wheels at possibly different speeds is a consequence of the capacities of the gear and the other parts of the differential. The organization of the differential cannot be represented as an adding up of influences nor is the manner in which the gear manifests its capacity in the context of the differential necessarily the same as the manner in which it manifests it in the drill press or some other machine.

(Hoover 2001, 55–6)

Perhaps it is so easy for certain contributions to slip into our census of the HM because we tend to focus on rules of composition like LoC above, involving some kind of addition, so we fall into thinking of the contributions as being like stones in a dry-stone wall: of course both the stones and the wall are there since the wall is nothing but the stack of stones. That's why I should like to stress that the vector addition of LoC is very different from simple addition and to cite Pissarides or Hoover, or the rules for calculating the flow of a current through a circuit. Capacitors contribute capacitance; resistors, resistance; and inductors, inductance. There's a formula for calculating the overall current in a simple circuit, but it's not as if these three contributions add up to it. For complicated circuits we proceed in steps. There is a series of rules that allow the reduction of a complicated circuit to a representative simple circuit; then the first formula comes into play.

3. A Powers Ontology

I have for a long time, along with other authors in this volume, been arguing that causal powers are not migrant workers that need a special permit for admission to our ontology. Nor are they isolated individuals. They come with retinues: families, attendants, friends, enemies, and coworkers. Some causal powers need to be triggered if they are to be exercised; some may need facilitating even once triggered; some can be inhibited so the contribution they produce is diminished or distorted; and even, if famous examples by metaphysicians are correct, an interference may stop them from being exercised although all the other conditions are right. So exactly what must be in place for the power to be exercised and the contribution to appear varies from case to case. Moreover, some powers are deterministic—they are always exercised when the conditions are right; some are probabilistic—they are exercised with a fixed probability; some may be erratic—sometimes they are exercised and sometimes not, but there's no fixed probability to it.

What really matters for the philosophy of science is to admit the three distinct categories: powers, their contributions or canonical exercisings, and the overall result that happens when they exercise. This can be consistent with different metaphysical accounts of what powers are, many of which will be represented in this volume. I have tried to develop the basics of an account that makes immediate sense of what I see happening in scientific practice. With that end in mind I identify powers by their canonical contributions. Different canonical contributions, different powers. This means that, like John Pemberton (2011), I am committed to a very great many causal powers indeed. The Scientific Revolutionaries mocked Aristotelian natural philosophy for multiplying powers in this way. But just where is the bite in that? Many philosophers of science take parsimony to be an epistemic virtue. But I would urge that we heed the arguments of Larry Laudan (2004) that none of those things usually called 'epistemic virtues' in philosophy of science are knowledge conducive. Of course they may be virtues, but in that case there are a great many other virtues that matter, and many often matter more than parsimony, as Helen Longino (1995) argues when she offers a list that includes novelty, ontological heterogeneity, mutuality of interaction, applicability to human needs, and diffusion or decentralization of power.

Nor need we be troubled by the Molière-type scorn of the scientific revolutionaries: "What makes heavy bodies fall?" "Gravity!" "And what is gravity?" Well, in part, I answer, just as they scoffed, "That which makes heavy bodies fall." This tight circle of explanation and identification does not make science ridiculous, or useless. Heavy bodies fall in part because the earth has a power of gravitational attraction, a power of a very specific kind, and gravitational attraction is, in part, the power to contribute a force of a very specific strength and direction. We mustn't confuse explanation with the ability to predict and to mold the world to our purposes. The advance of mechanics did not rest in breaking this explanatory circle but rather in a variety of key scientific tasks:

T1:   Learning to identify what the contributions are. (In the case of gravity, $a_G = GM/r^2$.)

T2:   Learning how to recognize when the causal power is there. For instance, it seems an object with a mass (M) always has the power of gravitational attraction. My recent buying experience suggests that it takes a great deal more knowledge than I have to tell if a dishwasher really has the power to get ordinary dinner dishes clean. But even I can tell what to plant in order to grow daffodils rather than oak trees.

T3: Learning the right conditions for the power to be successful in producing the contribution, and whether the production will be deterministic, probabilistic, or totally chancy. This includes learning to recognize interferences when we see them even though the theory does not provide a catalog of them.

T4: Learning other powers that will also make contributions to the outcomes we care about.

T5: Learning rules of composition.

T6: Learning telltale signs that other factors than the contributions covered in our theories are present that may influence the outcomes in question.

That's enough about ontology. It is now time to turn to the MRL view.

4. Mill–Ramsey–Lewis: An Objection and a Rescue

In the hands of most of its defenders the MRL view has the exact opposite aim to the aim of this paper and many in this volume. We aim to defend powers and their retinue. MRL, to eliminate them, and all else that smacks of modality, like causes, necessity, potentiality, and possibility. There are just the facts, no causal or necessitating relations among them, nothing that makes them hold, no reason they hold; just the facts in the order and arrangements in which they actually occur. What then of the *laws* of nature? According to my colleagues Craig Callender and Jonathan Cohen, "The heart of the Mill–Ramsey–Lewis approach to lawhood is to say that a true generalization is a law if and only if it is an axiom of all the 'Best Systems'—axiomatic systematizations that best balance strength and simplicity" (Cohen and Callender 2010, 433). Strength and simplicity in deriving the facts.

Of course if the views defended in this volume are correct, powers and their exercisings are actual. They will be among the facts so the MRL view will not get off the ground. But the MRL view presupposes that all the facts there actually are fall into some special kind. They are just those that appear in the HM. So let me begin by explaining some doubts about the very idea of an HM, which arise from the fact that it is generally not very clear what is supposed to be in this mosaic and why. I know that it is supposed to exclude most of what I see in the world around me, happenings that fall in the philosophical category of singular causings: pushings, pullings, smotherings, boostings, insultings, encouragings, and indefinitely many more. I take it that it is also meant to exclude causal powers and everything that falls into the more abstract categories connected with them, categories that are so essential to the way I—and much of modern science—understand and manage the world around me, categories like *interfere*, *inhibit*, *facilitate*, and *trigger*.

There are four kinds of reasons for worry about the idea of the HM: (1) The difficulty of identifying reasonable criteria for sorting what is supposed to be in from what is out. (2) The difficulty of identifying the special characteristics that are supposed to give whatever these features are their ontological privilege. Why are they to be regarded as the native inhabitants whereas the features that live in my neighborhood have to earn their right to live here? (3) The usual candidates do not have any higher epistemic status than many facts about causal powers. Many of the features that those who employ the concept of the HM let in are from high physics, like the value of a metric tensor at space–time points. Suppose we take observability as a mark of high epistemic status. These certainly aren't observable. And even the features that Hume claimed to have impressions of are no more observable than the lapping up of the milk by G. E. M. Anscombe's cat (Anscombe 1971). Nor are they any more readily measurable than capacities or causal powers—that was the point of the title of my book, *Nature's Capacities and Their Measurement* (1989), where there are extended discussions of how to measure powers. Nor are we generally justified in being more certain about them. It is far easier to be mistaken about what values physics quantities take on than about whether the cat is lapping up the milk; and we know we can also be mistaken about even the most immediate sensations, like pains. Finally, the concepts that pick out the features that the Humean border guards are loathe to let in are no more unintelligible, no harder to define, than those they prefer. They are only harder to define if you disallow all the concepts one would employ in characterizing them, just as it is difficult to define 'triangle' if the concept of a straight line is forbidden. (4) I think the Humean border guards cheat, as I shall explain in more detail in section 5. They often let in lots and lots of powers, contributions, interferences, and the like. They just give them names that sound OK.

Despite misgivings about the very idea, in order to pursue other concerns about the MRL view in a powerless world, I shall assume from here on that we do have some clear sense of what the HM consists in, and whatever that involves, it disallows powers and the whole retinue that accompanies them, like contributions, exercisings, interferences, and enhancers. With Dr. Seuss's *Sneetches* in mind (Dr. Seuss 1961), I propose to call the facts that are supposed to be in the HM, whatsoever they are, *gold star* facts.

In discussing the MRL view, I turn to the Cohen and Callender (C&C) account of it because theirs sidesteps some well-known difficulties. First, although they follow the convention of talking about a balance of coverage and simplicity, they acknowledge that there may be other virtues that one might demand from a set of laws as well or instead, certain mathematical constraints perhaps, or fruitfulness or maybe some of the virtues that Longino describes, like heterogeneity and social usefulness.

The major C&C addition, though, is to make the best system relative to a 'distinguished set of kinds,' where what will be the best axiomatic systemization of one set of kinds will not be the best for all others. This solves two problems in one fell swoop. First it acknowledges that what is a simple axiom system depends on the choice of basic kinds: Axioms about green and blue things look very complicated if grue and bleen are taken as basic kinds. Second, it allows laws to the special sciences, that is laws "in terms of kinds that cannot be understood as the fundamental natural kinds and that couldn't be laws when written in terms of the fundamental natural kinds" (Cohen and Callender 2009, 10). This is important because C&C, like me, "don't put much stock" in the strategy of capturing special science generalizations as corollaries entailed by statements of regularities involving "fundamental natural kinds" (2009, 11). I naturally think this is a big step forward because it fits more closely with how we actually make correct predictions in science, technology, and daily life.

Though they make this particular improvement in the MRL view, C&C maintain a further standard requirement that seems to me unmotivated from a 'Humean' point of view: the requirement that the axiom system should itself consist of true generalizations. The HM is supposed to contain the facts and nothing but the facts. As Helen Beebee puts it, laws are supposed to provide for "particular matters of fact that obtain" (2000, 572). It is an additional piece of metaphysics to suppose that there are true generalizations about the facts in the HM, let alone that these true generalizations will encompass the mass of matters of fact that our sciences can predict. If I am right, they will not. I have just been arguing that the analytic sciences make heavy use of laws about contributions in order to derive gold star facts; and laws about contributions do not report regularities in the HM. Nor do laws of composition, which are equally essential to the derivations. So I think the requirement that laws be true generalizations is far too restrictive. If we keep it, the best theory by MRL standards in the domains where the analytic method is employed successfully will likely be a very poor one.

The MRL view has many well-known defenses and there are many well-known objections to it, including the two that the C&C version avoids. I want to raise three difficulties that arise specifically from the assumption that the world consists entirely of gold star facts and no others, particularly not facts involving powers and their retinue. These problems are general but to make them easier to see I shall set them in the context of my caricature theory CT. Imagine a simple pretend world, W, that consists of situations consisting only of charged compact masses behaving in accord with CT. I take it that an overall acceleration is a gold star feature, as are charge, mass, and separation. But the power of gravity, the power of Coulomb repulsion and attraction, and their separate contributions to overall acceleration are not. So none of the 'laws' in CT state regularities in the HM. This is unsatisfactory for three related reasons.

(1) The results we get when we use CT are 100% reliable, and they are not lucky guesses. They rely on a system that works, and works all the time, for predicting accelerations. Yet they cannot count as laws on the MRL view.

(2) Are there any regularities in W? There are of course counterfactual regularities: one for every possible arrangement of masses and charges as input and the acceleration of each particle as output. But counterfactual regularities are not regularities in the HM. So whether there are any depends on what arrangements

actually occur and with what frequency. Imagine that one arrangement, β, which results in the set of accelerations A, occurs twice and all the others only once in the history of W. Is the true claim 'Whenever β, then A' to count as a law? That looks to depend on how the balance of strength and simplicity is made. But this is odd since all these arrangements are much the same except for the accident of one having a doppelgänger.[1]

(3) The issue about which, if any, of the regularities that hold are to be counted as laws raises another issue that frequently comes up in discussions of MRL. It is generally supposed that if it is to be an adequate account of laws, the MRL view should deliver something like the items we write down in our best theories. But then, across a wide variety of scientific areas where the analytic method has proved successful—those like physics, economics, and engineering—that means claims like those in CT, which are precluded by MRL.

How damaging are these objections? That will depend on more fundamental views about laws, for instance, that laws of nature are what support the successful practices of the sciences, so that our account should admit as laws enough to make sense of why the practices that work so well can do so. When it comes to meeting that demand, it seems these three objections make real trouble for MRL in any field that successfully employs the analytic method.

There are though two simple changes that can fix these problems and still allow that laws are the best way to encode the facts, deriving as many as possible in the simplest way. First is to give up on the demand for only gold star facts and allow power related facts into the world, yet still demand that laws express true generalizations that best balance simplicity and coverage of the facts.[2] The second is to admit only gold star facts but to give up on the demand that laws express true generalizations. Rather take laws to be the best way to systematize the facts by allowing for their derivation, best in the sense of providing most coverage in the simplest way.

This latter seems a reasonable strategy to try from a 'Humean' point of view because the requirement that the laws be true is at any rate hard to motivate from a point of view in which there is no governance of nature, just one event after another after another—and C&C themselves stress that MRL is a non-governing view—indeed, the best of these (2009). From a governance point of view I can see why laws have to be true (though perhaps not why they have to be reports of regularities). But what is the reason either for truth or for supposing that theories must consist of regularity claims if theories are just ways of organizing gold star events, or of predicting some from

---

[1] It seems especially odd from the point of view of CT since, from that point of view, they all hold for the same reasons—because of the laws of CT. Following the warnings of Helen Beebee (2000) though, we must be careful how much force we give this consideration. The MRL view starts out from the assumption that there are just the gold star facts and any patterns they happen to have. Laws just summarize that efficiently. So starting from an MRL point of view, whatever regularities there are do not hold for the same reasons since there are no reasons that regularities hold. They just do.

[2] See Demarest (Chapter 4, this volume) for an exploration of this route.

others? I don't mean to suggest that they should be false but rather that good devices for organizing the facts and providing for their derivation need not be candidates for truth at all. As Helen Beebee (2000) warns, we must be careful not to import into the reasoning of 'Humeans' demands and assumptions that sit uncomfortably with the basic ideas of the 'Humean' point of view. So I propose on behalf of the MRL view a more instrumentalist stance. Theories are there to derive gold star facts from other gold star facts. How they do so is open. The best theories are the ones that predict the most in the simplest way.[3] That's that.

The instrument in the case of our caricature mechanics theory CT would work like this. To predict the acceleration in a given situation, look to see the arrangement of masses and charges in that situation. Use LoG and CL to write down functions of the form GM/r^2 and $\varepsilon q_1 q_2 / r^2 m$ for all the pairs. Predict the acceleration that occurs in that situation the vector sum of these. That is, do just what we do, but don't make any claims about LoG and CL being true generalizations. They are just part of an efficient instrument for prediction.[4]

5. Causal Powers and Their Markers

I don't in the end think this will work though. The reason is familiar: individual causal powers, their specific triggers, interferers, inhibitors—the whole retinue of powers-related items that matter to the production of an outcome—do not in general reduce to gold start facts, and we need these as inputs if we are to hope to get the right outputs using our instrument for prediction. The concern is the same as Wilfrid Sellars's worries about the manifest, as opposed to the scientific, image. Some predictions can be based entirely on facts in the manifest image but others require facts from the scientific image to be added in. All people will die but only those with a certain genetic

---

[3] Of course there will always be the standard problems of how to measure breadth and what counts as 'simple.'

[4] C&C think we do not need talk of causal powers, so presumably they will feel that my rescue attempt is not needed in the first place. I find two specific claims they make in aid of their avoidance of causal powers. (1) Once MRL admits relativization to different sets of kinds, special science laws can be admitted. So that motivation for causal powers disappears. I don't see how that saves the day, though, since laws in the special sciences are not true generalizations—unless we take them to be true generalizations involving the successful exercise of a power and the obtaining of its contribution. And anyway, this is no special problem for the special sciences: It is a problem wherever the analytic method is employed. (Harvey Brown has argued, in conversation, that that's okay since basic physics—space–time theory, general theory of relativity—does not employ the analytic method. I take it that this is in line with the view of John Earman and others that basic physics is what's really true and basic physics simply assumes values of certain quantities at space–time points—quantities that are acceptable from a 'Humean point of view.' I of course dispute that basic physics can predict, even in principle, most of what even I can predict in practice.) (2) 'True generalizations' need not be true reports of exceptionless regularities. After all, many generic claims— "Bees sting," "Frenchmen eat horse-meat"—are *true* but do not report exceptionless regularities. I am not optimistic about their hope here for two reasons. First, many of these are true, I maintain, because they are correct ascriptions of causal powers, and this will include a very great many of the laws of the special sciences. Second, I suspect that the appropriate semantics for many others will also involve features not in the HM.

structure will be subject to Tay-Sachs disease. If we insist on looking only at facts in the manifest image, we will lose a lot of predictive capacity, and especially the ability to make the bulk of the very precise predictions we depend on in modern life. Similarly, I argue, we lose huge predictive capacity if we refuse to look at features that fall into the categories picked out by power concepts.

Too much focus on the simple world of my simple mechanical world W may obscure this. The only things in that world are particles and the only features that can be relevant to the targeted outcome, acceleration, in that world are all covered by my caricature theory: mass, charge, separation. This simple pretend world is far from the blowsy reality in which we actually live, where the wind blows objects about and charges that are at first moving in readily calculable trajectories, say at the Stanford Linear Accelerator, can get unpredictably disrupted by small earthquakes. In particular the example makes a number of special assumptions:

A1:   A power of a given type occurs if and only if some specific kind of gold star feature occurs. For example, the power to produce a contribution of size GM/r^2 to the acceleration of an object occurs in systems that have mass M and are situated at a distance r from the object.

A2:   Nothing can interfere with the exercise of a power once it is present and properly triggered.

A3:   There is a law of combination for all contributions.

A4:   Nothing affects the outcome except the exercisings of the powers listed.

These all matter because we are trying to use our theory as an instrument that directs us how to start with only gold star features as input to arrive at different gold star features as output. We can use whatever graphic language we want to describe the instrument, including talk of powers and the like, but we must be sure to restrict the input to facts involving only gold star features.

Using the analytic method in the conventional way, it looks as if our theories lead us to proceed like this:

Chain of Inference: Gold star input (like mass, charge) $\rightarrow$ *powers* (like gravity, Coulomb attraction and repulsion) and *triggers* $\rightarrow$ *contributions* (like GM/r^2, $\varepsilon q_1 q_2/r^2 m$) $\rightarrow$ *composed contribution* (like the vector sum of the contributions listed) $\rightarrow$ gold star output (like the actual acceleration).

On an instrumentalist interpretation, the theory provides instructions for how to proceed from each step to the next. The italics show concepts in which the instructions are couched. The instructions at step 1 might look like this: "If a system has mass M and is separated from another by r then write down 'the system has the *power* of gravity'; if it has charge q, write down that it has the *power* of Coulomb attraction or repulsion." In our case there are no instructions for moving from gold star inputs to triggers since we suppose that neither gravity nor Coulomb attraction and repulsion require triggers in order to be exercised. Step 2, represented in the second arrow, might look like this: "If you have written down that the power of gravity obtains, then write down as a contribution to the acceleration of any object a distance r away, GM/r^2. If you have written down that a Coulomb power obtains, then write down $\varepsilon q_1 q_2/r^2 m$ as a contribution to the acceleration of any object a distance r away." Step 3, represented in the third arrow, says to vector add these contributions to the acceleration of each object. And step 4 says to predict the result of the vector addition as the final acceleration of the objects.

We will end up deriving a correct acceleration if each step is reliable, which will depend on each arrow being secure. The first arrow is secured by A1, the second by A2, the third by A3, and the fourth by A4. The problem is that for many cases, at least one of the arrows will fail to be secure unless we input not just gold star features, but also facts about powers and their retinues. Powers do not function as just a turn of phrase used in the instructions. They have to be there in the facts that we input at the very start or our derivations will not lead us to true results.

The problem is not, though, that we make mistakes in predicting. Surely that is ineliminable in science. It is that we do so unnecessarily if we do not allow ourselves to input facts about causal powers and how they operate. And we also lose one of the central guides we have about when not to make predictions.

You can find a number of possible examples of this latter in the metaphysics literature on conditional analyses of dispositions, which is rich in proposed counterexamples to A2. If those examples work, they provide cases where the power is in place and properly triggered but the canonical contribution is not produced. The second arrow in our inference chain is broken. The point is that we can often tell that there is something in the situation that will interfere with the exercise of the power, and if we write that down, our instructions should tell us that we are not in a good position to predict outcomes. But we are not allowed to write it down if we restrict our input facts to gold star facts.

We could write it down within Humean bounds if every interference has a gold star base without which it cannot occur AND if our theory has instructions that recognize those and say "Don't predict if this occurs." But I don't think we have very strong reason to think the first is true; as to the second, inspection of our most successful theories shows how hard these are to find and articulate. But doing so matters or we will make wrong predictions we could avoid. That is why I include T6 among the central tasks of science that make power knowledge useful: "Learning telltale signs that other factors than the contributions covered in our theories are present that may influence the outcomes in question."

We have exactly the same sort of problem in philosophy of science with A1, which I want to look at it in more detail since it has had far less attention in the powers/dispositions literature.

If A1 is true then for each power (like gravity, G), there is some gold star feature (like mass, M) that is a certain mark that that power (G) occurs. Many will suppose that there must be such gold star features because powers need a causal base. I don't know good arguments for this. One doesn't have to go so far as some powers advocate in saying that gold star features are nothing but clusters of powers in order to think, as I do, that they are at least as occurrent as whatever the HM is populated with.

Of course causal powers are not much use to us if we do not have some way of figuring out that they are there short of waiting for them to make their contribution. As I indicated in T2, finding markers for them is one of the important tasks of science: Witness the two laws LoG and CL or the experts' ability to tell a nasturtium seed by looking. Sometimes the markers will be substructures, and sometimes we don't find them but build them.

You can see one of my favorite examples pictured in Cartwright and Hardie (2012, 77). I have a wonderful pencil sharpener, designed by Rube Goldberg. You don't turn a crank to sharpen the pencil but rather fly a kite. Flying a kite does not usually have the power to sharpen pencils. But you can see a clear set of markers for this causal power there in the Rube Goldberg design: the kite is attached to a string that goes under one pulley and over a second and is tied at the opposite end to a small, easily sliding door of a cage containing moths. When the door lifts, the moths fly out and eat flannel lying on a scale, and so on till a rotating knife eventually sharpens the pencil.

I use this example to underline that many causal powers are derivative. They are there because something else is, often something we would think of as a substructure. And often the substructure not only ensures the presence of the causal power but can provide a marker for us that it is there. That however does not imply that the substructure that guarantees the presence of the causal power can be sufficiently characterized in terms of gold star features.

Consider the Rube Goldberg pencil sharpener. An essential part of the sharpening apparatus is the pair of pulleys that the kite string passes under and over. The Rube Goldberg machine does not have the power to sharpen pencils by flying kites without these pulleys—and certain features of them. Most notably that they have the power to ensure that the range of downward forces exerted by normal kite flyings produces an upward contribution to the force on the little door larger than the net effect of all the downward pulling contributions on the door. That is not a gold star feature. There are gold star features that are markers for this next-level-down power: There's the double pulley setup; the wheels are nylon; the rope is galvanized wire; the slides on the little door are oiled; the little door is made of bamboo; the rope is firmly attached at both ends; I live in a very windy neighborhood; etc. But—here again a familiar point—any list like this is defeasible. These are markers for the causal power, not a set of features that constitute it nor a set that is either necessary or sufficient for the causal power to obtain.

Recall among my initial concerns about the HM my complaint that I feel that 'Humeans' often cheat. They suppose that because a term appears in proper science or technology, because it is well-understood, because it is regularly employed, and because it figures in successful prediction that it is not a causal power term. Names of simple machines, like 'pulley' and 'lever', are a prime example. A lever is something that, when balanced on a fulcrum, has the causal power to contribute an upward force F on an object a distance D from the fulcrum of size $F = F'D'/D$ when a total downward force of F' is exerted a distance D' on the other side of the fulcrum. And to the extent that there are true regularities in the offing they are of the form, "A lever will contribute an upward force on an object a distance D from the fulcrum of $F = F'D'/D$ when a total downward force of F' is exerted a distance D' on the other side of the fulcrum if this causal power is successfully executed."

In cases where assumptions analogous to A1 hold, there is a temptation to take the gold star features that are sufficient for the causal power to hold as what constitutes the power. It is in this context that Richard Corry suggests, if I understand him, that, once we have secured a place for contributions, we might be able to slim down the powers ontology by eliminating the causal power and making do just with the gold star features that are sufficient for it.[5] But that seems to require that causal powers can be reduced away to gold star features. I hope I filled in enough of an argument to show that this strategy won't work for the Rube Goldberg machine, and this machine may be unusual, but with respect to the connection between powers and the gold star features that might mark them, it is not atypical. Corry's proposal also supposes that A2 can be relied on. So inferring contributions directly from gold star markers for powers, without putting the step through powers in between, coalesces two arrows in the Chain of Inference for the analytic method into one; correlatively, it conceals two places where the move from gold star facts to the presence of a contribution can fail. If we ignore these two, we will be in danger of making predictions that won't be borne out.

Moreover, I am not at all sure that it works for classical mechanics, from which my caricature is drawn. The rules that take you from the gold star descriptions to causal powers are what used to be called 'bridge principles.' Do we really want to assume

---

[5] Corry says,

> One indication of the difference between Cartwright's position and the one I am advocating here can be seen by noting that nothing in my argument requires level (1) of Cartwright's hierarchy. Recall that level (1) contains dispositional properties, including dispositions to produce causal influences. We should only posit level (1) as a distinct, irreducible ontological category if we think that these dispositions are irreducibly dispositional in the way that Ellis and Lierse describe. But nothing in our discussion so far requires this. In particular, given the existence of influences at level (2), one could choose to analyse the disposition 'to have a causal influence of type X in circumstances C' in terms of a conditional just as Humeans do—the only difference being that the conditional will mention elements at levels (2) and (3) instead of just the Humean level (3). If we take this route, we can do without the kinds of thing that Cartwright, Ellis and Lierse all seem to agree are necessary: irreducible causal powers, capacities and the like. Now I am not suggesting that we should take this route—I am personally rather fond of causal powers, and there may be other good reasons for endorsing them—my point is that nobody seems to have noticed this possibility.   (Corry 2009, 180)

that every time there is a contribution to acceleration, that there is a source of that, a force, of a type that appears at the front end of a bridge principle? A 100% association between that specific contribution and some gold star features that allow us to write down just the right force function? Must there be something else than the power or force itself without which a force cannot obtain? Surely robust scientific realists should resist this assumption. It is just a special case of reducing a theoretical feature to other ones deemed more acceptable. A robust realism would suggest that forces themselves are real since they are the heart of the theory. They are not simply a shorthand way of talking about something else.

This probably brings to mind issues of supervenience. Do theoretical features supervene on observational ones? Do causal powers and their relatives supervene on gold star features? I have never seen convincing arguments that they do, in either case. And supervenience carries the wrong suggestions: that the causal action is at the base level, with features at the higher level accommodating to that. But as a realist about both theoretical features and about causal powers, I take it that just the reverse is the case. Heavy bodies fall because they are subject to the power of gravitational attraction. Even if the force of gravity does supervene on the presence of the earth, the laws of nature are written in terms of the powers we call forces. At any rate we do not need to take a view here on supervenience because it is not enough to rescue the MRL view. So let's return in conclusion to my instrumentalist rescue attempt.

6. Why Instrumentalism Will Not Rescue MRL

I say that supervenience is not enough for the instrumentalist rescue of MRL. What is needed is something stronger: real bridge principles. Every occurrence of a causal power needs not just a supervenience base in the HM. That base must also fall under some kind which is linked by a bridge principle with that kind of causal power, so that whenever that kind of gold star feature occurs, so too does the related kind of causal power.

Why? Because the theory is supposed to provide an instrument for deriving gold star facts from other gold star facts, and nothing more than other gold star facts. Suppose that, contrary to my worries, power features do after all always supervene on some gold star features or other. That means that every situation fixes something that 'should be' written down as input in order to get the process of prediction under way. But that's of no use if there is no device in the instrument that dictates what this is. There has to be a rule available in the instrument that describes these gold star features and instructs us what to do next when we see them. But if my claims have been correct, those are just the kinds of rules we don't have nearly enough of. Powers generally do not reduce to gold star features. And at any rate it is contributions we need for our analytic-method calculation, and they depend not just on the presence of the power but on the right facts about triggers, interferences, masks, and the like, none of which is generally reducible to the gold star features allowed in the HM.

7. Conclusion

My conclusion is a mere simple summary in two sentences of what has come before. I see no way to rescue MRL from admitting causal powers and their relatives if the scientific theories they reconstruct are to be of serious use, even for predicting results in the HM. And anyway, there's nothing wrong with the causal power family to begin with.

3

Saving the Scientific Phenomena
What Powers Can and Cannot Do

Anjan Chakravartty

1. Dispositions, Laws, and Scientific Practice

Causal powers or dispositions are familiar in philosophy from discussions of the metaphysics of properties, but increasingly, recent philosophy of science has found room for the concept in discussions of scientific knowledge. This shared fascination is no accident, for the concept is often implicated in discussions of the idea of laws of nature, and the topic of laws is one that is shared between metaphysics (where the subject matter is often laws in general) and the philosophy of science (where the subject matter is often specific laws). The metaphysician wonders whether there is anything in the world that answers to the description 'law of nature', and the philosopher of science wonders whether there is anything in common between the mathematical expressions and other generalizations about parameters, properties, and behaviors of certain kinds of entities and processes that merits a unified treatment. In both cases, a philosophical question is posed regarding whether there are things in the world that are properly called laws, to which all the things called laws in scientific practice (that is, law statements) might apply. It is in grappling with this question that the concept of dispositions naturally arises, as something that might explain why the sorts of phenomenal regularities that many associate with laws are found in nature.

Even more recent discussions have presented further motivation for the concept of dispositions in observations to the effect that many law statements do not appear to describe regularities at all, strictly speaking. That is, many law statements appear to describe regularities that break down when the conditions under which they are typically found do not apply. Arguably, some law statements in fundamental physics are about strict regularities (consider the originally intended scope of Newton's second law of motion, $F = ma$), whereas others are understood to be more tightly constrained to particular circumstances ('water boils at 100°C' is true only so long as water is at sea level, does not contain significant concentrations of solutes, and various other conditions are met). Some have thus sought to explicate the concept of law by appealing to metaphysical facts underlying fickle regularities: facts that might explain why there are regularities, where they occur, and why they break down elsewhere. These deeper metaphysical facts putatively concern dispositions possessed by things in the world, which may then figure in explanations of why these things behave in certain ways under certain conditions, and why they do not when conditions are varied in certain ways. This is, of course, an ancient idea, but one that has come to prominence again in the form of a number of modern interpretations.[1]

My aim in this chapter is to focus on some recent arguments for the reality of dispositions that have arisen in the context of these sorts of philosophical considerations. More specifically, I will focus on arguments based on considerations of certain aspects of scientific *practice*. In recent decades, a number of authors have claimed that realism about causal powers or dispositions (and with respect to more or less synonymous notions such as capacities, propensities, and tendencies) follows from a careful study of specific activities performed by working scientists. What is striking about these arguments is that unlike the more widespread considerations just mentioned, they are not part and parcel of the project of grappling with the idea of laws of nature. Rather, and intriguingly, dispositional realism is here viewed as a commitment that is entailed or strongly suggested by the ways in which scientific knowledge is employed by scientists in the course of scientific, as opposed to philosophical, work. The commitment to dispositions is described as a consequence of taking scientific practice seriously. In the remainder of this chapter, I will consider the idea that taking science seriously requires us to be dispositional realists, and I will argue that while this is not the case, a similarly motivated consideration may yet provide a compelling reason to be a realist about dispositions after all.

In section 2, I offer a clarification of what it means to be a realist about dispositions, which will serve as an essential probative tool in the analysis to follow. In section 3, I consider the general argumentative strategy suggested by recent authors for producing dispositional realism from an examination of scientific practice. Next, in sections 4 and 5, I consider the two main exemplifications of this strategy—an argument from scientific explanation, and an argument from scientific abstraction, respectively. In both cases I will argue that the inference to dispositional realism is, in fact, independent of the science adduced, and is instead a function of some substantive philosophical commitments, such as views regarding what sort of balance is most appropriate between ontological commitment, on the one hand, and explanatory power, on the other. In section 6, I will sketch a case for why, nonetheless, a scientistic consideration of the nature of property identity points in the direction of dispositional realism after all, and I will conclude in section 7 with some brief thoughts on the nature of the dialectic between dispositional realists and antirealists.

---

[1] For some notable examples, see Cartwright (1989), Ellis (2001), and Bird (2007a). There are further motivations in the literature. Chakravartty (2007), for example, argues that dispositions furnish a powerful unificatory framework for the conceptual foundations of scientific realism.

To begin, then, what is a causal power or disposition, and what does it mean to be a realist about them?

2. Dispositional Realism: Two Contrasts

I will use the modern term 'disposition' henceforth as a proxy for the various terms that are commonly used in more or less synonymous ways in this context, including 'capacity', 'propensity', and 'tendency'. To be fair, some authors in the literature distinguish these terms in subtle ways, but these fine-grained distinctions are immaterial for present purposes, and I will ignore them here. This benign neglect is licensed by the shared connotation of all of these terms, which is my primary focus presently: all of these terms have the common connotation of a *causal power*, commonly associated with Aristotle and scholastic philosophy more broadly, and in various ways opposed by the new mechanism of seventeenth- and eighteenth-century natural philosophy. Having gestured vaguely in the direction of Aristotelianism and scholasticism, however, it is still somewhat unclear what it means to be a realist about dispositions today. This ambiguity, I believe, has its source in the fact that the concept of a disposition is commonly described in two different ways, by means of two different contrasts, and these two contrasts and the modes of description that flow from them are not equivalent. Thus, at the risk of being tediously conscientious, let me describe these contrasts with some care, if only for the sake of clarity.

Dispositions, or dispositional properties, are often introduced by means of a contrast with so-called 'categorical' properties. The difference is usually explicated in terms of how these respective properties are described. Dispositions are described in terms of what happens to things under certain conditions, and categorical properties are described without reference to any happenings or conditions. Canonical examples of dispositions are thus properties like fragility and solubility, which are described in terms of what happens to certain things when they are treated roughly and placed in solvents, respectively. On the other hand, categorical properties are described in terms of static features of things, such as their dimensions (for example, length and volume), their shapes (square, cylindrical), and configurations or arrangements (such as molecular structure). So here we have one common contrast in the context of dispositions, and one may, of course, if one is so inclined, interpret this distinction as marking an ontological difference between two different kinds of properties.

Interestingly, however, the distinction between the dispositional and the categorical has no implications for the issue of realism about dispositions *all by itself*, because even if one is content to talk about dispositional properties, it is possible to give this talk a purely linguistic (as opposed to an ontological) interpretation. An excellent exemplar of this approach is J. L. Mackie (1973, ch. 4), who held that dispositional ascription is merely a style of property description. That is to say, it does not make reference to a separate ontological category of properties. Rather, all dispositional descriptions are co-extensive with categorical descriptions; for example, 'soluble', a predicate naming a putatively dispositional property, actually labels a given molecular structure, where 'molecular structure' is a predicate naming a categorical property. On Mackie's view, only categorical properties are real, but one can describe them in different ways. One may employ both categorical and dispositional descriptions, but this by itself does not reveal anything about ontology per se. It reveals only a distinction regarding predicates. Therefore, a linguistic acceptance of dispositional predicates must be distinguished from an ontological acceptance of dispositional properties, and this leads me to a second contrast.

A second way in which dispositions may be characterized is by means of a contrast with so-called 'occurrent' properties. The term 'occurrent' is used in different ways, reflecting different connotations, but as I will use it here, an occurrent property is one that genuinely exists, and thus, anyone who accepts this contrast is thereby an antirealist about dispositions. On such a view, dispositional ascription is merely elliptical for reference to categorical properties, and as I have described it, this is precisely Mackie's view. Conversely, realists regard dispositions as genuinely occurrent properties. That is, they deny the contention that the terms 'dispositional' and 'occurrent' are mutually exclusive labels. For the realist, it follows that the use of dispositional predicates is not merely a linguistic device; rather, it has genuine ontological significance. Unlike the contrast between the dispositional and the categorical, which can be interpreted in different ways—either as indicating the existence of two different ontological categories of property, or as indicating merely a distinction between two different kinds of predicates—the contrast between the dispositional and the occurrent represents an unambiguously ontological claim. Whereas the first contrast may be accepted by both realists and antirealists about dispositions, *modulo* different interpretations of dispositional language, the second contrast is accepted by the dispositional antirealist only.

I have belabored the point about these two different contrasts with respect to dispositional ascription because, as we shall see, a number of recent arguments for the reality of dispositions have not paid sufficient attention to it. As a consequence, or so I will maintain, the force of these arguments is not what their proponents contend. With this suggestion in mind, let us turn now to the idea of a scientific practice-based argument for dispositional realism.

3. Arguments for Dispositional Realism

Arguments typically adduced in favor of dispositional realism are well known from a number of longstanding disputes in metaphysics. They appeal to the idea that one's ability to explain certain facts about the world is significantly enhanced by adding dispositions to one's ontology, and that having this explanatory power is a good thing—an epistemological virtue. For example, why do objects (including here the referents of both count nouns and mass nouns) behave in law-like or regular ways in similar circumstances? Answer: they are disposed to do so, in virtue of their dispositional properties; these causal powers thus explanatorily ground law-like regularities. The idea that having such explanations is epistemologically virtuous, however, is demonstrably contestable. Indeed, historically, empiricists have contested it. On the commonly invoked Humean view (to pick a broad theme out of many more specific variations), there is no *want* or *need* of an explanation of law-like regularities. In response to a request for an explanation of this sort, one should simply accept that there is really nothing to be said. Perhaps there is no *want* of an explanation because there are no necessary connections between distinct existences (as per Hume). Perhaps there is no *need* of an explanation because the putative *explanans*—involving the concept of a disposition—is too mysterious or occult to function as an illuminating explanation.

These historically celebrated arguments between dispositional realists and anti-realists are well established, and my own considered view is that they have reached an impasse. I will not argue for this assertion here, but mention it simply to distinguish these arguments from the ones I will focus on presently. Interestingly, arguments from recent philosophy of science for the reality of dispositions take a somewhat different form than the traditional metaphysical arguments. These more recent arguments are generally presented, either explicitly or implicitly, as *transcendental* arguments.[2] Recall the general form of an argument of this type, which proceeds from two premises to a conclusion. The first premise, P_1, is typically a claim that is uncontroversial, readily accepted, or perhaps even undeniable. The second premise, P_2, is the claim that in order that P_1 be possible or conceivable, some other more controversial claim, Q, must be true. The conclusion, then, is Q. The arguments that I am interested in here, based on considerations of scientific practice, exemplify the general form of a transcendental argument in just the way one might expect: P_1 is typically an uncontroversial claim about how scientific knowledge is used, or how some activity is performed in scientific practice; P_2 is the claim that in order for it to be possible that we do these things, there must be dispositions. The conclusion, then, is dispositional realism.

These arguments from scientific practice come in two families, and I will consider them in turn.[3] The first comprises arguments regarding dispositional ascription in the context of scientific explanation, and the second comprises arguments regarding the use and nature of abstractions in scientific practice. If either one of these arguments could establish an ontological commitment to dispositions, it would succeed where traditional arguments have failed, to break what would seem to be an apparent deadlock in the dispute between dispositional realists and antirealists. Let us turn to this possibility now.

---

[2] For a more detailed diagnosis along these lines, see Clarke (2010).

[3] Williams (2011a) identifies 'the argument from science' more specifically with an argument for ungrounded dispositions based on descriptions of elementary particles in physics. My own phrasing here is intended more generically, to cover arguments of a more general form.

4. Arguments from Scientific Explanation

The first argument from scientific practice turns on how dispositions are often invoked in the course of scientific explanation. Two varieties of this argument have emerged, the first of which I will call the Dispositional Regress argument; though expressed by a number of authors, it finds especially forceful exposition in the work of Brian Ellis (2001). The basic idea is that we often appeal to dispositions in giving scientific explanations, which is clearly a central feature of scientific practice. And though one may think that one can discharge these appeals to dispositions by means of further explanations citing categorical properties instead, this simply leads to appeals to yet further explanatory dispositions. Consequently and ultimately, the appeal to dispositions cannot be discharged.

Perhaps the most transparent way to see how this argument works is to consider an example. Here is one that Ellis (2001, 15–16) himself uses: one might hope to explain an empirical fact regarding, say, the brittleness of a particular crystal, in terms of its internal planar structure—a categorical property. But this does not explain why the crystal is brittle, one might reasonably contend, unless one adds to the description the fact that the crystal is *disposed* to crack along certain of these internal planes: namely, the cleavage planes. Of course, one might hope to dissolve this talk of dispositions into talk of the lesser electromagnetic bonding forces between the cleavage planes in comparison to other planes in the internal structure of the crystal, where the determinate values of these forces are conceived as categorical properties. But again, one might contend, this does not explain anything by itself, unless one adds some information about the dispositions of attraction that hold between charged particles. As Ellis (2001, 116) puts it: "there never seems to be any point at which causal powers can just drop out of the account." Thus, in the absence of an appeal to dispositions, one would not be able to explain the phenomenon of brittleness.

The Dispositional Regress argument is seductive, but on reflection, it is incapable of doing the work for which it is intended. Let us grant for the sake of argument that there are scientific-explanatory contexts in which dispositional ascription is indispensable. Even granting this substantive claim, closer scrutiny reveals that the transcendental argument for dispositional realism here has no force, because, as one may recall, the dispositional skeptic is at liberty to use dispositional language where it is convenient. On the skeptic's view, the use of dispositional language commits the user of such language, at best, to an acceptance of dispositional predicates, not dispositional properties. If one is determined to do so, dispositional description can always be taken as elliptical for categorical description, whether one knows the relevant categorical description or not. As a result, the Dispositional Regress argument is ineffective as an argument for dispositional realism. It attempts to promote an ontological acceptance of dispositions as a necessary condition for scientific explanation, but instead, the best it can do is establish the necessity of a *linguistic* acceptance of dispositional predicates.

A second argument for dispositional realism arising from considerations of scientific explanation is due to Nancy Cartwright (2009). I will call it the Dispositional Exercise argument, and it begins with the observation that certain kinds of 'composite' phenomena are often explained in terms of the 'exercise' of dispositions whose associated manifestations are not realized. The relevant senses of 'composite' and 'exercise' here are, again, most easily illuminated by means of an example. Here is one that Cartwright (2009, 151–5) herself uses: imagine two negatively charged particles whose gravitational attraction is exactly balanced by their Coulomb repulsion. Here we have a composite phenomenon, combining both gravitational and electrostatic forces. In this case, one might reasonably say that both the disposition for attraction associated with the gravitational force and the disposition for repulsion associated with the electrostatic force are exercised, even though, as a consequence of the fact that the two forces are equal and opposite, there is no manifest motion.

This idea that dispositions can be exercised (that is, in some sense activated) in the absence of a corresponding manifestation (the manifestations generally associated with the dispositions ascribed in the current example are resulting motions) is intriguing. Cartwright maintains that if one does not appeal to the notion of dispositions exercising without manifesting, one simply cannot explain what is going on in composite phenomena such as that described in the example of the two particles. It would be a bizarre thing to suggest, for example, that both motions typically associated with the relevant dispositions—a movement together as a result of the attraction and a movement apart as a result of the repulsion—are actually *manifested*, given that there is no actual movement. And thus, so the argument goes, in order to explain what is happening in such cases, one must appeal to the existence of dispositions, which are the only sorts of properties capable of producing this interesting behavior of exercising without manifesting.

As in the case of the Dispositional Regress argument, there is something alluring about the Dispositional Exercise argument. On reflection, however, it too is revealed as ineffective. There is no question that for a dispositional realist, the description of the case of the two particles just given may seem entirely natural. On closer scrutiny, however, it seems undeniable that this description simply begs the question against the dispositional antirealist. After all, no such skeptic would be tempted even to say that both motions are manifested, because no such skeptic would agree that there are dispositions here to be manifested in the first place! That is to say, the explanatory context in which one cites dispositions exercising in the absence of their characteristic manifestations does not even arise for the antirealist. Such a person is content with a Humean description of the phenomena: there are no dispositions, or exercisings, or manifestings; there is only one state of affairs followed by another. When there is a net force, there is a motion. When there is no net force, there is no motion. That, for the Humean, is the end of the story—there is simply nothing more to be said by way of explanation.

No doubt, in both the case of the Dispositional Exercise argument and that of the Dispositional Regress argument, there is more that could be said. Dispositional realists will complain that the antirealist responses I have sketched above are unsatisfactory, for they antecedently regard dispositional antirealism as an unsatisfactory position. My point in discussing the Dispositional Exercise and Regress arguments here, however, is simply to note that they do not establish any further grounds for belief in dispositional properties than the traditional arguments they are intended to supplement. I will return to this moral shortly.

5. Arguments from Scientific Abstraction

Let us now turn to a second family of scientific practice-based arguments for the reality of dispositions: what I earlier referred to as arguments from scientific abstraction. The term 'abstraction' has the same connotation here as that found in much contemporary literature on scientific modeling. The basic idea is that to abstract is to extract certain features of a target system of interest in the world, and build only these features into a model of that system, ignoring others that may be relevant to its behavior. What is interesting about this notion of abstraction in the present context is how some philosophers of science have derived from it an argument for dispositional realism. Once again, it is a transcendental argument. It suggests that the efficacy of abstraction in scientific practice would be inconceivable, if in fact there were no dispositions.

The first instance of this argument from abstraction is due to Roy Bhaskar (1978), but it has been developed significantly by others since. Bhaskar maintained that scientists commonly generate knowledge of causal laws under 'closed' (for example, laboratory) conditions, in order effectively to shield the systems under study from potentially interfering factors, so that they can study causal relationships between a few isolated parameters. In other words, they abstract from the world. The very worth of this activity requires, however, that what scientists learn under closed conditions be exportable to the world more generally. Bhaskar offers little indication of how an ontological commitment to dispositions would help to explain how or why causal knowledge generated in the laboratory is exportable, however. Two decades later, echoing similar insights by Cartwright, Andreas Hüttemann (1998) argued that physical laws are generally abstract and thus only describe behaviors of isolated systems. It is common scientific practice nonetheless, he noted, to apply such laws to non-isolated systems, and it would be impossible to explain this practice unless both sorts of systems have dispositions. The key notion here is that of 'application'; one cannot explain how abstract laws are applicable to non-abstract conditions without assuming that these laws make reference to dispositions. Once again, however, one might ask: why is that?

There would appear to be two serious difficulties with the idea that the existence of dispositions makes such exportation or application possible. The first is that often such exportation and application *is not* possible. Consider a simple example. The fact that one might dissolve a teaspoon of salt in a glass of water in the laboratory does not entail that one will be able to apply successfully the lawful relations discovered there in other contexts. Whether this knowledge can be applied successfully elsewhere depends on whether the conditions elsewhere are sufficiently similar to the conditions one finds in the laboratory. Since, generally, dispositions are only manifested (or exercised, for that matter) in certain conditions, there is nothing about a dispositional ontology that guarantees the general applicability of abstract laws, and thus, invoking an ontology of dispositions does not provide any obvious answer to the question of how or why abstraction is a successful scientific practice.

The second difficulty with the idea that dispositions are somehow required to account for the efficacy of abstraction is that even in cases where real-world settings *are* sufficiently similar to closed laboratory settings, it is hardly obvious that an assumption that there are dispositions present is necessary to account for the success of the relevant abstractions. Presumably, for the dispositional antirealist, the presence of categorical properties could serve exactly the same end. Whether one regards the term 'solubility' as labeling an occurrent disposition or simply a given molecular structure— either way—the problem of induction is the same! That is to say, the question of whether external conditions are sufficiently similar to the conditions under which scientific knowledge is formulated is one that must be answered in either case. Imagine that under laboratory conditions one discovers that salt dissolves; in some other circumstances, it will also dissolve, and in yet others, it will not. Whether the properties involved are dispositional has no bearing on the inductive challenge of working out which circumstances are which.

Cartwright (2009) suggests that the ability to plan our endeavors, make predictions, manipulate phenomena, and consequently, to make good policy decisions of great importance to ourselves and our environment, depends on the presupposition that we have knowledge of occurrent dispositions. As we have just noted, however, there is nothing here to suggest that one could not do all of these things if there were only categorical properties instead. Indeed, Gilbert Ryle (1949) made a similar point sixty years ago when he described dispositional ascriptions as "inference tickets," because their function, he said, is simply to indicate that we are licensed to make certain inferences about what will happen to things with certain categorical properties in a variety of circumstances. Scientific abstraction, it seems, provides no telling argument for the reality of dispositions.

6. An Argument from Coherence: Property Identity

Where does this leave us? I have argued that considerations of scientific practice do not suggest that we must or should invoke dispositions in the world in order to make sense of phenomena like explanation or the use of abstractions. I have suggested instead that it is only in virtue of the philosophical intuitions one invokes in interpreting these scientific practices that one is able to determine how to read their ontological significance. This is not the last word, however. Even though I suspect that, ultimately, at the level of fundamental intuitions, there may be an irresolvable impasse between the dispositional realist and antirealist in connection with the usual metaphysical arguments for and against dispositions, I believe that there is one previously under-appreciated sense in which the realist about dispositions has a surprising advantage.

As a philosopher of science, one might be forgiven for taking an interest in the question of what properties of scientific interest are, precisely. This is ultimately a question about the natures of these properties, or their identity. What is it that makes electric charge the property that it is? What is it that makes the fitness of an allele the property that it is? One answer to this sort of question, proposed by a number of authors (though differing somewhat in the details), is that what makes a property the property that it is, are the dispositions it confers on the things that have it.[4] On this view, it is dispositions that constitute property identity; one may thus call it a dispositional essentialist view of property identity. If entities having negative charge are disposed to repel other entities with negative charge, and to attract entities with positive charge, then these dispositions are part of the nature of charge—they constitute (in part, since negative charge is also associated with other dispositions) the identity of charge.

Clearly, the dispositional antirealist cannot approve of the idea of dispositional essentialism, the most obvious reason being its appeal to dispositions in the service of ontology. Additionally, there may be further concern here regarding the fact that dispositional essentialism has the consequence that laws of nature are strongly neces-sary, since if one were to imagine different laws, then, given dispositional essentialism, these different laws could not concern the same properties.[5] For example, given that the attraction of positive charges is one of the dispositions conferred by negative charge, and that this disposition is part of what it is to be negative charge, it follows that laws concerning such attractive behaviors by entities with negative charge are metaphysically necessary—they are laws in all possible worlds in which there is negative charge. This conflicts with a common philosophical intuition that laws such as those concerning the behaviors of objects with negative charge might have been different—that there are possible worlds in which charged objects behave in slightly or radically different ways than in the actual world. If one has this intuition, the dispositional essentialist view will seem unacceptable thereby.

It is here that the dispositional realist can employ dispositional essentialism to good effect in her dispute with the dispositional antirealist. If one rejects dispositional essentialism, how is one to understand the identities of properties instead? The rival, dispositional antirealist view is that what makes a property the property that it is, is something primitive: a 'quiddity'. In other words, negative charge is something that is ultimately unknowable—its identity is primitive; there is nothing more that can be said about it. (For simplicity's sake, I will leave aside here the so-called 'double aspect' view according to which property identity is a function of both dispositions and quiddity.)

---

[4] For example, see Shoemaker (1980), Swoyer (1982), and Chakravartty (2007, ch. 5).

[5] I say "strongly necessary" here to distinguish the metaphysical necessity intended from weaker forms of "nomic necessity" associated with laws by Dretske (1977), Tooley (1977), and Armstrong (1983).

This appeal to quiddities accommodates the intuition of some philosophers that one and the same property might have figured in different laws of nature, but in doing so, it has the consequence that *any* nomic profile *at all* is compatible with the identity of a given property: for any given nomic profile, there is a possible world in which any given property has it. Once one detaches the identity of a property from the dispositions it confers, it follows that there is a possible world in which it has any causal profile one might imagine, so long as its quiddity remains the same.

If this is conceived as a purely metaphysical issue, I am not convinced that there are any non-question-begging ways to resolve this dispute between the dispositional essentialist and the dispositional antirealist about property identity. Very quickly one finds oneself mired in fundamentally opposed intuitions concerning what is more or less ontologically reasonable or satisfying, with little hope of progress. Qua philosopher or metaphysician of science, however, it seems that there *is* a promising way forward here, because from a scientistic perspective, the rejection of dispositional essentialism and the adoption of quiddities seems a bizarre way to make sense of our ordinary talk of properties, let alone property talk in the scientific domain. This, I think, leaves the dispositional antirealist in a very uncomfortable position. She may persist in claiming that what makes a property the property that it is, is something primitive. But is it not the very aim of the sciences to tell us about what the natural world is like? This, I will now contend, generates a kind of pragmatic incoherence on the part of the dispositional antirealist in the context of the sciences.

Dispositional antirealism is the default *empiricist* position in this area of the philosophy of science, and the empiricist typically champions empirical science as the paradigm or exemplary form of inquiry into the nature of the world. In considering the question of property identity, however, as we have seen, the dispositional antirealist is driven to claim that the natures of properties investigated by the sciences are entirely unempirical! This seems an obviously jarring combination of views. In order to avoid this apparently incoherent combination, one might think that the dispositional antirealist should simply avoid the trap of invoking quiddities, and instead say nothing at all about property identity. That is, one might think that the dispositional antirealist should refrain from saying anything at all about what makes negative charge the property that it is. But this sort of quietism also seems deeply anti-scientistic. It does not sit well with the idea of championing an empirical approach to understanding nature either. So once again, incoherence threatens.

What if instead of invoking quiddities or remaining silent, the dispositional antirealist were to grant that fixing the identities of properties in terms of the dispositions they confer is the most empirically satisfying account of property identity, but maintain that this sort of dispositional ascription must be understood in a deflationary manner— that is, in merely linguistic terms, as I suggested one might do earlier? But this is no good either. What would dispositional ascription here be elliptical *for*? If it is elliptical for quiddities, then one is back where one started. On the other hand, if dispositional ascription is merely an inference ticket, this would make the natures of properties in the world a function of human inferential practices, which surely sounds too much like idealism for any contemporary philosopher of science to accept.

Once the question of property identity has been raised, I cannot see a way forward for the dispositional antirealist in the context of the sciences. Conversely, if what makes properties like charge or the fitness of an allele the properties that they are has something to do with their causal powers or dispositions, then the natures of properties of scientific interest are things that can be investigated by the sciences after all. This, it seems, is the only means by which the empiricist-minded philosopher of science can avoid pragmatic incoherence: by accepting the very reality of dispositions that she has traditionally denied.

7. The Dialectic of Dispositions

I began this chapter by noting how some recent work in the philosophy of science has invoked dispositions in the course of interpreting scientific knowledge. Most commonly these appeals are intertwined with the project of explicating the concept of laws of nature, but a distinct vein of argument presents a putative requirement for dispositional realism in connection with certain scientific practices. I have attempted to show that contrary to such thinking, scientific practice does not, by itself, serve as the basis for an argument favoring an ontological commitment to dispositions. It is simply a mistake, I believe, to think that one can derive such fine-grained ontology from the use of dispositional ascription in scientific explanation and in the context of scientific abstraction. This is not to say, however, that one should not make such commitments. Indeed, though I have made no attempt to argue for it here, I believe that this case study of dispositions in scientific practice is indicative of a more general moral: by itself, scientific practice does not yield *any* ontology *at all* unless one is willing to adopt some philosophical lenses through which to interpret its outputs. Just as practices of scientific explanation and abstraction underdetermine the choice between realism and antirealism about dispositions, scientific practice in general underdetermines ontology more generally.

Longstanding, traditional arguments between dispositional realists and empiricists who reject the reality of dispositions have, I think, run their course, and fundamental disagreements stemming from clashes of deep-seated intuition are unlikely to be resolved. These intuitions inform considerations of what sorts of entities (like dispositions) are acceptable candidates for ontological theorizing, and whether the explanatory power they may contribute to philosophical analysis justifies their admission. I submit that the only real hope of progress here resides in the demonstration of some self-undermining incoherence on the part of one side or the other. I have sketched one such demonstration: the natural deference paid by empiricists to the sciences as the paradigm of inquiry into the natural world undermines their natural antipathy towards the notion of a disposition. This contention is infused with irony: the traditional empiricist worry is that dispositions are mysterious or occult, but in the context of property identity, it appears that one must value dispositions for being empirically accessible instead. It is in this way that a scientistic principle—the regard for empirical investigation as a gold standard for claims about the world—comes to undermine dispositional antirealism in the scientific domain. Thus it seems that powers can do some valuable work in saving the scientific phenomena after all.

The underdetermination of ontology by science generally, and the pragmatic incoherence of the rejection of an ontology of dispositions by empiricist skeptics in particular, take philosophical discussions of these issues beyond the traditional dialectic between dispositional realists and antirealists. Previously, faced with the traditional dialectic, many philosophers were apt to question whether those interested in the study of *scientific* knowledge should engage in theorizing about dispositions at all. For after all, one might contend that metaphysical issues concerning philosophical concepts that are not referenced explicitly in descriptions comprising scientific law statements are not subjects of genuine concern for the philosopher of science. In light of the underdetermination of ontology by science, however, this ban on the metaphysics of science is hopeless if we are to understand what scientific knowledge is knowledge *of*. And if I am correct in my contention that there is a form of pragmatic incoherence that is inherent to the rejection of dispositions by empiricist philosophers of science, it would seem that a modicum of metaphysical theorizing about the nature and role of dispositions in this context is unavoidable.

Among those who have always known that these and other issues in the metaphysics of science are central to a thorough philosophical consideration of scientific knowledge, there have always been healthy debates concerning precisely *which* metaphysic (at the relevant extra-scientific level of discourse) is most defensible. The conclusions of this chapter, if sound, open up to scrutiny a new set of issues with significant import for this discussion. Debates between those attracted to and repelled by realism about dispositions have traditionally focused on the explanatory power of the concept: whether it has any at all; and if so, the extent of this power. I have argued that although careful considerations of scientific practice do not take us beyond traditional clashes of intuition in these regards, careful considerations of our accounts of the aims and scope of scientific knowledge may yield progress nonetheless. A commitment to dispositional realism here does not represent the sort of gain in dubious explanatory power that one may enjoy simply in return for ontological profligacy. Rather, it represents an ontological commitment that is maximally consistent with a view of the sciences according to which they are our best hopes for learning whatever contingent truths about the natural world as may be within our grasp.

Acknowledgments

I am grateful to Jon Jacobs and the crew for the excellent workshop "Putting Powers to Work" at St. Louis University, for which many of these thoughts were prepared, and by means of which they were significantly improved. Some aspects of this chapter were also presented to helpful audiences at the annual meetings of the British Society for the Philosophy of Science, the Canadian Society for the History and Philosophy of Science, and the Eastern Division of the American Philosophical Association, as well as at colloquiums at the Universities of Alberta, Buffalo, and Cologne.

4

Powerful Properties, Powerless Laws

Heather Demarest

1. Introduction

In debates about the fundamental ontology and the laws of nature, two opposing metaphysical pictures loom large: the Humean picture and the anti-Humean picture. When it comes to the fundamental ontology—the most basic stuff out of which everything else is made—Humeans defend an austere fundamental ontology. They claim that, at bottom, the world is made up of only categorical (non-modal) properties distributed through spacetime. Anti-Humeans, on the other hand, defend a rich fundamental ontology. They claim that, at bottom, the world includes at least some modal entities. One example of a modal entity is a fundamental dispositional property, called a *potency*. I will have much more to say about potencies below. When it comes to the laws of nature, the most popular Humean account is the *Best System Account* (BSA). According to the BSA, laws are not fundamental, and they do not govern the world but merely systematize it. By contrast, according to several anti-Humean accounts, laws have metaphysical power because they govern the world.

I argue that the best scientific package is anti-Humean in its ontology, but Humean in its laws. This is because potencies and the best system account of laws complement each other surprisingly well. If there are potencies, then the BSA is the most plausible account of the laws of nature. Conversely, if the BSA is the correct theory of laws, then formulating the laws in terms of potencies rather than categorical properties avoids three serious objections: the mismatch objection, the impoverished world objection, and the metaphysical 'oomph' objection. I argue that combining anti-Humean properties with Humean laws into a *Potency-Best System Account of Laws* is a powerful and science-friendly account—something that people on both sides should be able to appreciate.

2. The Categorical Best System Account

I will begin by presenting the traditional, categorical best system account of the laws of nature, made famous by David Lewis,[1] which consists of two pieces. The first is a fundamental ontology of categorical properties and spatiotemporal relations, referred to by Lewis as the *Humean mosaic*.[2]

The second piece of Lewis's best system is a set of true statements that summarize and systematize the distribution of those properties and relations. These statements often take the form of universal generalizations, such as '$F = ma$.' Systematizations can be simple, informative, both, or neither. For instance, a long list of every property's instantiation—one mass at (t_1, x_1, y_1, z_1), one charge at (t_2, x_2, y_2, z_2), etc.—is informative, but not very simple, while the single statement, "all instantiations of mass move closer together throughout time, all else equal," is simple, but not very informative. Then, Lewis postulates that the basic laws of nature are the axioms of the systematization that best balances simplicity and informativeness.[3,4]

Lewis adds the further constraint that the laws reference only the *perfectly natural* properties and relations. Perfect naturalness is a primitive feature of Lewis's theory and corresponds roughly to other authors' notions of universals, sparse properties, or elite properties (see Armstrong 1978 and Lewis 1983a). Lewis has in mind properties like mass and charge when he talks of perfectly natural properties, though below I will question whether he is justified in assuming that the properties of our basic physics match up with the perfectly natural properties. To see why naturalness is necessary for Lewis, consider 'F,' the predicate which stands for the property applying

---

[1] This account is often called the 'MRL' account for its early proponents, Mill, Ramsey, and Lewis. The account is developed further and in different directions by various authors such as Helen Beebee (2000), Barry Loewer (2007), Markus Schrenk (2008), and Jonathan Cohen and Craig Callender (2009).

[2] The crucial idea behind a fundamental ontology is a metaphysical one: what is the minimum amount of stuff needed to guarantee the existence of the entire world? (A useful, much-used metaphor is to consider what God would have to create, in order to thereby create the entire universe.) For instance, suppose a table is nothing over and above atoms arranged table-wise. Then, the atoms are more fundamental than the table, and the existence of the atoms, along with their properties and relations, is sufficient for the table's existence. Thus, when the Humean postulates a fundamental ontology of purely categorical (non-modal) properties and relations in spacetime, she has to show how all the other features of the world, such as the laws of nature (but also tables, minds, causation, etc.) depend upon that ontology. There is a vast and fascinating literature on fundamentality and the related notion of ground, but the particular details will not be relevant here. For more, see Bennett (2004), Koslicki (2012), and Schaffer (2009).

[3] Throughout this chapter, I will refer to such *scientifically fundamental* laws as 'basic laws,' and I will reserve the term 'fundamental' for those things that are *ontologically* basic. Note that according to the best system account, the basic laws are not fundamental, because they supervene (or depend) on the fundamental Humean mosaic.

[4] Two caveats: First, if the world is chancy, then Lewis argues the best system will have to balance simplicity, informativeness, and *fit*. In this chapter, I will bracket all issues relating to chance, treating the world as a deterministic system. For more, see Lewis (1983a, 1994) and Elga (2004). Second, Lewis hopes that one system will emerge as the clear winner, though he also tells us what to do if two or more theories tie for the best in balancing simplicity and informativeness, but these details will not be relevant here.

to all and only objects at worlds where a given systematization holds. Then, the laws of the universe could be summarized by the axiom: '$(\forall x)Fx$.' Since this simple and (arguably) informative axiom would be 'best,' it also would trivialize the BSA. Therefore, Lewis stipulates the perfect naturalness constraint, eliminating such an axiom from eligibility.[5]

2.1. Science-Friendliness

In the scientific quest to discover the laws of nature, scientists routinely look for simple formulas that predict a wide range of phenomena. This emphasis on simplicity and informativeness is mirrored in the desiderata for the best system account, which lends the BSA additional credibility. According to Cohen and Callender:

> [The best system account] states that laws are the generalizations that result from a trade-off between the competing virtues of simplicity and informativeness. Scientists certainly see themselves as engaged in the project of finding such generalizations. . . . [I]t is clear especially since Newton that scientists have sought general but simple principles applicable to systems with very general features. Virtually every science textbook contains frequent appeal to simple principles that cover a vast array of phenomena in the field. Even philosophers skeptical of laws recognize that scientific theorizing is a process of carefully balancing simplicity and strength (e.g. Cartwright, 1983, 144). And in many cases the result of this process is a set of fundamental principles [basic laws] that are taken to describe the essence of a theory.
>
> (Cohen and Callender 2009, 3)

But, as Lewis pointed out, simplicity and informativeness are only well-defined *relative* to a set of predicates. Since scientists do not have direct access to these perfectly natural properties, they postulate the existence of properties based on how well those properties systematize. What then, is the systematization *of*? Ned Hall articulates a popular way of thinking about the project that I endorse:

> The primary aim of physics—its first order of business, as it were—is to account for motions, or more generally for change of spatial configurations of things over time. Put another way, there is one Fundamental Why-Question for physics: Why are things located where they are, when they are? (Hall 2010, 29)[6]

On this picture, particle trajectories through spacetime are the explananda, the phenomena to be predicted or captured by a theory. And, scientific theories include references to properties. So, the question naturally arises: how do the properties referenced by these theories relate to Lewis's perfectly natural properties? I take up this question in the next section and argue that the relation is a tenuous one.

---

[5] Not all defenders of the best system account accept perfectly natural properties—see, for instance, Loewer (2007) and Cohen and Callender (2009). For an illuminating discussion of several such accounts, see Eddon and Meacham (2015).

[6] It is not clear whether Hall endorses this way of thinking about physics, but his perspicuous presentation of the view is worth repeating here.

2.2. The Mismatch Objection

While the best system account is faithful to scientists' concern with simplicity and informativeness, its insistence on a fundamental ontology of perfectly natural, categorical properties makes it vulnerable to a 'mismatch' objection.[7] Suppose, the argument goes, that our best scientists have arrived at a very simple, very informative final theory of everything (TOE). But, suppose further, that this theory is formulated in terms which reference properties that differ from Lewis's perfectly natural properties—call them 'TOE' properties. We can easily imagine that in such a situation, the best system (i.e. the simplest), most informative system *restricted to terms that pick out perfectly natural properties*, is intuitively much less simple and/or much less informative than the TOE, which is not so restricted.

To see why, consider again Hall's characterization of the TOE: *The theory that summarizes, as simply and informatively as possible, the trajectories of particles.* In order to do that, scientists appeal to the properties that make for the best systematization, in this case, the TOE properties, and what they have straightforward access to is the trajectories (Figure 4.1).

But, if Lewis is right, then the real laws of nature do not systematize the trajectories, but rather, the distribution of perfectly natural properties in spacetime (Figure 4.2).

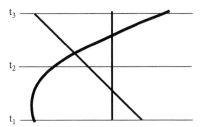

Figure 4.1. Trajectories of particles through spacetime

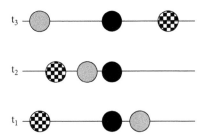

Figure 4.2. Distribution of perfectly natural properties

[7] Bas van Fraassen (1989, 53) introduces a version of this objection. Lewis (2009) acknowledges this version, but does little to address it. See also Loewer (2007), Cohen and Callender (2009), and Hall (2010).

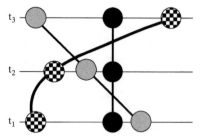

Figure 4.3. The BSA hopes for a match between the TOE properties, which figure in theories of trajectories, and the perfectly natural properties, which figure in the BSA

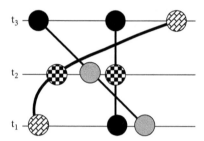

Figure 4.4. But, a mismatch is not only possible, but also undetectable. One pattern of trajectories is compatible with vastly many different distributions of categorical properties

Lewis hopes that the systematization of the perfectly natural properties matches up with the trajectories. However, there is no guarantee—not even a probabilistic argument—that they match up in just the right way. Furthermore, two worlds with the very same particle trajectories, and thus the same TOE laws and TOE properties, on the Humean view, could have radically different distributions of categorical properties (Figures 4.3 and 4.4).

In the two scenarios in Figures 4.3 and 4.4, the TOE yields the same laws while the BSA yields different laws. This is because categorical properties bear no necessary connections to the behavior of the objects that instantiate them. Thus, for every world in which the TOE does match the BSA, there are many, many more worlds in which it does not, and there is mismatch.

What is even worse for the Humean, is that when there is such a mismatch, it seems that the simple, informative TOE is a better candidate for the real laws of nature than the complicated, uninformative BSA. After all, on the Humean picture, the laws are supervenient entities, postulated to capture actual scientific practice in a way that is faithful to the Humean picture of the world. The introduction of perfect naturalness is merely a way to deal with the triviality objection. We then have two competing intuitions. On the one hand, it is plausible that the laws of nature systematize the distribution of the fundamental properties. On the other hand, it seems that the laws of nature should systematize particle trajectories as simply and informatively as possible.

What the mismatch objection shows is that the Humean is not entitled to demand *both*. And, if our theory of laws is motivated by actual, scientific practice, we ought to prefer the TOE to the BSA—a serious strike against the categorical-BSA.

It is important to see why the mismatch objection isn't just a skeptical argument. Of course, there is no guarantee, and indeed, there should be no such guarantee, that our best science will describe the actual world perfectly. The world can always conspire against us to make good theories seem bad, and vice versa. However, this objection goes further by alleging that Lewis's best system gets things wrong, even granting perfect knowledge of the categorical base. This is because the distribution of perfectly natural properties might be quite complicated to systematize, as in Figure 4.4., while a systematization of particle trajectories—even if that systematization is in terms of non-perfectly natural properties—could be very simple and informative. Since the Lewisian places so much importance on simplicity, informativeness, and science-friendliness, while de-emphasizing extraneous metaphysical commitments, by the Lewisian's own lights, the TOE properties begin to look like better candidates than the perfectly natural properties for formulating the laws of nature.

2.3. Impoverished Worlds Objection

One well-known objection to the best system account arises for laws of nature in impoverished worlds (see, for example, Tooley 1977, Carroll 1994, and Beebee 2000). Consider, for example, a world in which there is only one particle, which happens to instantiate mass.[8] Such a particle will behave inertially for all time. Therefore, according to the BSA, there is one law at this world: all massive particles travel inertially for all time. But, intuitively, the law should say that massive particles attract other massive particles and behave inertially only in the absence of other massive particles. Ordinary counterfactuals lend support to this objection. If that particle were in the presence of one other particle which happened to be massive, it would not behave inertially.

Defenders of the BSA try to minimize the force of this objection by pointing out that our world is not impoverished (see, for example, Loewer 2007 and Hall 2010). And intuitions about worlds like ours matter more than our intuitions about other worlds. If the BSA gave the wrong result for the *actual* world, that would be a problem, but it only does so for other, exotic worlds. Another response is to distinguish between statements that are *laws in* other worlds and statements that are merely *true of* other worlds. The statements that systematize world *A* give the laws that are *laws in A*. Statements that are laws of other worlds may be *true of A*, even if they are not *laws in A*. So, the Humean can say that the statement 'massive particles attract one another, all else equal' is *true of* the impoverished world, even though it is not a *law in* that world.

---

[8] Here, and throughout the chapter, I use toy-physics examples. The behavior of Newtonian mass is easier to understand than quantum mechanics, though I have every reason to think my arguments work just as well with Bohmian mechanics, for example.

These responses help, but are far from satisfactory. While I care *more* about the laws at the actual world than at impoverished worlds, as a metaphysician I care about the laws at impoverished worlds too. A good theory of lawhood should give the right results for what the laws are in *any* world. As for the *law in/true of* distinction, it is of no help with counterfactuals. The impoverished world will have many different, incompatible statements true of it, and if we relied on them for counterfactuals, they would yield different counterfactuals. But, surely there is a fact of the matter about what the massive particle would do, were it to encounter another massive particle. The Humean is not able to accommodate that fact with a straightforward appeal to the laws. I argue below that the dispositionalist can.

2.4. Metaphysical Oomph Objection

Some philosophers, such as Fred Dretske, Michael Tooley, David Armstrong, and Tim Maudlin, argue that the laws have very important metaphysical work to do, and the categorical-BSA is not equipped for such work. According to this objection, some parts of the world are fundamentally *powerful* (see Dretske 1977, Tooley 1977, Armstrong 1983, and Maudlin 2007). The laws provide a kind of 'oomph' that governs, or produces, the behavior of the particles in the world. But other philosophers, such as Barry Loewer and Jenann Ismael (personal communication), think that intuitions about governance and production need not be taken seriously. One reason is because these notions are often obscure or mysterious. Thus, before I argue that the categorical-BSA is ill-equipped to account for governance or production, I would like to make these notions more precise. I suggest that metaphysical power is best thought of as *dynamic, metaphysical dependence.*

There are many entities in the actual world and they are related by a variety of metaphysical dependence relations. For instance, the following are plausible candidates for such dependence:

- A mountain is related to the atoms that compose it by the metaphysical dependence relation of constitution—the mountain depends on the atoms.

- The truth of the proposition that it is raining is related to the fact that it is raining by the metaphysical dependence relation of truthmaking—the true proposition depends on the fact.

- A mind is related to a brain by the metaphysical dependence relation of realization—the mind depends on the brain.

Suppose the world does contain dynamic, metaphysical power. This power is best captured by the metaphysical dependence relations of governance and production. Both relate entities or events at one time to entities or events at an earlier time. Governance does so via the laws, while production does so via dispositional properties.

Governance: The behavior of entities or events (at least partly) dynamically, metaphysically depends on the laws of nature.

Production: The behavior of entities or events (at least partly) dynamically, meta-physically depends on properties.

Note that the ontology of the categorical-BSA does acknowledge some metaphysical dependence relations. For instance, the laws of nature, as statements that systematize the distribution of properties in spacetime, metaphysically depend on the distribution of properties in spacetime. However, the ontology of the categorical-BSA does not support any kind of *dynamic* metaphysical dependence. This is because the fundamental base includes the entire Humean mosaic of categorical properties: past, present, and future, with no metaphysical dependence relations between states at different times. Of course, from the laws and the state at a time, the Humean can *predict* the future states, but the laws are themselves metaphysically derived from those future states, so there can be no dynamic metaphysical dependence. This lack of powers should come as no surprise to the defender of the categorical-BSA, since the Humean mosaic is postulated with this requirement explicitly in mind (see Lewis 1983a, Beebee 2000, Loewer 2007, Cohen and Callender 2009, and Bird 2007a).

It is no use for the Humean to appeal to a theory of causation. Since Humean causation ultimately depends on the Humean mosaic, it does not exhibit dynamic metaphysical dependence either. For the Humean, nothing short of the entire mosaic is sufficient to guarantee the entire mosaic. Some Humeans argue that their account of causation can explain our experience of macroscopic 'oomph.'[9] But Humean causation is a higher-order phenomenon, and does nothing to accommodate production (or governance) at the fundamental level. More importantly, the *experience* of production is different from the intuition that the world, fundamentally, is produced.

The intuition that there is production (or governance), fundamentally, in the world, is strong enough that any theory which denies it is biting a substantial bullet. Helen Beebee (2000, 593) argues that even so, "the Ramsey–Lewis view does justice to enough of our intuitions about the laws of nature to be a viable alternative." That may be, but I think that the defender of the BSA can do even better. By exchanging purely categorical properties for potencies, as I argue we should, the best system account of laws *can* accommodate our intuition that there is fundamental, metaphysical 'oomph' in our world.

3. Potencies: Fundamental Dispositional Properties

Many philosophers argue that the fundamental properties are *dispositional*.[10] Dispositional properties are necessarily connected to the behavior of the objects that instantiate them. Take, for instance, the property of having mass. If mass is *categorical*, then massive objects in different possible worlds can behave very differently, attracting

---

[9] In personal communications, David Albert, Jenann Ismael, and Barry Loewer take this experience as illusory—or at least reducible to something that does not include 'oomph.'

[10] See, for example, Ellis and Lierse (1994), Mumford (1998), Bird (2007a), and Jacobs (2011).

each other in some worlds (like ours), repelling each other in other worlds, and neither attracting nor repelling in still others. However, if mass is *dispositional* in the way I think it is, then the property of having mass is necessarily connected to the behavior of the objects that instantiate it. Thus, any massive object, in any world, is disposed to attract other massive objects.[11]

In what follows, I will rely on Alexander Bird's (2007a) characterization of fundamental dispositional properties, as presented in *Nature's Metaphysics*, though my conclusions should generalize to many other dispositionalist accounts. My account of potency-BSA can be thought of as elaborating on Bird's suggestion that it is possible to derive universal generalizations from potencies.[12] Since dispositions can exist at any level (fragile vases or massy electrons) and for a wide variety of properties, as gerrymandered as you like, Bird (2007a, 45) introduces a new term, *potency*, that is defined as follows:

Potency: A fundamental, sparse property with a dispositional essence.[13]

Potencies can be thought of as dispositional versions of Lewis's perfectly natural properties. They are fundamental, so they are not made up out of anything else—they are on the 'ground floor' of the world.[14] They are sparse, and as I will argue below, correspond to the scientific kinds that appear in our best physical theories. The dispositional essence of a potency is the necessary connection between the property and the behavior of objects that instantiate it.[15,16]

---

[11] I will set aside the interesting and important debate about whether the categorical/dispositional distinction can be successfully drawn, or whether all properties must be both qualitative and dispositional. For more on this, see Martin and Heil (1999), and Jacobs (2011).

[12] Bird argues that the regularities of a best system account can be derived from potencies via the following entailment: $\Box(\forall x)(Px \leftrightarrow (Sx \,\Box\!\!\rightarrow\, Mx))$ entails $(\forall x)(Px\&Sx) \rightarrow Mx))$, where P is a potency, S is a stimulus condition, and M is a manifestation. Unfortunately, Bird does not elaborate on what it is that metaphysically grounds the biconditional. I do not rely on counterfactuals in deriving the laws of nature from potencies, and doubt whether Bird's formulation succeeds. Nevertheless, I take my account to be very much in the same spirit as Bird's. I fill in the details of just what a potency best system account should look like, and why we should prefer it.

[13] Though the arguments in this chapter won't depend on the answer, another interesting question is whether to treat the potencies of 1 kg, 2 kg, etc., as one (determinable) potency with infinitely many determinates, or as an infinite number of different potencies. I am inclined to agree with Jessica Wilson (2010), who argues that the fundamental properties are best thought of as determinables. Additionally, I will address only briefly the very complex issues of component forces.

[14] While some, for example G. K. Chesterton, have objected to the coherence of fundamental dispositions, the literature is full of excellent replies, and I need not repeat those arguments here. For a particularly nice reply, see Bird (2007b).

[15] Several defenders of dispositional properties have moved from talk of dispositions and stimulus conditions (situations) to *mutual manifestation partners*. Thus, rather than think of one instance of mass as the disposition and another instance of mass as the stimulus condition (situation), it is more accurate to think of both instantiations of mass as participating equally in the interaction. When two masses are near each other, they both manifest mutual repulsion. Singling out one as the disposition and the other as stimulus is merely an artifact of our particular interests. I think this is a promising idea and my conclusions in this chapter should carry over to such a picture.

[16] Schrenk (2010) argues that the connections between these properties cannot be necessary because other conditions—namely, antidotes—can always intervene, altering the dynamic dependence. Thus, a more

Three things to note. First, even though the potencies are metaphysically more fundamental than the behavior of the particles that instantiate them, the behavior of particles across worlds is sufficient to individuate potencies (i.e. no potencies have the same essential dispositions). Second, while this connection entails certain counterfactuals (how objects *would* behave in different circumstances), those counterfactuals depend upon the nature of the particles involved, how they are arranged, and what potencies they instantiate, so I reject any attempt to analyze potencies in terms of counterfactuals. The metaphysical direction of explanation runs the other way. Third, potencies are purely deterministic. I see no reason why propensities—chancy dispositional properties—could not be integrated into the potency-BSA, but I leave that development for a future paper.

A potency's dispositional essence, plus the stimulus condition or external situation, determines the behavior of any particle instantiating it. I will turn to the question of *how* this determination works in section 4.4. Sometimes this behavior is the instantiation of a further potency, as when a moving charge induces a magnetic field, and sometimes this behavior is simply a modified trajectory through space(time).[17]

3.1. Potencies are Science-Friendly

Since potencies often do not exist in isolation, and are typically exposed to many stimulus conditions, it can be quite difficult to determine just how the particles that instantiate them will behave. Luckily, the effects of stimulus conditions get weaker with distance, and often can be shielded. Thus, while the gravitational contribution from Alpha Centauri has some effect on massive particles on earth, that effect is insignificant relative to the gravitational effect of the earth's mass. Similarly, because oppositely charged stimulus conditions have opposite effects on a charged particle, they can be used to shield one another. Scientists rely on these features to carefully construct experimental setups in which a single potency's characteristic behavior can be observed.

To illustrate this phenomenon, consider a representative physics experiment, which measures gravitational attraction at very small distances.[18] In such an experiment, the physicists place two masses very close to each other and measure the force between

---

careful formulation would only posit a necessary connection when all factors in the potency as well as its stimulus condition were accounted for. Such a formulation has not been forthcoming in the literature, so for the purposes of this chapter, I rely on the standard formulation. But I happily acknowledge there is work to be done on this front to capture the true nature of the essential power that, say, masses have to attract one another.

[17] Alexander Bird offers some arguments for thinking spatiotemporal relations are also potencies, see Bird (2007a, ch. 7), but I doubt such a view could be metaphysically complete, so I assume that spatiotemporal relations are not potencies. For arguments that spatiotemporal relations cannot be potencies, see Ellis (2010).

[18] These details are from an experiment performed at the University of Colorado by Long et al. (2003).

them by how much they deflect the springs to which they are attached. Because the force of gravity is so weak, especially when compared to the electromagnetic forces, the biggest challenge of the experiment is to screen off as many outside effects as possible. Thus, the experiments are performed in a deep basement, in the dark, at night, and only during breaks in the traffic outside. This careful screening-off procedure is evidence that the physicists aim to discover the characteristic behavior (manifestation) of a specific *kind* of property (disposition). Cartwright (1999) describes a similar process in the case of measuring charge:

> To say it is in [the electrons'] nature to experience a force . . . is to say at least that they would experience this force if only the right conditions occur for the power to exercise itself 'on its own', for instance, if they have very small masses so that gravitational effects are negligible.
>
> (Cartwright 1999, 82)

By repeated applications of this procedure in different areas of fundamental physics, each potency can be ever more effectively isolated and its characteristic behavior in various conditions discovered. Why think these properties are dispositional rather than categorical? Scientists need only perform a relatively small number of experiments on a single kind of particle before they feel confident that they have captured its true nature, or, in my terms, the essential dispositions of its potencies. As Cartwright (1999) argues,

> For example, we measure, successfully, we think, the charge or mass of an electron in a given experiment. Now we think we know the charge or mass of all electrons; we need not go on measuring hundreds of thousands. In so doing we are making what looks to be a kind of essentialist assumption: the charge or mass of a fundamental particle is not a variable quantity but is characteristic of the particle so long as it continues to be the kind of particle it is.
>
> (Cartwright 1999, 85)

I argued in section 2.1 that when scientists formulate their systematic theories, they use simplicity and strength as standards for success. In this section, I gave reasons to think that when scientists investigate the nature of the fundamental properties, they look for dispositional essences, or what it is that things *do* in different situations. Thus, just as the best system account is a science-friendly account of the laws of nature, potencies constitute a science-friendly ontology.

4. Potency-Best System Account of Basic Laws

In this section, I combine potencies with the best system account of basic laws. I use Lewis's best system account of laws as a template, replacing his perfectly natural categorical properties with sparse, dispositional properties (i.e. with potencies). The other crucial difference is that I systematize the potencies in many possible worlds, not just one. More specifically:

Potency-BSA: The basic laws of nature at w are the axioms of the simplest, most informative, true systematization of all w-potency-distributions, where a w-potency-distribution is a possible distribution of only potencies appearing in w.[19]

For example, if a world, w_1, contains a possible distribution of the potency of mass, then the laws of w_1 must systematize all possible distributions of mass. Since the possible distributions of mass are determined by the potencies and not the laws, there is no threat of circularity. If another world, w_2 contains a possible distribution of the potencies of mass and charge, then the laws of w_2 must systematize all possible distributions of mass, all possible distributions of charge, and all possible distributions of both mass and charge. Thus, any systematization that fails to reference those potencies fails to be an eligible candidate for lawhood. In the same way that Lewis's perfectly natural, categorical-BSA rules out a trivial best system, so does the potency-BSA—in this case '$(\forall x)Px$,' where P is the potency had by all and only objects satisfying a given systematization. And, as I will show below, this account does not succumb to the three objections discussed above.

4.1. Why Systematize Properties in non-Actual Worlds?

Recall that every Humean version of the BSA systematizes the properties of the actual world. But, with the introduction of potencies, properties that are primitively modal, there is no additional cost to include other possible distributions in our systematization. As discussed above, the initial distribution of potencies determines the later distributions (by *production*, which I discuss below). Because the laws include systematizations of all the ways in which initial configurations of dispositional properties can evolve, it allows us to characterize the laws of nature without including any actual, but accidental generalizations, and without omitting any non-actual, but lawful regularities.

Why can't the Humean systematize the distribution of properties in non-actual worlds? First, the Humean would need a way of characterizing the other worlds. Granting that, the Humean would need to identify the right set of worlds to systematize for the laws. Choosing only those worlds at which the laws of nature hold would be obviously circular since the systematization is meant to ground the laws, not the other way around. On the other hand, the Humean cannot systematize all of the worlds that instantiate the perfectly natural properties found in the actual world, as I do with potencies, because it would include too many worlds. Since the categorical properties are not connected to the behaviors of the particles that instantiate them, they can appear in vastly more combinations than potencies. Therefore, the laws would have to systematize worlds that differed in radical ways from each other. There would be no non-trivial regularities between such disparate worlds, and thus, no BSA laws.

---

[19] David Albert (2000) persuasively argues that an additional, low-entropy restriction on possible initial distributions is necessary to recover the special science laws. But for the purposes of this chapter, I am concerned only with the basic laws of nature.

Therefore, the only reasonable option for the Humean is to systematize the distribution of properties in the actual world.

4.2. A Potency-BSA Matches our TOE

Let us return to the mismatch objection. Suppose, again, that our best scientists have arrived at a very simple, very informative final theory of everything (TOE) that correctly predicts as wide a range of empirical data as scientists can test. What are our reasons for thinking such a theory will match the potency-BSA?

Recall that potencies—primitive, sparse properties with unique dispositional essences—are necessarily connected to the behavior of the particles that instantiate them. So, almost any permutation of potencies will affect the trajectories of particles, unlike in the case of categorical properties, as we saw in section 2.2. This is where the ontology of potencies and the best system account of laws complement each other so well. Since the scientists' TOE systematizes the trajectories of particles, and since the trajectories of particles are *produced by* the potencies, we have good reason to think that a simple, informative TOE will appeal to those potencies.

By positing an ontology of potencies, we have ruled out the vast majority of ways in which a best system could fail to match our TOE. However, there is still no guarantee (again, nor *should* there be) that the trajectories of the particles will yield enough information for scientists to uniquely identify every potency. For instance, if there are only a few potencies instantiated in only a few different kinds of situations, scientists would not be able to fully capture their modal profiles, and thus, their theory of everything would fall short of the best system.

However, there is reason to think that a complex world like ours is not impoverished in this way. Nature, it seems, eventually gets around to displaying all different kinds of behavior. And, if nature is not forthcoming, scientists perform experiments specifically designed to test for potencies in stimulus conditions that rarely occur on their own. For instance, scientists are able to perform experiments at very high energies which arose naturally only just after the Big Bang. Thus, the defender of the potency-BSA need not worry—beyond the unavoidable skeptical worries—that science fails to capture the genuine laws of nature. Similarly, there is good reason to think that a best system account that systematizes only the actual world, and that referred to potencies rather than categorical properties, would match the potency-BSA as well—another way of saying that actual scientists systematize actual behavior that is determined by the potencies.

4.3. Impoverished Worlds and the Potency-BSA

Since the potency-BSA systematizes the distribution of potencies in all possible worlds that contain the same potencies, an impoverished world will receive the same systematization as a complex world. Consider, again, a world with a single massive particle, traveling inertially for all time. The laws of this world will systematize not just this world, but all worlds that contain mass. Therefore, it will be a law that all massive particles attract each other, and NOT that they always travel inertially. Furthermore, even without developing a theory of how counterfactuals depend upon the potencies and laws, it is easy to see that *if* that single particle *were* near another massive particle, it *would* experience attraction toward that particle. Therefore, the potency-BSA laws are intuitively correct in impoverished worlds, and they yield the right counterfactuals for those worlds.

Of course, scientists of such a world would be in a kind of skeptical scenario, and thus unlikley to *arrive at* the correct account of the laws. Analogously, if our world turns out to be impoverished, we would be in a similar, unfortunate situation. But, this is the correct result—the laws of nature are not guaranteed to be epistemically accessible. The potency-BSA, and not the traditional BSA, secures the intuitively correct result in impoverished worlds, whether or not inhabitants of those worlds know it.

4.4. *Potencies do Metaphysical Work*

There is a very deep and interesting question about just how it is that a potency produces its characteristic behavior. Many philosophers, such as Bird, avoid this metaphysical question by appealing to counterfactuals. But while counterfactuals can tell us *what* behavior results from a configuration of potencies, they cannot tell us *how* that behavior results. Nevertheless, Bird (2007a, 200) claims, "Mumford and I agree that the existence of regularities in nature, the truth of counterfactuals, and the possibility of explanation are explained by the potencies."

So, Bird claims that the potencies are explanatory, but he says very little to illuminate how this explanation is supposed to go. Stipulating a biconditional between potencies and counterfactuals does not tell us how it is that the potencies *explain* the behavior of particles—even if those counterfactuals can be used to derive regularities. Entailment falls short of metaphysical explanation. To see this, consider that Lewis's best system account of laws entails facts about how particles behave. Despite this, the laws do not (metaphysically) explain the behavior of particles. On the contrary, it is the distribution of properties that explains the categorical-BSA laws.

I think the most promising solution is to appeal to *production*—dynamic, metaphysical dependence. According to my view, the fundamental ground includes spacetime and an initial arrangement of particles and potencies. And the subsequent behavior of the particles (further potency instantiations as well as trajectories through spacetime) is dynamically, metaphysically dependent upon that base. Since the potency-BSA systematizes those trajectories, the laws of nature are not fundamental, and do not govern, but rather depend upon the behavior of the particles and potencies. To summarize what (metaphysically) explains what: on my view, the initial distribution of particles and their potencies dynamically ground the subsequent behaviors of particles and subsequent property instantiations. And, all of the possible initial distributions and evolutions determine the (metaphysically inert) laws.[20]

If the fundamental properties are potencies, they can do the metaphysical heavy lifting many have thought had to be done by the laws of nature. The intuition about metaphysical 'oomph' is that the behavior of particles in our universe is not primitive but, rather, is produced (or governed) in a systematic way. One option is to locate this power in *governing* laws of nature, which 'push and pull' the particles around. But, if the fundamental properties turn out to be dispositional, rather than categorical, then the potencies are a natural place to locate metaphysical power,[21] as they *produce* the behavior. If the potencies bear the metaphysical responsibility for the behavior of particles, then the laws of nature are no longer needed for this role. This makes a best system account, which eschews just such a role, perfectly suited to a fundamental ontology of dispositional properties.[22] Thus, we can reconcile the thought that 'oomph' is needed in the world while retaining the BSA and its tight connection to scientific practice.

5. Conclusion

In this chapter, I have argued that a best system account of laws and an ontology of fundamental dispositional properties are well-suited to each other. Physicists test for potencies, and formulate laws that systematize trajectories, while maximizing simplicity and strength. This makes an ontology of potencies and best system laws science-friendly. In addition, my potency-BSA can avoid three objections that plague the categorical-BSA. Because potencies are necessarily connected to the behavior of the particles that instantiate them, the potency-BSA avoids the mismatch objection.

[20] Much more could be said about such a relation. For instance, each arrangement of particles and their potencies is probably best explained in terms of the previous (or in the limit) arrangement of particles and their potencies, perhaps just in the past light cone of the arrangement in question.

[21] Indeed, Bird (2007a, 46) takes potencies and powers to be the same thing: "potencies just are their dispositional powers." Mumford (1998) and Bird (2007a) agree that governing laws are superfluous with an ontology of potencies.

[22] Markus Schrenk (2012) objects,

> if nature equips properties with their own (causal) essences then what would be the point of a Lewisean best system analysis? Most causal roles and, thus, causal laws would anyway already be fixed by the properties' essences and, so, a best system competition would at best deliver exactly those already given laws and roles.   (Schrenk 2012, 8)

But, while laws of nature are, indeed, fixed by dispositional essences, they are distinct from them. The difficulties that beset attempts to state dispositional essences do not beset similar attempts to state the laws of nature. For instance, even if the potencies are restricted to include only mass, there is a great deal of controversy as to what the dispositions are. Are masses simply disposed to attract one another, with perhaps a meta-disposition for how those massive attractions add to or subtract from one another? Or are there separate dispositions for each particular possible mass-instantiation distribution? If, instead, the laws systematize the possible distributions of potencies throughout spacetime, there is the possibility of 'backsolving' to arrive at the potencies. And, it is likely that this is exactly what metaphysicians do when they discuss dispositions such as mass and charge. But, of course, the metaphysical direction of explanation need not point the same way as the epistemic one.

Because the potency-BSA systematizes all worlds with the relevant potencies, rather than just one, it avoids the impoverished worlds objection. Finally, I have argued that potencies can play the metaphysical role of production traditionally reserved for governing laws of nature. So it makes sense to think that the laws of nature are metaphysically inert, just as they are in a best system account. Thus, I hope to have shown that potencies and the best system account of laws complement each other nicely and make for a promising picture of the fundamental ontology and the laws of nature.

Acknowledgments

I would like thank Zachary Miller, Jonathan Jacobs, Barry Loewer, Jonathan Schaffer, Branden Fitelson, Jenann Ismael, Barbara Vetter, Markus Schrenk, Jenn Wang, Marco Dees, Tom Donaldson, and the audiences at Rutgers University and at the "Putting Powers to Work" conference at St. Louis University.

PART II

Causation and Modality

5

Aristotelian Powers at Work

Reciprocity without Symmetry in Causation

Anna Marmodoro

1. Introduction

This chapter puts powers to work by developing a broadly Aristotelian account of causation,[1] built around the fundamental idea that causation is the exercise of causal powers.[2] What is distinctive about the ontology underpinning this account of causation is that it takes the manifestation of a power to be the activated state of the very same power, and not the occurrence of a new power.[3] Furthermore on this account, there are no lonely powers; all powers have partner-powers.[4] Each partner-power serves as a necessary condition for the existence and manifestation of the other.[5] Thus another distinctive feature of the account is that each power is individuated, jointly, by the type of activity its manifestation is and the type of partner-powers it can have.[6]

What does this view commit one to, when it comes to explaining causation in terms of causal powers? First, it offers a realist theory of causation that, as we shall see, does not reify the mutual activation of the causal partner-powers into a relation.

---

[1] The chapter develops, in an original way, Aristotelian insights on causation and causal powers, but does not discuss these exegetically.

[2] The view that causation is the mutual activation of causal powers is gaining consensus in contemporary power metaphysics. In fact, activation of causal powers is *all there is* to alternative power-based accounts of causation in contemporary metaphysics. See, for example, Heil, Chapter 7 in this volume; Mumford and Anjum, Chapter 6 in this volume; and Martin (2008). My account adds that the activation of causal powers is their activity (i.e. a process in time).

[3] For example, Mumford and Anjum (2011) and Bird (2007a) hold this view.

[4] The view that powers have manifestation partners is gaining consensus among contemporary power metaphysicians; see, for example, Martin (1993b, 2008), and Martin's contribution to Armstrong et al. (1996); Mumford and Anjum (2011); Heil (2003), and Chapter 7 in this volume. I argue in my book manuscript with the working title *Power Structuralism in Ancient Ontologies*, in progress, that this is a view that in fact stems from Heraclitus, on to Plato, and develops into a theory of active and passive mutual partners in Aristotle.

[5] A power can have two or more partner-powers. The account can become more complex by entertaining powers whose partners are in some possible worlds but not in every possible world in which the powers exist.

[6] The type of activity and the partner-power(s) are not two independent individuation principles.

Second, from the fact that powers depend for their activation and their exercise on the activation and exercise of their mutual partner-powers, it follows that there is reciprocity in causation. The reciprocity may be illustrated for example with a causal scenario where A causes B to become hotter. A's power to heat is activated; it manifests by heating B up. But A's heating up B can take place only if B's power to be heated is activated too, and manifests itself in B's getting hotter. A's heating and B's being heated are mutually dependent in a variety of ways, and each activity lasts as long as the other lasts.

If causation is mutual activation of causal powers, one might think that there is an important feature to causation that is left out in this account, namely that causation has a direction and is thus asymmetric. My analysis of the mutually manifesting causal powers is different from others advanced in the contemporary debate, in that it explains the intuition that there is direction in causation; and this direction is metaphysically underpinned by a distinction of roles between causal agent and patient. Hence, the view that causation is the mutual activation of causal powers does not commit one to giving up causal agency. Yet, is it the powers, or the substances that possess them, that are causally efficacious? At the most fundamental level, it is powers that are causally activated; derivatively, at the macro-level, we can say that the substances, constituted by the powers, are the agents of causal action.

2. Powers and Manifestations

I shall begin with a very brief account of the nature of causal powers.[7] On my account, a power is the potentiality to bring about a change, or the activity of bringing about that change. Nothing inert or impotent is needed in the power's nature to anchor the power to reality.[8] To put the point concisely, one may say that all there is to a power is its powerfulness, that is, what it can do or is doing.

In this connection, it is somewhat unclear to say that a power is potentially its actuality (which is an expression Aristotle introduced), because this can be read in two ways: that the potentiality is for the power's *activation*; or that the potentiality is for the power's *activity* when it is being exercised. It is the second meaning that I intend. The point may be clarified by way of contrast with a widely shared view in contemporary metaphysics. On my account the powerfulness of a power is its capacity to actively engage in an activity (whether this activity is a doing or a suffering, as we shall see below). By contrast, many contemporary power ontologists take the powerfulness of a

---

[7] Although I am concerned in this chapter with the fundamental powers in the ontology, I will sometimes speak of powers generally, when I believe that my corresponding claims apply to all powers. (I assume that a defense of my generalizations will be needed only if counterexamples are supplied.)

[8] See, for example, Bird (2007a), Holton (1999), Shoemaker (1984), Mellor (1974). Contrast this with views on which a power has a categorical basis (e.g. Armstrong et al. 1996; Armstrong 1997, 80; Armstrong 2000, 13–14; Armstrong 2004, 138–9; Ellis 2010).

power to be its readiness to get activated, that is, to instantaneously 'jump' into another power, which is the causal effect.[9]

How does a power get to do what it can do? What does the exercise of its power-fulness consist in? On my account when a power is activated, it engages in the activity it is for, or it suffers the activity of its power-partner. Take for example a pile of books on a table with a glass tabletop, and imagine that we keep adding books to the pile: as the pile of books exercises increasing pressure on the glass tabletop, the glass 'suffers' the pressure (where pressuring is the activity of the heavy pile) and eventually breaks (where breaking is the activity of the fragile glass).

A power that is engaged in the activity it is for (e.g. the magnetic power of a magnet attracting some metal) is in a different state than when it is in potentiality (not attracting any metal). On my view, the activation of a power is an *internal* 'transition' from one state to another of the very same power: its manifestation is not the occurrence of a new power; rather it is simply a different state of the original power: an activated state.[10] This view of the activation of powers sets my account apart from other power ontologies that share the commitment that all there is to a power is its powerfulness.[11]

There are two issues on which I hereby take a position. First, there is the question of whether 'pure' power ontologies of the kind I endorse (where there is nothing cat-egorical anchoring the powers to reality) are committed to a *world of mere potentiality*. I argue they need not be so committed. Second, there is the question of whether powers

---

[9] For example, Mumford and Anjum (2011) and Bird (2007a) hold this view.

[10] Depending on the ontological assumptions in play, one may think that for powers that suffer change their activation is either the qualitative change of the same power or the generation of a new power. Whether the power that suffers the partner-power's activity is considered, when manifesting, numerically the same power or not as before manifesting, depends on how finely or coarsely a power is individuated. If the individuation of powers is fine-grained, the power is numerically different (for example, one may think that the rising heat of the pot on the stove involves the generation of distinct powers in it). If the individuation of powers is coarse-grained, the power remains numerically the same, and it only gets altered (the heat simply increases).

[11] C. B. Martin (2008) takes the directedness of a power toward its manifestation to be intrinsic to the power; but his position differs from mine in that he does not make the manifestation of a power a different state of the power itself; see for example his Two-Triangles Model:

> You should not think of disposition partners jointly *causing* the manifestation. Instead, the coming together of the disposition partner *is* the mutual manifestation: the partnering and the manifestation are identical. This partnering-manifestation identity is seen most clearly with cases such as the following. You have two triangle-shaped slips of paper that, when placed together appropriately, form a square. It is not that the partnering of the triangles *causes* the manifestation of the square, but rather that the partnering *is* the manifestation.
>
> (Martin 2008, 51, emphasis in the original)

This is an important difference between the view that I am proposing and Martin's, in that for him, although the directedness is intrinsic to what has it (the powers), what it is directed toward (the manifestation) is not intrinsic to what has it (the power itself). With reference to the example in the quote above, the square is not intrinsic to either of the triangles that constitute it. By contrast, on my view the power that is directed towards heating is activated when it is in fact heating something. Heating is the exercise of the powerfulness of the power to heat, which is a state attained by the power to heat.

have an *essentially relational nature*. I argue that they do not; powers are monadic properties ontologically dependent on various types of circumstances.

2.1. Is There Only Potentiality in a World of 'Pure' Powers?

Is the account of powers I am proposing prey to the criticism that if all fundamental properties are powers, as described above, all there is or can be at the bedrock of reality is potential, and that change is simply a transition from one potential state of the world to another such state? The concern has been raised for many contemporary power ontologies; one expression of it is the Always Packing Argument.[12] David Armstrong (1997, 80) formulates it thus: "Given purely dispositionalist accounts of properties, particulars would seem to be always re-packing their bags as they change properties, yet never taking a journey from potency to act."

The Always Packing Argument raises difficulties for the position held by contemporary power ontologists whereby the activation of a power in potentiality is merely an instantaneous 'jump' to its manifestation, which is another power in potentiality. A theory of powers that did not allow powers when activated to exercise their powerfulness would be rather odd indeed—yet, this seems the position that some power ontologists are committed to, when claiming that the manifestation of a power is merely a new power in potentiality.[13] It is this conception of the power's manifestation that commits one to a network of powers in potentiality, where nothing ever is actual. This is the complaint that Armstrong's argument voices: that there is no actuality in the ontology. There is no journey from potency to act, not because nothing happens in a world of 'pure' powers; powers do in fact manifest, but the manifestation is an instantaneous transition to another power in potentiality. The exercise of powers on other powers is not reified (i.e. it is not part of the ontology). In other words, in such an ontology change is not defined in terms of potency and act, but only in terms of potency to potency. My account avoids a commitment to worlds of mere potentiality: the manifestation of a power, that is, its transition from potentiality to actuality, is a transition the power makes to its own activated state. A power in potentiality is numerically the same power when manifesting. (The activated power may cause further powers to come about, but this is not what the manifestation of the original power consists in.)

John Heil raised additional objections against an ontology of 'pure' powers only, with his Domino Argument, which is similar and yet different from Armstrong's Always Packing Argument. Heil writes:

Despite its appeal in some quarters, many philosophers have been struck by the thought that a properties-as-powers view leads to a debilitating regress. Suppose *A*s are nothing more than powers to produce *B*s, *B*s are nothing more than powers to produce *C*s, *C*s are nothing more

---

[12] The expression "always packing, never traveling" is first used by Molnar (2003, 173).

[13] Contrast this with, for example, Mumford and Anjum: "The manifestation of a power will . . . be itself a *further* power or cluster of powers." (2011, 5, my emphasis)

than powers to produce *D*s . . . and so on for every concrete spatiotemporal thing. How is this supposed to work? Imagine a row of dominos arranged so that, when the first domino topples, it topples the second, which topples the third, and so on. Now imagine that *all there is* to the first domino is a power to topple the second domino, and *all there is* to the second domino is a power to be toppled and a power to topple the third domino, and so on. If all there is to a domino is a power to topple or be toppled by an adjacent domino, *nothing happens: no domino topples because there is nothing—no thing—to topple.*   (Heil 2003, 98, my emphasis)

We saw that the Always Packing Argument assumes that the world is a sequence of powers in potentiality getting constantly replaced, upon being manifested, by other powers in potentiality; there is nothing but powers in potentiality in the world. But the Domino Argument does not question how a power will take the journey from potency to act, if all there is to a thing or to the ontology is potency. Rather, it questions how a power can take the journey from potency to act *if all there is to the thing a power will act on is potentiality.* This is a concern, not about the fact that powers never take a journey from potentiality to actuality, but about their journey having no destination as it were. In other words, the question is whether there is an object *at all* when all there is to its constitution are pure powers in potentiality.

Are mere collections of powers in potentiality *no thing* at all? I submit that there is no metaphysical impediment to the existence of things constituted of pure powers in potentiality.[14] On the other hand, such a circumstance could not arise in our world. To explain why I do not find the Domino Argument to be an objection to pandispositionalism, and why I do not think that it describes what our world would be like if things are indeed constituted of pure powers only, I need to briefly address the question of the constitution of things in an ontology of only pure powers *in potentiality*.

First let me say that I agree with Heil that there are no objects that are constituted of the power to topple something else and the power to be toppled. After all, powers cannot be toppled! But these are not the powers that dominos consist of. The power to topple is a complex power, consisting of simpler powers, and ultimately, of fundamental powers; nor is the power to topple a power that exists on its own, but rather it belongs to objects that have many other powers in addition to the power to topple. For contemporary physics, the fundamental powers are mass, spin, and charge. Elementary particles are combinations of these powers. Thus, an electron consists of 0.5 mass, –1 charge, and ½ spin. That an electron repels another electron is a result of the powers that comprise them. The powers electrons have to light up the night result from powers that they acquire when they function within larger structures, possibly including many types of entities. Now, if one was to ask the core question Heil asks, namely whether such a thing as an electron exists as a thing composed of these three powers (mass, charge, spin), if they happen to be in potentiality only, my answer is "yes." Even if the electron is not interacting with anything else, and the three powers that constitute it are only in potentiality, there is no obstacle to understanding its

---

[14] I argue for this claim in my book manuscript *Power Structuralism in Ancient Ontologies* (unpublished).

existence, and the readiness of its powers to be activated by its environment. Similarly, consider photons, which make the case even clearer: they consist of 0 mass, 0 charge, and 1 spin. They are, to adapt a term from biology, monopotent (i.e. one power only constitutes them). And yet, even photons are entities.

On the other hand, as a matter of fact, things in our world are not combinations of powers in potentiality only. Fundamental powers of elementary particles are continuously manifesting in their environment, given the presence of the ambient gravitational force in the universe, but also of the other fundamental forces. In complex objects, powers are continuously manifesting in the presence of other powers in the same object; for instance, the gravitational and electromagnetic powers of physical parts of a domino manifest in the presence of such powers of the other parts of the domino etc.[15] In the case of powers such as the power to topple, they presuppose structural constitutional complexity of the object that possesses them—size, shape, weight, hardness, etc. Many of these powers of a domino will be constantly activated, manifesting in the presence of the other powers of the domino, even if the power to topple is not. In short, there is a domino there to be toppled.

To recapitulate, the commitment I make with the claim that all there is to a power is its powerfulness (which is shared by a number of contemporary power metaphysicians) is not uncontroversial; it has brought about in some quarters the worry that is expressed in the Always Packing Argument by David Armstrong, and in the Domino Argument by John Heil. I address these concerns, on the one hand, by reifying in my ontology the state of activation of powers; and on the other hand, by showing that there are always powers in the state of activation in the world.

2.2. Are Powers Monadic or Relational Properties?

Although it is a common (Aristotelian) assumption that powers are defined in terms of their manifestation, power ontologies that make the manifestation of a power be a further power thereby establish a network of polyadic relations; each power is defined in terms of its relation to something different from itself, namely other powers. Many hold this view; for example Alexander Bird: "The essence of a potency involves a relation to something else; if inertial mass is a potency then its essence involves a relation to a stimulus property (impressed force) and a manifestation property (acceleration)." (2007a, 107)[16]

I too follow the Aristotelian conception of a power as defined in terms of its manifestation, but on the view I am proposing this does not result in an account of powers as

---

[15] The four fundamental *forces*, the weak, strong, electromagnetism, and gravitation, are not additional powers for physicists. Rather, they are considered four fundamental *interactions*, explained as the emission and absorption of elementary particles. So, following my description above, the four fundamental interactions are emissions and absorptions of combinations of fundamental powers constituting elementary particles.

[16] See, for example, Bird (2007a, chs. 5–6); Psillos (2006), and my discussion of his paper in Marmodoro (2009).

polyadic relations. On my account the manifestation of a power is not another power the original power is related to, but another state of the same power. (For example, the power to heat manifests by heating up something, not by becoming a different power of heat—there is more to say below about causal reciprocity.) Furthermore, a manifesting power is described in terms of what it does, and this description makes reference to the type of effect the power brings about, namely to the activity that is suffered by the partner-power (e.g. heating). This indicates the type of dependence partner-powers have on each other. Yet, ontological dependence is not a polyadic relation, and powers are not relational properties. Rather, fundamental powers are *monadic* properties that are outwardly directed. This is a core Aristotelian intuition which I develop in section 3. But before examining the non-relational nature of powers, I will say more about which dependencies hold in my view among fundamental powers.

3. The Interdependencies among Fundamental Powers

In this section, I address the issue of which dependencies there are among fundamental powers, arguing that powers depend on other powers for their existence and activity.

3.1. Do Powers Depend on Other Powers for Their Existence?

Powers are defined in terms of what they do, when activated. We have in fact no other way of knowing a power than its operation on its partner-power. This is to say that there is *epistemological dependence* of the potential state of a power on its activated state. A consequence that follows is that powers are defined in terms of the type of partner-powers they can have, since this determines what they do.

Whether *lonely* powers (that is, powers without partner-powers) exist or not is ultimately a question of ontological parsimony. I favor parsimony, so I assume that powers with no partners do not exist even in potentiality. An argument could be made to allow for powers that have no partners in the actual world (so they cannot be manifested in it), but do in other possible worlds (so they can manifest in them). The position can become more complex if one distinguishes between degrees of similarity between the actual and the possible worlds, especially in relation to the physical laws of nature. Thus one could allow for lonely powers in the actual world which have partners in very similar worlds to the actual one, but not allow for lonely powers in the actual world if the only partners they have are in remotely different worlds. It is the latter possibility that threatens to overpopulate one's ontology, and thus one needs to guard against it. Instead of entering the slippery slope of possible world similarity, I assume as a rule of thumb for my ontology that the only lonely fundamental powers there are in the world are the ones that have partners in possible worlds with the same (relevant) physical laws as the actual world. So, suppose that there is a fundamental power that cannot manifest if the universe freezes over; on my view such a power is not to be banished from the ontology. Thus, my stance is that fundamental powers are *existentially dependent* on their partners in the actual world; or, if lonely, on their partners in physically similar possible worlds.

3.2. Do Powers Depend on Other Powers for Their Activation?

Most power ontologists recognize that powers can be either in potentiality or can be activated. Leaving aside for now the discussion of whether there are spontaneous manifestations of powers (to which I return later in this section), the activation of a power in potentiality needs to be somehow explained; there must be some trigger, stimulus, or obtaining condition that explains why a moment before the power was in potentiality and now it is activated. Consider the Stimulus Model for powers' activation, which might prima facie seem intuitively appealing; Heil, for example (2012), describes the model thus:

> Philosophers who have been attracted to an ontology of dispositions or powers, sometimes characterize powers as features of objects that manifest themselves in a particular way given a particular kind of 'trigger' or 'stimulus.' Alexander Bird (2007a), for instance, takes a disposition, D, to be characterizable by reference to a manifestation, M, resulting from D's being stimulated by S. (2012, 122)

Yet this model has attracted much critical discussion in recent literature. Heil (2012) develops an epistemological argument against the validity of the Stimulus Model: there are cases in which it seems impossible to tell (in a non-arbitrary way) which is which:

> Note, first, how poorly this way of thinking about dispositions fits with our examples, with, for instance, salt's dissolving in water. We have salt, water, and the salt's dissolving. Where do we locate D? In the salt? In the water? And where is S? Is S the salt, the water, or something else? (2012, 122)

Mumford and Anjum offer two additional arguments. The first is that the Stimulus Model does not allow for spontaneous manifestations, of which they think there are plenty of examples in nature; the second:

> is based more on a rejection of what can be called passivist accounts of nature (see Ellis 2001, 7). A passivist metaphysics is one in which there is no internal principle of change within things. They do not contain potentialities within them, for instance. Rather, they move or change only when they are pushed to do so from outside.... This general concern about passivism can be found in the specific instance of the stimulus-manifestation pair. The power itself is depicted as being on its own passive. It will produce no change unless it is stimulated to do so by the appropriate stimulus. But then this makes the stimulus look like the power: it is the element that has the power to produce change, while the power itself has, on this account, been rendered impotent. Something seems to have gone wrong with the account, therefore, as it disempowers the very powers it is supposed to explain. *The activation of the exercise of a power is 'explained' only by allotting responsibility entirely to this stimulus that is itself left unexplained*

and, furthermore, it is hard to see how it could be explained if the elements in the world are all said to be passive.

("What Tends to Be: Essays on the Dispositional Modality", unpublished; my emphasis)

Additionally, others have pointed out against the Stimulus Model that there is the danger of a regress ensuing if the stimuli have to be stimulated to stimulate the powers. I do not examine the aforementioned arguments in detail here, because I agree with the general stance taken, that we do not need to introduce a stimulus in order to explain the manifestation of a power. Rather, powers have other powers as their *manifestation partners*. Contrary to Bird, and with Heil, Mumford, and Anjum, among others, I hold that it is the 'coming together' in appropriate conditions of the partner-powers that accounts for their mutual activation. For example, the solubility of salt requires that salt be placed in solvent in order for it to dissolve.

It is of course difficult to draw a line between what in the environment is to count as the partner-power and what as enabling conditions. This difficulty has been explored extensively in the causality literature in recent decades, and so I will not engage here with it. I will only acknowledge here that there is a degree of contextual selectivity, whether pragmatic, given social circumstances, or scientific, given theoretical pursuits, which enters into the determination of partner-powers. For fundamental powers it is only the theoretical considerations that would enter into the distinction between partner-powers and enabling conditions.

4. Causal Powers are Relatives

Reality at the fundamental level is not a web of relations. Powers are not (polyadic) relational properties. Furthermore, there is no polyadic relation connecting a power in potentiality to its manifestation, since the manifestation is numerically the same power in a different state.[17] Nor is the essential nature of a power P a different power Q, to which P in potentiality is related; *P is one* with its essential nature (see Marmodoro 2009; 2013). The essence of power tells us what type of entity the power is, namely, of the sort that can do such and such type of activity to this or that type of thing. Finally, there is no polyadic relation connecting a power to its power-partners. Powers are ontologically dependent on their partners, but as we have seen, ontological dependence is not a polyadic relation.

Powers are monadic properties, but monadic properties of a special kind, which Aristotle called *pros ti*, literally, "toward something"; such properties are 'pointing toward something.' This 'pointing' is what we call nowadays the *directedness* of powers. The current translation in English of *pros ti* is "relative." Aristotle says: "All relatives are

---

[17] I am on this point in disagreement with Bird (2007a), and in agreement with Martin (2008, 12): "A disposition cannot be a relation to a manifestation." But Martin's justification for the view that dispositions or powers are not relations differs from mine: he thinks that dispositions cannot be relations because "a disposition can exist although its manifestation or even its reciprocal disposition partners, do not." (2008, 6)

spoken of in relation to correlatives that reciprocate. For example the slave is called slave of a master and the master is called master of a slave" (*Categories* 6b28–30).[18] He explains the directedness of relative properties thus:

We call *relatives* all such things as are said to be just what they are, *of* or *than* other things, or in some other way *in relation to* something else. For example, what is larger is called what it is *than* something else (it is called larger than something); and what is double is called what it is *of* something else (it is called double of something); similarly with all other such cases.

(*Categories* 6a36–b3)

The relation between relatives is not a linguistic or a semantic relation. It is an *ontological* relation, as he states clearly:

If there is no master, there is no slave either.... When there is a slave there is a master; and similarly with the others [*sc.* other relatives].... Also, each carries the other to destruction; for if there is not a double there is not a half, and if there is not a half there is not a double. So too with other such cases.   (*Categories* 7b6–22)

This is what 'binds' monadic properties into reciprocal pairs, for example being a master and being a slave: that they are ontologically interdependent. The 'pointing' nature of relatives is Aristotle's way of depicting ontological dependence. Aristotle explains (reductively) the ontological dependence between relatives as a counter-factual dependence (e.g. if there is no master there is no slave). If we apply this understanding of ontological dependence to the case of causal relata, it follows that taking causal relata as ontologically interdependent amounts to the view that there is no cause of activation or change if there is no patient of the activation or change.

So the ontological interdependencies of causal powers (as described in section 3) are not polyadic relations holding between them;[19] rather, they are mutual *conditions* that enable their respective existence and activity. A power p is manifesting when such and such a power $p\prime$ (where p does not equal $p\prime$) is satisfying such and such conditions (i.e. it exists, it is appropriately located, nothing impedes it, etc.).[20] For example, A's power (p) to heat requires B's capacity ($p\prime$) to get hotter, where B is in sufficient proximity to A with nothing in the way, in order for A to be able to achieve its manifestation, that is, heating.[21]

---

[18]   All quotations of Aristotle are from Aristotle (1984).

[19]   Typically when we provide an ontology for xRy, we take R to be an entity that exists between x and y. Either such an entity would belong to x and to y, or to neither but be somehow self-standing. With Aristotle, I hold that there is no entity that belongs to both x and y, when they are related, nor that exists between them.

[20]   This point is developed in section 6.

[21]   Because of this mutual dependence, partner-powers manifest themselves in activities that are *co-determined, co-varying, and co-extensive in time*. See Marmodoro (2006). It follows that if causation is explained in terms of causal powers, there is reciprocity in it in the sense that both causal partner-powers get activated, each 'facilitating' the activation and the activity of the other. This point is developed in section 6.

From the preceding discussion, three core conclusions follow. Powers are the metaphysical bedrock of reality. Powers are ontologically dependent other powers. Powers are monadic properties; not a network of polyadic relations.[22]

5. The Modality of Powers

In this section, I turn to the modality of powers. I take fundamental powers to be physical powers. Such powers are subject to a physical modality, which I do not associate with natural laws, but with the nature of things. In this I follow Aristotle's account of the essence of substances, especially as the thesis has been interpreted and developed by Kit Fine.[23] But my concern is not the nature of substances, but the nature of what there is in elemental ontology. Aristotle allows his account of 'nature' to extend to fundamental constituents of nature. As is well known, he thought that the primary elements in the world are earth, fire, air, and water. In explaining natural phenomena, he discusses the upward movement of fire in the cosmos and explains that the movement does not have its own source of normativity; rather, nature is the origin of the movement's normativity:

The term 'according to nature' is applied to all these things and also to the attributes which belong to them *in virtue of what they are* [that is, in virtue of their natures], for instance the upwards transference of fire—which [transference] is not a 'nature' nor 'has a nature' but is 'by nature' or 'according to nature' [namely, the nature of fire or the universe].

(Physics 192b35–193a2; my emphasis)

Accordingly, the normativity I attribute to physical powers has its source, on my account too, in the natures of the entities in the ontology.

I will start from the distinction Aristotle makes between three types of normativity, namely necessity, physical necessity, and chance,[24] and show that their explanation does not require three distinct primitive normative notions, but two. What distinguishes necessity from physical necessity is that unqualified necessity is not impeded; what is necessary is. By contrast, it is not the case that what is physically necessary is. Rather, it may, or may not be. By this I do not mean that somehow physical necessity fails to 'fire' sometimes, namely that it is somehow a 'faulty mechanism' of necessity. Rather, I mean that physical necessity does not determine what will come to be under any circumstances, come what may; it determines what will come to be *under specific circumstances*, only if and when such circumstances obtain. So, for instance, fire makes

---

[22] Bird (2007a) for example holds this view.

[23] Aristotle's grounding of necessity on the nature of things has been analyzed and explicated by Kit Fine (1994).

[24] "First then, we observe that some things always come to pass in the same way, and others for the most part. . . . But as there is a third class of events besides these two—events which all say are 'by chance'—it is plain that there is such a thing as chance and spontaneity." (*Physics* 196b10–15)

wood burn, unless the wood is wet. What is characteristic of the modality of things that happen according to nature is that it is a *defeasible* modality.

We could describe this type of physical modality as *conditional necessity*, in order to indicate that it is governed by obtaining circumstances. Thus, in the case of powers, the circumstances pertaining to their activation consist in the presence of their partner-powers, as well as of further conditions, including the absence of conditions which might impede the activation of the power (e.g. the wetness of the water). These are all empirically determinable coefficients for each power, which give the profile of the conditions that must obtain for the activation of each power. Aristotle too stresses the need for the obtaining of external circumstances for the activation of a potentiality:

[a thing] has the potentiality in question when the *passive object is present* and is *in a certain state*; if not it will not be able to act. To add the qualification "if nothing external prevents it" is not further necessary; for it has the potentiality . . . on certain conditions, among which will be the exclusion of external hindrances; for these are barred by some of the positive qualifications [for the potentiality in question].   (*Metaphysics* IX.5, 1048a15–20, my emphasis)

On the other hand, although physical necessity is governed by obtaining circumstances, if these circumstances are satisfied, the power *cannot fail* to get activated. The satisfaction of the external conditions, including the presence of the partner-power, necessitates the activation of the power.[25]

Stephen Mumford and Rani Anjum describe the modality of dispositions as follows, questioning whether we can use the notion of necessity to explicate the modality of powers, as I did above:

Dispositionality is a primitive, unanalyzable modality that is intermediate between pure possibility and necessity because of its special modal nature, no analysis that fails to invoke it can succeed. It will be subject to counterexamples because it will attempt to reduce dispositionality to something else, such as necessity, which thereby misses the subtlety and flexibility of dispositionality. In particular, it would miss the key element that dispositions can be subject to prevention and interference. This modal feature is essential to dispositionality: it is what makes it distinct from everything else.   (Mumford and Anjum 2011, 193)

I have argued that we can explain the modality of dispositionality using the notion of necessity, without sacrifice of the flexibility of dispositionality. On my account, necessity is qualified by the external circumstances required for the activation of a power. The account explains both the nature of the flexibility in the activation of a power, as determined by the obtaining or not of the external conditions, as well as the

---

[25] The account of physical modality I just offered, namely, conditional necessity, is to be distinguished from an Aristotelian notion that plays a different role in his metaphysical system, namely, hypothetical necessity. *Hypothetical necessity* is a requirement set by the form (or essence) of a thing, on account of what matter there is. Aristotle's example is a saw, which necessarily has to be made of iron, or something hard, if it is to serve the function of a saw (*Physics* II.9). Hypothetical necessity is an expression of a requirement, a necessary condition for a function to be served. It is not expressive of the normativity of a natural power. When conditions are satisfied, the function can be served. By contrast, conditional necessity describes the way that powers behave in nature—when conditions are satisfied, the powers manifest.

modal 'imperative' of the power's activation, when the external conditions do obtain. It shows that there is a normative pattern to the behavior of powers—what one might call "physical laws governing the powers"—that derives from the nature of the powers (and their bearers) and ensues in the necessity of the activation of a power, in the appropriate circumstances.[26]

Mumford made (in personal correspondence) the following reply to my proposed account of the modality of powers:

> Though I like explanations that are 'for the most part,' I'm not sure that it captures the dispositional modality. I think there can be quite significant dispositions that are a long way short of 'for the most part.' Consider the disposition of the contraceptive pill to cause thrombosis. This is medically significant and there is a clear tendency towards that outcome rather than all the other logical possibilities. But only 1 in 1000 women taking the pill get thrombosis so it falls well short of for the most part.

I do not think that this is an objection to the conception of conditional necessity that I developed earlier in this section, in order to explain physical normativity. Rather the opposite, since my account can well explain this phenomenon. To begin with, the example that Mumford gives can be described in a way that shows its compatibility with my explication. Although it is only 1 out of 1000 women taking the pill that gets thrombosis, and although this is a medically significant percentage, it is *not* a percentage that reflects the frequency of activation of the pill's power to cause thrombosis in women. The reason is that the pill is taken by selected women to activate the pill's power for contraceptive protection, rather than to activate the power to cause thrombosis. *These* women's bodily systems provide the appropriate external conditions for the contraceptive powers of the pill to be activated (in contrast to the conditions that would be provided by those not selected for the pill's use: prepubescent girls, post-menopause women, or men). But the adult women selected for the pill's use are not selected in order to activate the pill's power to cause thrombosis. The reason why the pill causes thrombosis in 1 out of 1000 women is that the physical state of the type of organism which that one woman has is the (only) type that satisfies the requisite conditions for the pill to cause thrombosis. If the pill were given selectively to women of this type, the statistics of the activation of the pill's disposition to cause thrombosis would be very different.

6. Causation Is the Mutual Activation of Two (or More) Causal Powers

In thinking about the mutual activation of causal powers, it seems natural or intuitive to think of it as a *transmission* of powerfulness between them. But transmission of

---

[26] Heil too finds a firm normative imperative in the activation of powers, when the circumstances are right, while allowing that circumstances might not facilitate the activation of a power: "Whether various reciprocal powers are on hand at a given time can be probabilistic, but, given the powers at *t*, causings at *t* are thoroughly deterministic." (2012, 125)

power—if we want to use this expression—shouldn't be thought of quantitatively in the account of what takes place in causation. Rather, powers are powerful because they can bring about qualitative change in other powers.

The idea that causation happens because of the passing around or transmission between properties can be traced back to an ancient Greek conception known in the literature as the Contagion Model of causation.[27] But this should not be read quantitatively.[28] Rather, their conception was that what was passed around was a qualitative state originating from the state of the source. Aristotle too talked of transmission between powers, when he talked of the 'form' of the active power being transmitted onto the passive power.[29] But, even for Aristotle, this is a figurative way of describing the mutual activation of powers, not quantitative (see Marmodoro 2013).

On the view I am proposing, the causal partner-powers are mutually activated from potentiality to activity. All there is to their causal 'interaction' is their *mutual and simultaneous manifestation* (e.g. heating and being heated). The power fulfilling the active causal role is activated, while the power fulfilling the passive causal role is activated, and, often, changes as well. There is no exchange between them, no transmission of anything, and no relation bridging the two.

The account I am proposing is thus to be contrasted with the Passing Around Model put forward by Mumford and Anjum (2011). They develop this model as an answer to the Always Packing Argument discussed in section 2.1, and introduce the model thus:

On reflection, the idea of causation as a passing around of powers, especially for a pandispo-sitionalist, starts to look extremely attractive (Mumford 2009a). Some examples will illustrate this. You come in from the cold and sit by the fire. You sit by the fire because it is hot, which for the pandispositionalist means that it has the power to warm your body. Causation occurs when the fire warms your body, changing it from cold to hot. Armstrong retorts that such causation, for pandispositionalism, consists in the mere passing around of powers. In the present case, that would mean that the heat of the fire, which consisted in it having the power to warm some other object, has been passed on to you. But that sounds quite right.

(Mumford and Anjum 2011, 5–6)

The position proposed by Mumford and Anjum is intuitively attractive, but raises a number of questions. How does 'passing on powers' take place, metaphysically? What is the mechanism of the transfer of powers such as, for example, the power to warm another object? It is also not clear, crucially, whether the first object loses the power that is passed on to the second object, or the power is duplicated. Related to the last question, what individuation criteria are in play for the token powers that are passed

[27] For an account of the model in ancient thought with particular reference to Aristotle, see, for example, Scaltsas (1989). The contagion model was also revived in early modern philosophy; see for reference O'Neill (1993, 44).

[28] The ancients experimented with quantitative readings of transmission too, but they were not success-ful or prevalent.

[29] See *Physics* 202a9–11.

on? Finally, how does this account explain what happens, in the case of a vase that breaks, in terms of a power that was passed on to the vase?

More generally, Mumford's and Anjum's proposed model raises the question of whether causation can be adequately accounted for in *quantitative* terms only, as their Passing Around Model appears to suggest. One might think that contemporary physics stirs our intuitions in that direction, offering a *particulate* account of causation in terms of the transfer of particles. To explain how elementary particles 'act' on one another, contemporary physics posits the existence of virtual particles whose role is to be force-carriers. (For our discussion I propose to think of virtual particles as pure quanta of powers, which are passed around from object to object.) Thus, elementary particles (e.g. protons) exert forces on each other by exchanging such virtual particles (e.g. gauge bosons). One might think that, thereby, contemporary physics does away with qualitative change in causation; that by introducing virtual particles to carry forces from particle to particle (e.g. to carry the electromagnetic force, or the weak, or the gravitational forces) contemporary physics has reduced causation to the addition or subtraction of force in the constitution of the particles, thereby eliminating the need to talk of qualitative effects of one particle on another. But this is not the case. Virtual particles of various types interact with one another *qualitatively*, too, and this cannot be accounted for in terms of force-carriers only. For instance, vector mesons can be produced by quark–antiquark annihilation in different *structural* arrangements (see, for example, Green 2003). In such cases, I contend, the constitutional additions or subtractions of particles, through force-carriers or collisions, is not sufficient to account for structural variation. As I understand it, the force-carriers achieve two things. They transfer token quantities of energy from one entity to another; and they bring (through their presence) the first entity in contact with the second. But this is not sufficient to explain qualitative change.

Rather, I submit that transfer of particles is a mechanism for attaining contact between objects, and even for transferring forms of energy from one object to another. But this only *sets up* the problem of causation, of how we get qualitative change from contact, plus more or less energy. Qualitative change is not reducible to quantitative change, although quantitative change can be accounted for as a type of qualitative change.

7. Each Instance of Causation Involves Two (or More) Manifestations

Following Aristotle, I take the view that when two causal partner-powers are mutually activated, their two manifestations occur *simultaneously* in one event, but they are two *different types* of activity. C. B. Martin's account is aligned with the one I am proposing, in that it, too, is Aristotelian, explaining causation through partner-powers that manifest reciprocally and simultaneously. He writes:

There is a surprising identity in causing and affecting. One must take the reciprocity of a reciprocal readiness partnerings as their mutual manifesting seriously and not ask for the action of a single readiness factor because there is no such action. Instead, actions are the reciprocal partnerings of a web or net of readinesses.   (Martin 2008, 22)

It is not a matter of two events, but of one and the same event—a reciprocal dispositional partnering as a mutual manifesting.   (Martin 2008, 46)

But there is an important difference between my Aristotelian account and Martin's. Martin sees the mutual manifestation of two powers as their mutual identification into a single event, and emphasizes that we should not seek to find the activity of a single power in a causing. But is this realistic? Is it true that the two powers *do the same thing*, as Martin (and also among others, Heil, Mumford, and Anjum) appear to think? Many counterexamples are available from our everyday experience: the stove *heats* while the pot *is heated*, the sense organ *hears* while the guitar *sounds*, etc.

8. Active and Passive Causal Roles

That causation has a direction is a generally shared common-sense intuition.[30] The orthodox view on the direction of causation has been that it reduces to the direction of time: causes occur prior to their effects. But the temporal view of the direction of causation has fallen into disfavor of late,[31] again,[32] and a number of alternatives have been suggested.[33] My account of causal agency is an alternative way, to the temporal one, of underpinning causal direction metaphysically. Those accounts of causation that do not draw the distinction between (the roles of) causal agent and patient of change provide no argument in support of their claim that causation needs to be symmetric with respect to the activation of powers; some merely appeal to the frequency in nature of changes that appear to be symmetric, for example Heil (2012):

The received view of causation might lead you to think that the water and the salt are related as agent and patient: the water, or maybe the water's enveloping the salt, causes the salt to dissolve. Perhaps the water possesses an 'active power' to dissolve salt, and salt, a complementary 'passive

---

[30] While there is general agreement that causation has a direction, people do disagree on what underpins metaphysically causal direction. See, for example, Schaffer (2008) for an excellent account of the spectrum of positions.

[31] Shaffer (2008) reckons six main arguments in the literature regarding the relation between the causal and temporal directions, and four conclude that they do not coincide.

[32] The first period of disfavor was brought about by Aristotle's theory.

[33] Other alternatives that Schaffer mentions are: "For instance, that the causal direction is the direction of *forking* (Reichenbach 1956, Horwich 1987, Papineau 1993, Dowe 2000), *overdetermination* (Lewis 1979), *independence* (Hausman 1998), and *manipulation* (von Wright 1975, Price 1991 and 1996, Woodward forthcoming [2003]). On these alternative views, the coincidence of the causal and temporal orders is merely a contingent feature of the actual world, or at least a typical feature of our patch of it" (Schaffer 2008).

power' to be dissolved by water. But look more closely at what happens when you stir salt into a glass of water. Certain chemical features of the salt interact with certain chemical features of the water (Ingthorsson 2002). This interaction is, or appears to be, continuous, not sequential; it is, or appears to be, symmetrical.   (Heil, 2012, 118)

In the case above, water dissolves salt and salt dissolves in water. In disagreement with Heil and Ingthorsson, I don't think that positing a symmetrical interaction between salt and water provides an adequate metaphysical description of what occurs. It is not true that what the water does to the salt and what the salt does to the water are actions of the same type. In the causal interaction of water and salt, polarized water molecules break the bond between the negative chloride ions and the positive sodium ions; whereas salt does not break the water molecules. This is what makes the chemical reaction asymmetrical. Heil's and Ingthorsson's account fails to capture the directionality of the causal process, which is underpinned by the different 'actions' of salt on water and water on salt respectively. The fact that water dissolves salt, but not vice versa, is scientifically informative. It expresses a law of nature. The law is no less informative because it governs an interaction between macro-level entities, such as water and salt, which do not figure at the micro-level (where it is the interactions between the fundamental powers that are operative). Talking of water dissolving salt conveys genuine scientific knowledge. It is the explanatory value in science of such statements about the causal processes in the world that justifies the existence of sciences over and above elementary physics. Chemistry, botany, biology, etc. produce scientific knowledge by discovering and formulating such laws as that water dissolves salt.[34] But as will be seen later in this section, I do not mean to, and should not be taken to be classifying causal asymmetry a macro-phenomenon.

From the asymmetry of causation follows the distinction between active and passive powers involved in a causal interaction.[35] There are various metaphysical differences between mutually manifesting partner-powers that can ground classifying their mutual activation as asymmetric; such metaphysical differences can also ground distinguishing between active and passive roles of powers.

---

[34] One might at this point ask: does water have the power to dissolve salt, or is this only an epiphenomenon of the micro-level powers of water's constituents? My claim is that water does have the power to dissolve salt, *for the same reasons for which we claim that water exists*. There are substances at the macro-level of reality, and these substances have powers. A full defense of this claim cannot be made within the limits of this chapter. But very briefly, consider the counter-intuitive consequence that if there were no substances, physics would be sufficient to explain the phenomena in the world. Can physics really offer adequate accounts for all macro-level phenomena? I do not believe it can, which is why I subscribe to an Aristotelian ontology of substances and their powers.

[35] Regarding the distinction between active and passive powers, as Heil notes, among contemporary metaphysicians, for example, Shoemaker (1980, 1998, 2007) draws a distinction along the same lines when talking of "forward-" and "backward-looking" "conditional powers." The distinction is rooted in a long-standing tradition: Plato (*Theaetetus*); Aristotle (*Physics, De Anima*); Locke (*Essay Concerning Human Understanding*); Leibniz (*Philosophical Essays*).

It follows that I hold that active and passive powers are not by nature such. Powers 'take on' an active or passive causal role when engaged in causal interaction.[36] These causal roles are the roles of the 'doer' and the 'sufferer.' A power is a doer when it is described as doing something on something else; and a sufferer when it is described as suffering the causal activity of another power.[37] As 'doer' and 'sufferer' are roles that powers play, rather than features of their natures, in some cases each causal partner power can be *both active and passive*. Thus for example a power (or its bearer) may be heating while being cooled, and hence changed, at the same time.[38]

From a metaphysical point of view, an important feature that can ground classifying a power as active is if the power is bringing about *change* in another power (or its bearer). If the power's activity brings about change (e.g. in the direction of a particle's spin), then the effect of the power's activity is a new power that is generated in the process. The attribution of active and passive roles is less clear if a power's activity does not bring about change, but the effect is only the activation of another; for example, resting a playing card against another, which activates the resistance and weight of each without changing them. Again the attribution of active and passive roles is less clear if the powers temporarily alter and then recover (e.g. when the repelling powers of two electrons are mutually affected as they approach each other), but recover after they pass one another.

The distinction between active and passive causal roles has been discussed in the literature with such examples as the two playing cards holding each other up (Heil, 2012), or the one of an ice cube in a glass of lemonade (Mumford 2007). On the back of such cases, Heil claims: "Considered ontologically, causes and effects take a back seat to causings. Causing is where the action is." (2012, 120) For Heil, causing is the single manifestation mutual partners achieve in causation. (Recall Martin's "surprising identity," discussed in section 7). Cases such as the two playing cards holding each

---

[36] I develop this view from an Aristotelian insight in *Physics* III 3. Although Aristotle's theory of causation might lead one to believe that there is a metaphysical distinction between active and passive powers, on my analysis of his theory, activity and passivity are roles that powers have in causal processes. In fact, I hold that Aristotle considers this the analysis of causation—namely, it is a *conceptual truth* that a power (or its bearer) that engages in a causal process is *doing* something which is *suffered* by another power (or its bearer).

[37] Can causal powers be activated neither as doers nor as sufferers? Do fundamental powers spontaneously become anything other than what they are? If they did, then this would not be an instance of doing or suffering. I submit that fundamental powers do not spontaneously become other than they are, but are governed by the conditions around them. For instance, alpha decay results from the counterbalancing of the electromagnetic and the nuclear forces; gamma decay results from a nucleus in an excited state, just as photon emission results from an electron that shifts to a lower energy level.

[38] For example, Heil claims that: "Examples of this kind [e.g. two playing cards propped against one another] ... arguably, they are by far the most common species of causal interaction" (2012, 119) and from this concludes that: "The causing here is a reciprocal, symmetrical, continuous affair." (ibid.) I argued above that there are difficulties with Heil's stance, and I here offered an alternative metaphysics for such cases, preserving the important point that causation has directionality. I return to a discussion of Heil's views later in this section.

other up are very common in nature and show that there is no ontological distinction between cause and effect (i.e. between the manifestation of the active power and the manifestation of the passive power). There is only one manifestation for both, and the fact that we call it "dissolving" or "being dissolved" (in the case of salt in water, as Heil sees it) is only a matter of "perspectivalism." He concludes: "The mistake is to allow these epistemological concerns to call the shots ontologically. . . . My suggestion is that a dispassionate look at the ontology of causation takes us to causings, the mutual manifestings of reciprocal powers or dispositions." (2012, 133)

I have argued in this chapter that although the differences between active and passive powers are functional roles powers are allotted in their mutual manifestations with their partners, the grounds for allotting these roles are not epistemological but metaphysical. For example, whether only one of the two powers changes, or changes more than the other, or alters temporarily, etc., can determine whether a power is classified as active or not. My position is that a variety of metaphysical differences between mutually manifesting partner-powers can become the ground of allotting activity or passivity to them, or both.

9. Conclusions

This chapter sketches the main tenets of a new account of the nature of fundamental properties. On the assumption that all properties at the fundamental level of reality are causal powers, the view this chapter advances is this: Reality at the bedrock (that is, at the level of what is physically fundamental) is a network of causal powers which are dependent on each other for their existence and manifestation. The dependence of fundamental powers on partner-powers for their existence and activity does not tease out different levels of fundamentality. The dependencies are horizontal, and do not ground different ontological levels in nature. A power can be in a state of potentiality, or in a state of activation; in the latter state, it co-manifests with its partner power in activities of what they are potentially powers to do. As I mentioned in section 2, I take a manifesting power to be in a state of activity, and thus to have temporal duration, rather than be an instantaneous transition from one power in potentiality to another. On my account, activated powers (e.g. weight) can last in time, because the activation of a power does not require that the power change into a numerically different power. Thus the world consists of powers in potentiality, powers that are going in and out of activity, and powers that are constantly activated in the presence of their partner-powers. The network of the interdependent fundamental powers in potentiality or in activation comprises a structure of powers, which is the ontological foundation of reality. The structure is not constituted of polyadic relations, but monadic relatives, which are the powers. I have derived this view from Aristotelian insights, and I call it *Power Structuralism*.

Acknowledgments

The research results presented in this chapter are part of my ongoing project *Power Structuralism in Ancient Ontologies*, supported by a starting investigator award (number 263484) from the European Research Council. Earlier versions of the chapter were presented in Oxford, the London School of Economics, Innsbruck, and Geneva. I am grateful for the feedback received from the audience on all these occasions. Thanks are also due to this volume's editor and the OUP anonymous readers, who provided very helpful comments on the penultimate draft.

6

Mutual Manifestation and Martin's Two Triangles

Rani Lill Anjum and Stephen Mumford

1. Triggers and Partners

C. B. Martin has offered an alternative to the old stimulus–response model of how to trigger a power. He calls it mutual manifestation. Instead of powers being inert and standing in need of a stimulus in order to act, Martin's new model suggests that powers act when they are matched with their reciprocal disposition partners. We will stick with the terminology of mutual manifestation partnership as this, and how it works, will be the key idea explored in this chapter.

What is the difference between the stimulus–response and mutual manifestation models? The stimulus–response model suggests that powers do nothing without being appropriately pushed to do so. They remain latent, awaiting their stimulus, and unless received such powers will never be exercised. Examples of powers or dispositions and their stimuli are well known. Being dropped triggers the manifestation of fragility; being placed in liquid triggers the manifestation of solubility; and, as an example of a mental disposition, being asked 'Snakker du norsk?' triggers someone's disposition to speak Norwegian, if they have it. The stimulus–response model of how powers reveal themselves should be regarded as problematic by anyone who professes realism about dispositions, especially a pandispositionalist. Powers are rendered impotent by this account. They do not and cannot do anything alone. They are intrinsically powerless, which is of course a perverse outcome for a theory of powers. Instead, they must wait until they are appropriately triggered by the stimulus. Hence, it is the stimulus that appears active and the power itself passive. That will suit some accounts of dispositions, especially those that reduce them away in other terms, such as in the conditional analysis or the categoricalist metaphysic. But realists about dispositions will want their powers to be genuinely powerful rather than inert and active rather than passive. Instead of searching for things done unto them, powers should be what do the doing. Pandispositionalists will in addition object that the account bifurcates reality. All properties should be treated the same and we should not ascribe something to the stimuli—activity—that is not ascribed to the powers. Powers and their stimuli should not be regarded as two different types of entity or quality. It may be possible to resist such a conclusion. Perhaps the stimulus is not qualitatively different from a power. A stimulus might just be the action of a prior power. But then we still have to account for how that prior power came to be stimulated. If we rely on the same stimulus–manifestation model, then the same question arises for it in turn. This is not to say automatically that an infinite regress occurs, but some fancy footwork would be needed to sidestep the danger (see Holton 1999).

How does the mutual manifestation model avoid these problems? In Martin's metaphysics, there is no ontological division between powers and their stimuli. Rather, manifestation arises from equal partnerships. The sugar cube and the liquid are equal partners, for instance, in the production of dissolving. We do not say that one partner is the (passive) power and the other is the (active) stimulus. Each is as active as the other. They produce something together that they could not have produced alone. There is, thus, no qualitative bifurcation of reality. All powers are in the same boat and, for a pandispositionalist, so are all properties. This solves the problems we identified for the stimulus–manifestation model: powers are active and there is no regressive account of their activation. And there is an intuitive appeal in the idea that the partnership is equal too. If one considers ice in a drink, both the ice and the drink seem to be doing things. The drink melts the ice, but the ice cools the drink. Would there be solid grounds for classifying either as active and the other passive? Energy transference theorists of causation might think so, but that would be theory-driven rather than guided by our intuitions (see Fair 1979 and Kistler 2006). Such a debate could be had, but if we are just considering for the moment what we think makes philosophical sense, then the idea of joint and equal partnering of powers seems to have the advantage.

How many partners do we need? Any number will do. In the case of the striking of a match, there may be many that are needed to produce burning. Friction, flammable material, and oxygen all add their powers to produce flame. Why not ten powers or a hundred? Some complex causal processes may indeed involve a vast number. But must there be at least two powers together? Now that we have done away with the idea of powers being passive and standing in need of stimuli, there seems nothing wrong in principle with even a single power doing its work. Some believe that there are spontaneously manifesting powers, radioactive decay being the most obvious purely physical example. We are used to it in the case of persons too; for some of them we describe as spontaneous, meaning that they are liable to get up and do something new for no particular reason. This of course does not count as a partnership, for there are no partners: just single powers. But the metaphysical picture of the mutual manifestation model already allows that powers in groups can produce their effects without any other kind of trigger. Whether we are taking a grouping of powers as our unit, or the unit consists of a single power that really has no further subdivision into components, power(s) is enough to do the work. But is it really enough? Some chemical reactions need catalysts to get going, for instance. On the mutual manifestation view, the catalyst would just be a further power to be added. Until it arrives, we have an incomplete partnering of powers with respect to the particular manifestation that interests us. Once it's there, it's just a further mutual manifestation partner that completes the partnership.

We thus see that Martin's theory of mutual manifestation partners gives us a better model of powers than the stimulus–response model. All partners are equal and active. Rather than thinking that a power is in need of external stimulus to do its work, we should think of powers as being released or unleashed, such as when the water is released from the tap (Mumford and Anjum 2011, 37).

There is more work that could be done to justify Martin's model, but the aim here is not to produce a definitive argument for mutual manifestation as a theory of dispositions. Rather, it is to consider and amend the account of mutual manifestation and possibly of causation that would come from Martin's view.

2. Triangles

Many have thought of there being some connection between powers and causation. Powers are often thought to produce their manifestations. Indeed, this is the reason we think of it as perverse if the stimulus–response model leaves our powers powerless. We will now set that problem aside and go with the idea that powers do indeed produce their manifestations. But how do they do so? And would this give us a theory of causation or of something else?

In his chapter on causation, Martin (2008) says the following:

> You should not think of disposition partners jointly *causing* the manifestation. Instead, the coming together of the disposition partners is the mutual manifestation: the partnering and the manifestation are identical. This partnering-manifestation identity is seen most clearly with cases such as the following. You have two triangle-shaped slips of paper that, when placed together appropriately, form a square. It is not that the partnering of the triangles *causes* the manifestation of the square, but rather that the partnering is the manifestation.
>
> (Martin 2008, 51)

Despite the title of the chapter from which this comes (*Causation*), it is very clear from the quotation that Martin does not see himself as offering a theory of causation in terms of powers. It is, rather, an alternative to causation. If the world is a world of powers, and we have the correct account of manifestation in terms of mutual partnerships, then it seems he is telling us that we would not need causation besides. This is effectively an eliminativism about causation. A world of powers, on the Martin account, is not a world of causation. But how could that be? Martin's suggestion is that the manifestation just is the partnered powers. When they come together, they don't do something to produce the manifestation, they just *are* the manifestation. As two triangles suitably arranged form a square (Figure 6.1), so too the powers suitably arranged are the manifestation.

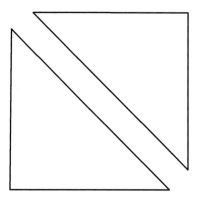

Figure 6.1. Martin's (2008) two triangles

One of the reasons certain philosophers find an ontology of real powers attractive is the work powers can do in one's general metaphysics (Molnar 2003, 186), solving a host of thorny philosophical problems. Causation may be among them. It is without doubt one of the greatest philosophical problems of all. Martin's account of mutual manifestation seems to be offering a relatively simple solution to the problem. It suggests that one only needs powers, suitably arranged, hence manifesting, and one needs no further philosophical theory of causation. Gone would be one of the most difficult and discussed problems in the subject area. How realistic is Martin's ambition?

We will argue that Martin's own model of mutual manifestation is not adequate to account for causation in the eliminativist way that he suggests. But we do not wish to be misunderstood. The project of accounting for causes in terms of powers is one that we fully support (Mumford and Anjum 2011). To succeed, however, the theory requires the correct account of mutual manifestation. Martin's two triangles model suggests that there is no causation over and above the right mereological composition of the component parts or powers. If we look more closely at the composition of causes, however, we see that it is quite implausible to suggest that it would always consist in the mere addition of the component powers. There are more complex rules of composition that can involve interaction and alteration of those powers. Causation can thus involve the production of genuine novelty, which mereology alone does not deliver.

We cannot hope to eliminate the notion of cause from our philosophical lexicon, therefore. The notion that causation brings something to the world, over and above the mere coupling of disposition partners, for instance, remains sound. There are facts of causal production over and above the positioning of powers. This seemed to be a feature of the world that Martin was denying. Nor do we believe that causes are reducible to powers. The notion of a power is a notion of something that is productive: of its manifestations. But production is itself a causal notion (Mumford and Anjum 2011, 8). Our concepts of power and cause thus look too closely connected to allow the prospect of a reductive analysis. We still think that a dispositional theory of causation has much to recommend it. It tells us that dispositions tend towards their effects, for instance, but never necessitate them, even in the cases where they succeed in producing them. And we can take power to be a slightly broader concept than cause, which explains also properties, laws, and events. But this is still a theory; not an analysis.

We will proceed to justify our claim, but there should be one caveat before we do so. It is not clear exactly what Martin intended the scope of his account to be. We offer an eliminativist interpretation of the passage quoted. He urged that in those cases we take it that the partnered powers just are the manifestation: they do not cause the manifestation. This is a theory, as he calls it, of 'partnering-manifestation identity.' One could hold that without being committed to the more ambitious thesis of disposition-partnerings eliminating the concept of causation altogether. Martin could just have been saying that powers do not cause their manifestations: when suitably partnered, they instead are their manifestations. So causation is not found here, but it might be found elsewhere in the world and another account of something else entirely would have to provide it. This would be a far more modest claim on Martin's part. Unfortunately, Martin's account (2008, ch. 5) is insufficiently detailed to allow a definitive interpretation. We cannot be sure that Martin was offering his claim as a bold eliminativist one or the more modest one we have outlined. We suspect the former though accept we may be mistaken. We will nevertheless proceed to consider the ambitious eliminativist thesis while conceding that it might not have been Martin's.

3. Time and Process

We will begin by pointing out two inadequacies of Martin's model for mutual manifestation. We accept that mutual manifestation itself is a better account of how powers come to exercise than is the stimulus–response model, but that should not lead us to think of it yet as perfectly adequate. We have elsewhere (Mumford and Anjum, forthcoming) drawn attention to two ways in which the image of two triangles forming a square is an imperfect analogy. In the first place, when the two triangles are placed together in the right arrangement they form a square instantly. We know, however, that when mutual manifestation partners are brought together it takes time for them to produce their full manifestation. The analogy fails because it suggests that powers produce their manifestations instantaneously.

The relation between powers, causation, and time is a troublesome and contested one. It has become rather orthodox to follow Hume (1978) on this issue and assume that causes are temporally prior to their effects. Martin's account seems an improvement on that, if our aim is to use it as a theory of causation. Partnered powers causally produce their effects and Martin's two triangles analogy suggests that they do so immediately. There is, thus, no temporal gap between the powers coming together— or being together—and the manifestation occurring. The account suggests Hume is wrong, therefore, to commit to temporal priority for causes. We agree that Hume was wrong. We agree that there is no gap in time between powers being suitably partnered and them acting. But that does not tell the full story. Partnered powers may start to act instantly, with no temporal gap, but that does not mean that they have their full effect instantly, as Kant recognized (1921). It often does take time for powers to do their work, even if they start doing so immediately. Hence, the sugar may start to dissolve as soon as it is in contact with the water, but it still takes maybe a minute or so until it is all dissolved. The earth may gravitationally attract a rock that has been rolled over a cliff edge, but it still takes some seconds for the ground and rock to collide. And you may speak Norwegian as soon as you are with fellow Norwegian speakers, but clearly doing so takes time. Indeed, speaking Norwegian is not something that could be done at an instant.

What is happening in such cases? Martin (2008) starts his chapter on causality by criticizing the two-event model of causation. He is right to do so. The account suggests that causation is a relation—one that Hume tells us is impossible to observe—between two events. In its place, we suggest we understand causation as involving continuous processes that are extended through time involving changes of properties. The sugar's dissolving in liquid is one such process. The process may have a beginning and an end, but it is not as if we go straight from one to the other with nothing in between. Rather, the process goes through every intermediate stage between. The soluble and solvent powers, when partnered, issue in a natural process that can run its course, unless it is prevented or interfered with. Similarly, the rock that falls from the cliff, gravitationally attracted by the ground, goes through every space time point (continuum many if space time is dense) before it reaches the ground and rests. And speaking a language, like many other disposition manifestations, has to be process-like. It is necessarily extended through time, for one cannot have spoken a language at just one instant unless that were during such a process of speaking.

It seems that we have independent reasons for thinking that the manifestations of at least some powers are in processes, therefore, quite apart from anything we say about causation. But it can be noted that exactly the same can be said of causation and this gives encouragement to the project of grounding a theory of causation in the exercising of powers. Kant gives us an example. We ignite the stove so as to warm the room. The wood and the flame are brought together to cause heat. They do so immediately. Unlike Hume, Kant was quite ready to allow that causes were simultaneous with their effects: the ball causing a hollow in the cushion upon which it rests being his most famous example (1921, A203). In the stove example, however, Kant notes that it takes time for the stove to have its full effect. It is capable of heating the room to a temperature of 25°C, let us suppose. But it could take an hour for it to do so. Kant's claim of simultaneity of cause and effect is not threatened by this. Simultaneous does not entail instantaneous. The room is heated, and will be so while ever the powers of the flame are exercising, so we have simultaneity, but the whole thing is extended through time.

The analogy is inadequate, then. Martin's example, to accurately reflect the way mutual manifestation works, would have to suggest that the triangles, once together, took time to gradually become a square, through a continuous process of change. Even cases of causation that look to be instant may be like this: it is just that the gradual change is a very quick one. When billiard balls collide, for example, and the cue ball causes the object ball to move, the causation seems to be going on exactly at the time they touch. This may look to be an instant matter, but physical theory tells us that the balls slightly squash into each other and then the object ball springs away. It is too fast for the unaided eye to detect, but it is process-like nevertheless.

4. Emergence

The second way in which Martin's analogy is inadequate is that it fails to allow for the production of genuinely novel phenomena. The status of emergentism is philosophically contentious, it need barely be said, but we do not need even strong emergence to show that there is something inadequate in Martin's model of composition. It seems very implausible to suggest that when we bring two or more powers together then what we are left with is merely a mereological sum of such powers. Instead, some kind of transformation looks to be incontestable.

To see this, one need only look at what happens when powers of things get combined in the sort of way Martin envisages. If we put together the powers of sodium, for instance, with the powers of chlorine, in the sort of way Martin puts together his two triangular cards, we do not get just their sum. It is hard to argue, then, that the partnered powers are identical with the manifestation. Sodium has a power to ignite spontaneously in water. Chlorine is poisonous. As Rothschild (2006, 153) points out, when we bring together these two substances with their various powers, we do not get something that is both poisonous and explosive. Instead, the two substances transform to become sodium chloride, that is, salt: something that has the powers of being soluble, tasty, and in the right quantities to be a contributor to human health. This is no simple mereological sum of the powers of the parts. Some powers of the parts are no longer found in the whole and some powers of the whole are not found among the parts.

Shoemaker (1980) provides another example, which perhaps better illustrates how powers can be put together to form new ones. Hardness is a power to resist deformity and being knife-shaped involves various powers that we need not specify (but Shoemaker indeed thinks this property is a cluster of powers as he is arguing for pandispositionalism in this chapter). Only once we bring together these two distinct powers do we get something new: a power to cut, which each of the constituent powers did not alone have. This gives us a kind of power emergence only insofar as there is a power at the level of the whole that is not to be found in the constituent powers making up that whole.

These examples raise questions of interpretation. It might be alleged that we do not have genuine mutual manifestation in these cases. They really are about the addition or composing of powers and in that sense not really cases of causation. But that is exactly the point. They are not genuine cases of mutual manifestation either. It is not as if these powers are exercising together to produce a manifestation. And what this shows is that Martin's two triangles model of mutual manifestation is on the wrong track. It does not suffice to account for the transformative nature of causation, where partnered powers produce some process of change. When we strike a match, flame is ignited and this seems a genuine change to the extent that you cannot claim a flame is just a suitable arrangement of the powers of friction—when the match is rubbed against the matchbox—and flammability of the match tip. And nor does Martin's model account for the emergent nature of powers through component powers, as in the cases of sodium chloride and the knife's power to cut.

Martin's model instead seems to be one of mereological summing together with some element of spatiotemporal arrangement. There are after all many arrangements in which the two triangles do not form a square. But where they are suitably arranged, there is still arguably no serious transformation occurring of the kind we think is to be found in the mutual manifestations of powers and in causation. The shape of the square is entirely explicable in terms of the shapes of the two parts. No novelty is produced. It is arguable, however, that in cases of causation we do have such novelty. It is as if, to adapt Martin's analogy, our two triangles could come together to form a circle rather than a square. How is that possible? Within the restrictions of Martin's model it is not. But Martin's model assumes that the partnered powers are left unchanged as a result of their partnership. The triangles remain triangles even while they are forming a square. It is only because they remain triangles that they are able to do this. If they turned into hexagons, for instance, they wouldn't be able to. We should focus in the remainder on how this transformation is possible and how it can sit with the theory of powers in general.

5. Nonlinearity

A linear system is one in which an output is proportional to its inputs. Martin's model for mutual manifestation, if the two triangles is a faithful analogy, is a linear system. The area of the square 'produced' is simply the addition of the areas of the two constituent triangles. Addition is a linear function. This would be fine if it were not the case that many causal interactions are nonlinear. The output is not simply the addition of inputs, but would have to be captured by a different and transformative function. If we plot on a graph the causal influence of sunshine on health, for example, we would find that it produced a curve rather than a straight line. Lack of sunshine is very unhealthy. A certain quantity is healthy because it delivers the essential vitamin D that, among other things, protects against cancer. But too much sunshine is again unhealthy because it dries the skin and contains ultraviolet radiation that is a carcinogen. Many causal systems are likely to be nonlinear. We will not speculate as to how many because counting in such cases may be meaningless. Perhaps it is sufficient to say that there are at least some, possibly many, nonlinear causal interactions and Martin's model of mutual-manifestation-as-identity cannot account for them. In other words, and keeping the issue of causation separate, there seem to be cases of mutual manifestation that cannot simply be identity because what is produced is a nonlinear function of the inputted powers.

How can we philosophically explain nonlinearity? We already have hints, but the answer we give will leave us with a problem in relation to our theory of powers, which we address in due course. The way we explain it is in terms of the powers interacting when they are partnered and undergoing a transformation, and it is for this reason that mutual manifestation involves a change that is more than just mereological summing.

Elsewhere, we provide an illustration of how this kind of interaction of powers could occur (Mumford and Anjum, forthcoming). It concerns the volume produced during conversations. A typical conversation between two people would be conducted at around 60 decibels (dB). But we cannot assume that the volume of multiple conversations would simply be the addition of single conversations. If those conversations are held within a confined space, such as a drinks party within a room, then the conversations begin to affect each other. In order to be heard above all the other conversations, one conversing pair might raise their voices and talk at something like 63 to 70 dB, which they would not have done if they were in the room alone. (Note that the decibel scale is itself not additive but logarithmic: a conversation of 70 dB would be around twice as loud as one of 60 dB.) What the illustration shows, then, is that being within a mutual manifestation partnership actually changes the contribution made by one or more of the contributing elements. The noise produced by the whole drinks party is greater than the sum noises of each of the individual conversations had they been conducted in private: because they are brought together in such a way that they start to interact, affecting each other's contributions. Being together and working together affects the output of the parts. We thus have to consider nonlinear systems holistically for they really will produce more (or sometimes less) than the sum of their parts. Martin's two triangles model does not show this as a possibility.

Our example—drinks party conversations—of course involves human agency. The guests of the drinks party want to hear their partners speak and want to be heard by them so they intentionally raise their voices. Many nonlinear systems will not involve conscious agents, however, so will this illustration suffice for the non-mental realm? We claim that it does because even in non-conscious, non-mental systems, the same principle applies: namely that the individual components interact and affect each other's outputs. We give three simple examples, the first from biology and the other two from the non-biological world.

The biological case concerns the watering of plants in a limited space. At first, when we water the seeds, there may be a rapid growth of the plants in response to provision of water. But there comes a point where the plants start to crowd each other out. Their root systems grow and require more water but they are competing with the growing root systems of their neighbors. And the leafy foliage will have grown but will now be competing for light with the leaves of other plants, affecting the ability to photosynthesize. The rate of growth is negatively affected, therefore, such that the same degree of watering starts to produce a diminishing return in terms of growth rate. If we plot growth rate against watering, therefore, we get the curve that is indicative of a nonlinear interaction.

Now two non-biological examples, which concern familiar dispositional properties. The first is the common example of solubility and concerns rate of dissolving. When the sugar is first placed in the liquid, dissolving occurs quickly. But the more sugar goes into solution the more saturated the liquid becomes. The less solvent power the liquid has, therefore, and this slows the rate of dissolution of the remaining solid sugar. Here we have a clear interaction of the powers when they mutually manifest. The solvent changes the sugar by dissolving it—and using up its power of solubility—while the sugar also can exhaust the solvent power of the liquid. Being involved in the mutual partnership thus affects the powers involved. They are not left unchanged as a result of their partnership, as Martin's model suggests. They are transformed. At the end of the process, both powers have spent themselves and we are left with a solute: a substance in solution. A second example concerns the burning of wood. At first, when ignited, the wood burns slowly as the fire takes hold. Then it grows and the subsequent flame and heat produced rise rapidly. But as it does so, it uses up the supply of flammable material that fuels it. The flames gradually die down and the temperature drops. If we plot the heat produced by the fire we get a curve, therefore, and this is precisely because the fire interacts with its fuel, reducing it over time and thus having less to burn. The two mutual manifestation partners—the powers of the fire and its fuel—change as a result of their partnership.

We have an explanation of the nonlinearity of mutual manifestation, therefore, which on our account is also an explanation of how causal systems can be nonlinear, and if correct this is enough to show us why Martin's account of mutual manifestation is inadequate. But there remains a problem. It could be argued that there is a price for this account because it appears to be inconsistent with a central tenet of disposition theory, namely that the identity of a power is determined by its manifestation. We will now proceed, therefore, to tackle this problem and we believe there is a solution.

6. Contribution and Identity

The identity of a power appears to be determined by its manifestation. Thus, it is that a power's manifestation is dissolving that makes the power solubility, it is that a power's manifestation is stretching that makes the power elasticity, and it is that a power's manifestation is jumping that makes it the power to jump. The latter example makes the point apparent. All powers are power *to* something. In well-known and commonplace examples we have a specific term for the power, such as fragility and solubility, where it is through knowing the concept that we understand what it is a power towards. But in other cases we don't have a specific term and then have to use the explicit dispositional vocabulary, calling it a disposition to *x* or a power to *y*, where the values of x and y determine the identity of the disposition. There are yet other cases where the manifestation type is even further hidden and would require some theoretical basis to understand, as in the cases of spin, charge, and mass. And there are cases such as being spherical that are, according to the pandispositionalist, powers, but where the manifestations towards which they dispose requires some work to find out, perhaps involving experimentation to discover.

The claim that the identity of a power is determined by its manifestation now faces two challenges, however. The first comes from the claim of polygeny: that effects are typically produced by many powers working together (Molnar 2003, 194). The second comes from nonlinearity, if the account we offered above is accurate, in which powers seem to change each others' manifestations. We will now explain how it is possible to retain the thesis that the identity of a power is fixed by its manifestation while accepting both polygeny and nonlinearity.

The problem created by polygeny is that most effects are typically produced by many different powers acting together, which is of course entirely consistent with a notion of mutual manifestation. Hence, the lighting of the match is caused by the flammable tip of the match, the fueling of the oxygen, the friction of the sandpaper, the dryness of the wood, and so on. But polygeny then threatens our claim that the manifestation determines the identity of the power because one of those powers—the friction of the sandpaper, for instance—could when combined with a different set of powers produce a different effect. The friction could wear down the rough surface of a piece of wood, for instance. It looks, therefore, as if the same power can produce different manifestations dependent upon the circumstances: which other powers it is partnered with.

Molnar, in seeing the pervasive nature of polygeny in causation, realized that this could pose a problem. It looks like the same power could produce lots of different effects depending on the situation within which it is placed. But Molnar also saw a way of avoiding this unpalatable conclusion. We should understand the manifestation of a particular power not to be the final effect that is produced for in the cases that cause us problems these are effects our original power can only produce with the cooperation of a number of other powers. Rather, the manifestation of the first power should be understood as a contribution towards the effect that the whole set of powers causes. And Molnar is then able to claim that the same power makes exactly the same contribution to any effect of which it is a part of the cause (2003, 194–6).[1] This solution has the disadvantage that it introduces a third element into the story: there will now be the power, its contribution/manifestation, and the final polygenic effect. But the third element seems inevitable once one accepts the polygeny of effects, as it seems one must, and equating the manifestation of a power with its contribution towards the effect has the distinct advantage that we can still allow the identity of a power to be fixed by its manifestation.

---

[1] For a more explicit discussion of the problem, see Mumford (2009a, 102–6).

Our discussion and revisions of Martin's account of mutual manifestation has now raised a further problem, however, which comes from the acceptance of nonlinear interactions. We could say that powers make exactly the same contributions to effects no matter which other mutual manifestation partners they are with. But we argued above that causation can be nonlinear and then we explained nonlinearity in terms of the contributing powers affecting each other. This, when we filled out the account, involved the powers mutually affecting each others' contributions. The output of a power—its manifestation—was altered as a result of its partnership. So where, then, does that leave the claim that a power's identity is fixed by its manifestation and its corollary that the same power will always make the same contribution to any causal situation of which it is a part?

Fortunately, it is possible to provide a solution that satisfies all our requirements. What we suggest, for meeting all our theoretical requirements while also being empirically plausible as an account of how powers compose, is that the identity of each power is given by its manifestation type. This will remain consistent for a power even if it is involved in a nonlinear causal interaction. What would alter in nonlinear cases of mutual manifestation would be the degree to which the power is manifested.

As a theoretical background to the making of this move, we should say that there is already a strong case for taking powers to be gradable (Manley and Wasserman 2007) and causation to be scalar (Moore 2003, 71). We take it that both powers and their effects can come in degrees. They have a magnitude: they are quantifiable. Hence, the power of elasticity is not merely elasticity *simpliciter* but, rather, anything that is elastic will have elasticity of some degree. Similarly for the manifestations of those powers. Elasticity can manifest itself in stretching, but the exact degree to which something stretches can vary according to the conditions and other mutual manifestation partners. The degree to which elasticity is manifested may thus vary, perhaps within a range that has an upper limit. Being heated will alter the degree to which something is elastic, for instance. Allowing such variation in magnitude clearly does not threaten the kind of identity condition that concerned us. We can still say that the manifestation-type fixes what the power is—whether it is fragility, attraction, spin, flammability, and so on—and then allow that the degree of manifestation is dependent on the mutual manifestation partnership in which the power participates. And this will be designed to include those nonlinear cases where the degree of manifestation is determined through interaction with other mutual manifestation partners. We contend, therefore, that the problems created by polygeny and nonlinearity can be answered without any damage to the theory of dispositions. Indeed, the powers ontology provides a rather attractive account of these issues.

7. Reckoning

We are now in a position to make a final reckoning and to summarize our findings. We argued that the notion of mutual manifestation—as an account of how powers come to be exercised—is a significant advance over the stimulus–response model. However, we need the correct account of mutual manifestation. Martin has given us the basic idea and he illustrated it with an analogy of two triangles forming a square. This, we said, was inadequate as it failed to accommodate some significant features of mutual manifestation. These features are also to be found in causation, which is significant for those of us who think that powers are a basis for causes. Partnered powers issue in processes that take time, we said, whereas Martin's illustration suggests that partnered partners are identical with their effects. We also said this was implausible for reasons we classified as emergentist. Resultant powers do not seem to be the mere mereological sum of their components. Third, we noted that mutual manifestation partnerships can result in nonlinear interactions and this suggests there is a genuine transformation in the production of a manifestation. We have just shown in the previous section that we can allow that interacting partnered powers can change the degree to which they manifest a power rather than change in their manifestation type.

If we are to sum up the problem with Martin's model of mutual manifestation we would say that it shows us something that is more like mereology than like causation. Martin urges that we do not think of partnered powers as causing their manifestation, but instead as being identical with their manifestation. Given what we have argued above, we think that this is precisely the point on which Martin is wrong. We should indeed think of the mutual manifestation as being caused by the component powers working together. To do so is to allow that powers produce something, which may be novel and a transformation of its causes into something else. There is no reason to resist such an image of the world.

7

Real Modalities

John Heil

1. Modal Modesty

We inhabit a universe pregnant with possibility. I can say with confidence that the gutters on my house might overflow during the next thunderstorm, but they could not be dislodged from the eaves by less than gale-force winds. If the houseplants are not watered, they would certainly die, and, were they to die, their leaves would turn brown and fall off.

Often in speaking thus, we mean only to be placing bets on how things are likely to turn out. Sometimes, however, we take ourselves to be saying something about what really *is* possible (even if not actual), what is not possible, what is inevitable, what *would* or *would not* happen were certain conditions to obtain: we take ourselves to be saying something about how matters stand *modally*. When this is our aim, what features of the universe are responsible for the truth or falsity of what we say?

I shall offer reasons for thinking that an ontology of interrelated powers or dispositionalities provides the resources requisite for an accounting of real modalities, truthmakers for important modal truths. Consideration of these reasons will, in addition, disclose surprising connections between dispositionality, on the one hand, and, on the other hand, causation and causal laws as these are commonly understood in philosophy.

My approach to these topics assumes 'modal fallibilism,' assumes we could be wrong in our modal beliefs. Fallibilism stands in contrast to the idea that we are in a position to discern possibilities from the armchair. We philosophers have lost sight of fallibilism, largely, no doubt, owing to the near universal acceptance of the apparatus of 'possible worlds' in discussions touching on modality.[1] It is easy to concoct alternative universes, universes that differ from the universe we inhabit in any respect we please.

---

[1] An important source for conceptions of possible worlds is the medieval thesis that an omniscient God could create any logically possible universe (see e.g. Grant 1974, 45–50). What is possible is what is logically possible, and what is logically possible is ascertainable a priori. Presently I shall suggest that there are good reasons to suppose that familiar conceptions of causal laws are traceable to the same source.

But what gives us the right to assume that any of these alternatives *are* genuinely possible?

Fallibilism treats modal truths as mind-independent, presuming that they reflect ways the universe could be, not merely our capacity to invent alternative universes. The question then is, what are the ways in question, what are the truthmakers for modal truths?

Progress on this topic will be hampered so long as we insist on framing answers in terms of received conceptions of laws and causation. Achieving clarity on these topics will reveal important connections among ontological categories widely taken to be independent. Although I do not anticipate agreement on all I have to say in what follows, I am hopeful that revisiting the historical roots of some of the doctrines we nowadays take for granted might lead to a heightened appreciation of the substantive nature of those doctrines, hence the extent to which each stands in need of a substantive defense.

2. Laws

Everyone—*almost* everyone—agrees that laws of nature are central to the scientific enterprise. But what exactly *are* laws? The thought that objects are governed by laws did not fall from the sky. A glance at the history of science[2] reveals that talk of laws of nature stems from late medieval considerations of God's omnipotence and the divine will, considerations aggressively promoted by the Church as replacements for an Aristotelian picture of nature as wholly self-governing. On the Aristotelian model, things behave as they do, not because they are governed by laws, but because they are as they are.

The alternative is to suppose that how things behave is not up to the things, but depends on something outside and independent of the things, on God's will, for instance, a will constrained only by principles of logic and God's benevolent nature. With the encouragement of the Church, a conception of a contingent universe, one universe among endless possible—because logically possible—universes, a universe administered by a divine lawmaker, became the default.

Two components of this conception stand out.

First, laws, God's decrees, are *external* to what they govern. It is no part of the nature of objects subject to the laws that objects with those natures behave as they do. Laws are independent of the character of objects over which they preside. God creates the objects and, in a distinct exercise of will, enacts the laws. Think of laws as

---

[2] As historically informed readers will quickly discover, my discussion of laws omits many important qualifications. My aim is not purely historical, however, but philosophical. For historical discussion see Grant (1974, 1981); Ruby (1986); Des Chene (1996); and Milton (1998). See van Fraassen (1989, 1–14) and Roberts (2008, ch. 1) for contemporary discussion.

expressions of God's nature, freely chosen principles on which God imposes His will on material bodies.[3]

Second, God, being omnipotent, *could* have willed that the laws be otherwise. The laws are, in this regard, contingent. God's power includes the power to create alternative universes, universes altogether different from the actual universe in every logically possible way.

In discussing the nature of laws today, mention of God's decrees sounds, well, *medieval*. The interesting point is that, although a conception of laws as contingent and external to what they govern had its source in contentious theological considerations, the demise of those considerations did not result in the demise of the conception. Philosophers altogether lacking in allegiances to Church doctrine are nevertheless happy to embrace a picture of the world according to which objects are governed by external, contingent laws. But if laws are not expressions of God's will, if laws are not God's decrees, what *are* they? Minus God, what could it mean to say that particles, for instance, are 'governed by' or 'obey' laws? Philosophers serious about metaphysics, have sought to answer this question by offering an assortment of God replacements.

Hume, an honest, if occasionally devious, ontologist, recognized that subtracting God from the picture was not merely a matter of adjusting a detail, it was in effect to forsake the picture. The subtraction of God meant abandonment of the idea that laws *govern*. Laws, Hume contends, are nothing more than true generalizations. This *F*'s being a *G* is an instance of a law, just in case all *F*'s are *G*'s.

Humeans of various stripes dominated the philosophical landscape of the twentieth century. Many influential philosophers were happy to embrace Hume's picture, pretending it to be metaphysically innocent. Others, David Armstrong for instance, endeavored to graft an element of necessity onto the Humean conception and thereby to resuscitate the governing character of laws (see, for example, Armstrong 1997). Laws, according to Armstrong, are higher-order universals of the form $N(F, G)$: the *F*'s necessitate the *G*'s. The obtaining of this law guarantees the truth of the corresponding Humean universal generalization—all *F*'s are *G*'s—but not vice versa.[4]

This treatment of laws upholds two central components of the theological picture. First, Armstrong's laws are *external* to what they govern. There is nothing in the *F*'s and *G*'s themselves that would require the *F*'s to necessitate the *G*'s. Returning to a theological idiom, God's creation of the first-order universals, the *F*'s and the *G*'s, in no respect constrains God's choice of which higher-order, necessitating universals

---

[3] There are two ways God might intervene in the course of nature. God might change the objects in some way, thereby affecting their capacities for action, or God might actively manipulate the objects. The latter, late medieval early modern conception is what I have in mind here.

[4] One immediate difficulty for any Humean conception of laws, including Armstrong's, is that universal generalizations taken to be implied by laws are rarely true. Nancy Cartwright has made much of the apparent fact that, taken as universal generalizations, even 'strict' laws of physics evidently 'lie' (Cartwright 1983; Cartwright 1999).

to create. Second, Armstrong's laws are *contingent*. Alternative universes include alternative distributions of higher-order universals.

Another approach to laws, recently championed by Marc Lange, explicates laws in terms of subjunctive and counterfactual conditionals (Lange 2009). If you want to know what laws physicists, or chemists, or biologists accept, look for the subjunctive and counterfactual judgments they embrace and exhibit an unwillingness to revise.

Lange's approach might well serve as a guide to *which* laws are accepted, but it remains curiously detached from the question as to what the truthmakers might be for those subjunctive and counterfactual conditionals. Invoking contrary-to-the-fact facts here would be ontologically evasive and ultimately unsatisfying.

Return to the original theological picture. That picture was meant to replace a broadly Aristotelian conception of the universe. On the Aristotelian conception, things do what they do owing to their various natures. Such a conception distances God from natural occurrences and, worse in the eyes of the Church, challenges God's omnipotence. If being an apple is a matter of being an object of a particular sort disposed to behave in particular ways in particular circumstances, God loses control of apples once He creates them. In electing to create objects of particular sorts, God would thereby elect to create objects with particular sorts of power, particular sorts of disposition to do this or that with particular sorts of reciprocal partner.[5] Any intervention in the natural order would require tampering with the nature of the objects—hence changing the very objects—affected. Left to itself, nature takes a definite course, unfolding with a kind of inevitability sharply at odds with the theological vision.

Removing powers from the objects and placing them in God solves the problem. Objects do as they are told, and what they are told depends exclusively on God's will. God might will any object to do anything at all consistent with the dictates of logic. Objects are governed, not by their own natures, but by external factors.[6]

It is one thing, however, to strip the objects of their powers and cede the powers to God, another matter altogether subsequently to delete God from the picture. Doing so leaves the objects waiting for Godot.

Once you abandon the idea that power resides exclusively in God, an obvious move would seem to be to return powers to the objects. Objects behave as they do, not because they are at the mercy of God's will. Objects do not wait passively to be set in motion. Objects behave as they do because they are as they are. What I have been calling the 'behavior' of objects would be better thought of as mutual manifestings of reciprocal dispositions: dispositions possessed by the objects. The manifestings of dispositions are wholly 'deterministic.' Simple Humean generalizations fail owing to vast complexities that come into play whenever objects interact.

---

[5] I use 'power' and 'disposition' interchangeably.

[6] Although my comments might suggest that powers were abandoned universally, powers were never in fact altogether abandoned. Aristotelian ideas survived until the scientific revolution and beyond.

You might sum this up by describing a position according to which objects are governed by laws as one in which there is a distinction between what something *is* (an apple, an electron, a black hole) and what it does or would do. The alternative is a conception according to which what something is determines—because it is inseparable from—what it does or would do in particular circumstances.

Suppose this is on the right track. Suppose powers—dispositions—are housed in the objects, suppose properties of objects dispose those objects to behave in various ways with various reciprocal disposition partners. Does this mean that we have dispensed with laws?

When scientists invoke laws they seem often to have in mind formulae, equations, principles. These are what Armstrong would call 'law statements,' statements that, if true, are made true by laws themselves, non-linguistic denizens of the universe. However, even philosophers who profess agreement with Armstrong on this point occasionally slip and speak of laws as being true or false (see, for example, Bird 2007a). Philosophers debate whether Newton's laws are true, for instance, or approximately true, or flatly false. This makes it sound as though laws are what I have suggested they are, formulae, equations, principles.

But if laws are formulae, equations, principles, what makes laws true when they are true? Here is one possibility. Laws, some laws, 'causal laws,' isolate the contribution powers or dispositions make to their possessors.[7] Take Newton's laws of motion. These might be thought to provide an accounting of the contribution mass makes to objects possessing mass. In that way, the laws tell us—indirectly—how objects would behave *qua* 'massy.' To be sure, objects with mass possess, as well, various other dispositions. How an object behaves in any given situation will depend on its ensemble of dispositions and on dispositions belonging to whatever interacts with the object.

3. Causation

Serious discussion of the ontology of powers and dispositionality has in recent years re-entered the philosophical mainstream.[8,9] Owing perhaps to a lingering Humean distrust of powers, philosophers have tended to flesh out conceptions of powers using resources afforded by prevailing models of causation and laws. The results have been uninspiring and ontologically tentative. We start with a worldview according to which

---

[7] The idea that laws tell us how 'idealized' objects would behave in 'idealized' circumstances could be seen as a special case of this conception.

[8] Material in this and the next three sections is based on Heil (2012, ch. 6).

[9] C.B. Martin (1993b; 1994; 1997; 2008) and Stephen Mumford (see e.g., Mumford 1994, 1998, and, most recently, Mumford and Anjum 2011) have been at the forefront in the revival of interest in powers. See also Ellis (2001), Molnar (2003), Bird (2007a) and essays contained in Handfield (2009) and Marmodoro (2010b). The position developed here has points of contact with these authors, but it differs from theirs in substantial respects. Thus, although my target in this chapter includes philosophers who have remained largely skeptical of powers, some of what I have to say bears directly on competing conceptions of powers and their relation to laws and to causation. See Heil (2003, chs. 8–11), Heil (2005, 2012).

objects are obedient subjects in a realm of laws. We then stir powers into the mix. But adding powers requires fundamental changes in the way we think about laws, about causation, and, in the end, about modality. Returning powers to the objects brings with it a package of interrelated commitments that philosophers have tended to evaluate piecemeal.

Take causation. On the received view, causation is an asymmetrical, nonreflexive relation among events. Some event, one billiard ball's striking another, causes a distinct event, a second billiard ball's rolling, or its rolling in a particular way. The whole affair reeks of contingency. It is easy to imagine a universe in which the second billiard ball fails to roll, rolls in a different manner, or, as Hume helpfully suggests, leaps off the table.

Consider a different case. You stir a spoonful of sugar into a cup of hot tea and the sugar dissolves. Sticking with the received view, the tea, or the tea's enveloping the sugar, causes the sugar to dissolve. The tea is the agent, the sugar the patient. Perhaps the tea has an 'active' or 'forward-looking' power to dissolve sugar, the sugar a 'passive,' 'backward-looking' power to be dissolved by tea (see Shoemaker 1980, 2001, 2007, 2011). At any rate, this is how it looks when you graft powers onto the received model of causation.

But look more closely at what happens when you stir sugar into a cup of tea. Chemical features of the sugar *interact with* chemical features of the tea (Ingthorsson 2002). This interaction is, or appears to be, continuous, not sequential; it is, or appears to be, symmetrical. Both the sugar and the tea work in concert to yield a certain result: the sugar's being dissolved in the tea.

One way to understand such cases would be to imagine that sugar and hot tea possess reciprocal powers or dispositions.[10] The sugar's dissolving is a *mutual manifestation* of dispositions of the tea and sugar. The result is something—sweetened tea—with new powers, new dispositions capable of further mutual manifestations with further reciprocal disposition partners.

We are trained to think of causation sequentially: a cause occurs, followed by an effect. In the case under consideration, the effect—the sugar's being dissolved in the tea—is the outcome of a dispositional process that is itself continuous and symmetrical.

Take two playing cards and prop them against one another so they stand upright on the table. The cards—with the help of the table—are mutually supporting: they remain upright. The cards work in concert with the table, the gravitational field, and assorted disposition partners to produce this result. But their working together and the result are not sequential. The cards' remaining upright is a continuous mutual manifesting of reciprocal powers possessed by the cards and the table.

Examples of this kind do not fit comfortably with the received model, yet, arguably, they are by far the most common species of causal interaction. We all depend for

---

[10] See Martin (1993b, 2008) and Martin's contribution to Armstrong et al. (1996); Heil (2003, 2012).

our existence on stable structures that we inhabit, move about in and on, and deploy. We count on our environment's maintaining a high level of stability. Stability would be impossible without massive cooperation, the mutual manifesting of countless reciprocal dispositions to hold things together, to preserve the status quo. Their holding together is an outcome, but one that temporally coincides with their manifesting themselves as they do. Causation in this case is a reciprocal, symmetrical, continuous affair.

What of familiar causal sequences commonly deployed to motivate the event-causation model? Return to the billiard balls. One billiard ball approaches another, stationary, billiard ball. The balls collide. The second billiard ball moves off in a particular way. This sequence can be described as one in which one event, the first billiard ball's striking the second, causes a distinct event, the second billiard ball's rolling across the table, but such a description is unperspicuous. When the first billiard ball makes contact with the second, *both* balls compress, then decompress. The trajectory of *both* balls is altered. This process is, or appears to be, continuous, symmetrical, reciprocal (Heumer and Kovitz 2003). Its outcome is a change in the velocity of *each* ball. This outcome resembles the outcome in the sugar and tea case. It results from a mutual manifesting of dispositions. In the playing card case, the outcome is simultaneous with the manifesting.

4. Dispositions

Several points here are worth emphasizing. First, manifestings are most often mutual manifestings of *many* reciprocal disposition partners. We are inclined to omit mention of most of these in our descriptions, relegating them to the status of 'background' conditions. This practice is unobjectionable in cases in which our interest lies in singling out particular aspects of an occurrence in assessing responsibility for particular outcomes (a spark, not the presence of oxygen, caused the fire), or in determining what you would need to add on a particular occasion to achieve a particular outcome (a charged battery, not a fully functioning drive train). But this way of talking cuts no ontological ice. Any outcome, even the status quo, turns on the cooperation of multitudinous reciprocal dispositions.

Second, the status quo is not a matter of dispositions waiting docilely to be manifested. The status quo is itself an ongoing mutual manifesting of countless dispositions, indeed many of the same dispositions that manifest themselves in new ways with the advent of new reciprocal partners.

Third, to the extent that it might be correct to recast causal sequences as mutual manifestings of reciprocal dispositions, it is important to see that one and the same kind of disposition is capable of manifesting itself differently with different kinds of reciprocal partner. Failure to appreciate this point has led to confusion in recent discussions of dispositions.

A ball's sphericality disposes the ball to roll. But it is also, in virtue of being spherical, that the ball is disposed to make a concave, circular impression in the carpet, and disposed to reflect light so as to look spherical. Rylean talk of single- and multi-track dispositions is confused from the outset. Dispositions, quite generally, are 'multi-track,' if this means that they would manifest themselves differently with different kinds of reciprocal partner. If you start with the thought that the diversity we find in the universe stems from varying combinations of a comparatively small number of different kinds of fundamental entity, then you will want dispositions to be capable of diverse manifestations with diverse kinds of reciprocal partner.

Philosophers who have been attracted to an ontology of dispositions sometimes characterize dispositions as features of objects that manifest themselves in a particular way given a particular kind of 'trigger' or 'stimulus.' Alexander Bird (2007a), for instance, takes a disposition, D, to be characterizable by reference to a manifestation, M, resulting from D's being stimulated by S:

$$S \rightarrow D \rightarrow M$$

Note, first, how poorly this way of thinking about dispositions fits with the examples discussed earlier, with, for instance, sugar's dissolving in a cup of tea. You have sugar, tea, and the sugar's dissolving. Where do you locate D? In the sugar? In the tea? And where is S? Is S the sugar, the tea, or something else?

Second, observe that dispositionality is being characterized causally. But by now it should be clear that this puts the cart before the horse. Once dispositions are on the scene, you have the resources needed to make sense of causation. Reversing the order of explanation requires pairing dispositionality with conceptions of causation and laws that have a role only in a universe stripped of dispositionality.

Third, note that by individuating dispositions Bird's way, you are bound to over-count. Suppose one and the same disposition manifests itself one way with one kind of reciprocal partner and another way with a different kind of partner. This, I think, is the norm, although it altogether eludes the individuative scheme implicit in the idea that a disposition can be pinned down in the manner suggested by Bird.

So where are we? The reinstatement of powers in the objects mandates a rejiggering of the prevailing conception of causation, a conception that had been tailored to a picture of a universe comprising passive objects governed by laws. It remains to be seen how dispositionality could yield an account of modality, the topic featured in the title of this chapter. One route from dispositionality to modality runs through causal indeterminacy.

5. Nondeterministic Causation

If you thought of causation as a relation among distinct events, and if you thought that there were more to causation than the correlation of types of event, you would want an account of the causal nexus.[11] What might it be for a cause to *bring about* its effect? One option would be to build *necessitation* into laws governing types of event. The C's necessitate the E's when there is a law to that effect. One selling point for such a view is that it makes it easy to understand cases of nondeterministic or probabilistic causation. You have probabilistic causation when the Cs (merely) make probable—or raise the probability of—occurrences of Es. In fact, it might be thought that you could understand *all* causation probabilistically. Deterministic cases are just those in which the probability of a C's causing an E is unity.

A conception of this kind is plausible, however, only so long as you think of laws as external to whatever they govern. The law manages somehow to ensure that Es occur in tandem with Cs with a certain probability. Once you relinquish this picture, however, matters are less clear. Suppose sugar were disposed to dissolve in tea, but only with a certain probability. This is, in fact, most likely *true* given that numerous additional factors are required for a dissolving. Pretend that it is not so, however, pretend that cases in which sugar fails to dissolve are not due to the presence—or absence—of some further factor, some 'hidden variable.'

Now consider a case in which the sugar *does* dissolve. Remember: we are pretending that the circumstances are *exactly the same* in cases in which the sugar dissolves and those in which it does not. In what way is a dissolving a *manifestation* of dispositions of the tea and the sugar? The dissolving *occurs*, but in what way are dispositions of the tea and sugar *responsible* for its occurring? When the sugar dissolves, in what way do the pertinent dispositions *produce* or *bring about* the dissolving?

If you feel nothing here, if you are not gripped by the problem, what I have said will not much matter. But if, like me, you *are* moved by the problem, if you regard it as close to unintelligible that in one case A and B occur without an occurrence of C and in another case A and B occur and are fully *responsible* for an occurrence of C, A and B *bring about* C, you will regard the production of C by A and B as deeply mysterious. *Laws* can be formulated in a probabilistic idiom, but the notion of probabilistic or nondeterministic causing or manifesting looks hopeless. There are probabilities of there *being* a particular kind of manifesting, perhaps, but not probabilistic manifestings.

The cognoscenti will scoff. Physics provides ample reason to think that the universe is not deterministic. This is not a matter of the occurrence of inconsequential micro-events that tend to 'cancel out' at the 'macro level.' Nondeterministic micro-processes can have cosmic outcomes. This suggests that, whatever effete philosophical qualms I or anyone else might have, we are going to need a working conception of nondeterministic causation.

The question is not whether the universe is deterministic, however. It certainly seems not to be. The question is where precisely to *locate* nondeterministic occurrences. One possibility is that causality—the manifesting of dispositions with reciprocal dispositional partners—itself is or can be nondeterministic. But this is not

---

[11] Topics addressed in this section are treated in more detail in Heil (2013, 2016).

the only possibility and, if my gut instincts are right, it is not a coherent possibility at all.

Begin with the idea that various occurrences are irreducibly nondeterministic: the decay of a radium atom, for instance. There is a certain probability that the atom will decay over a particular period of time. Probabilities are invoked in these cases, not owing to our ignorance of factors affecting the atom's decay. There are no such factors, no hidden variables. A propensity for spontaneous decay is, rather, built into the nature of the atom. You could think of the atom's decaying as the manifesting of a disposition the manifestation of which requires no reciprocal partner. Alternatively, when the atom decays, nothing *causes* it to decay. The atom decays *spontaneously*.

Suppose the atom is harnessed to a device that would ignite an explosive charge were the atom to decay, and suppose the atom decays, thereby causing the device to ignite the charge. The mistake would be to think that the atom's decaying introduces an attenuated kind of causation, *probabilistic* or *nondeterministic causation*. Doing so would be to mislocate the nexus of indeterminacy. There is no saying *when* the atom will decay. The atom's decay, when it occurs, is spontaneous, uncaused. But when the atom *does* decay, its manifesting itself as it does in concert with the explosive device, the surrounding oxygen, the gravitational field, and perhaps much else, is wholly deterministic, deterministic through and through.

The important point here is that, if you introduce spontaneous elements into an otherwise deterministic system, you introduce proliferating contingencies. The atom decays on Tuesday, but it might not have. This truth is made true by the nature of the atom. The charge's being ignited on Tuesday is contingent, its contingency traceable to the atom's spontaneous decay.

Contingency aside, what of non-spontaneous, *deterministic* manifestings? As a preliminary, let me point out that, just as it would be a mistake to attempt to explicate dispositionality in terms of causal necessitation, so it would be a mistake to set out to explicate the determinism exhibited by the manifestings of dispositions modally, to explicate it by reference to necessitation. Do the dispositions involved in the dissolving of sugar in tea necessitate the dissolving? The dispositions could all be on hand, yet the dissolving fail to occur owing to the presence of some further disposition, one that 'blocks' or 'diverts' this manifestation. Does this mean that the presence of the pertinent dispositions plus the *absence* of blocking dispositions necessitates the dissolving? Or perhaps the dispositions necessitate their manifestations *ceteris paribus*.[12]

The moral to draw from the difficulty of analyzing manifestings in modal terms is not that there is something fishy about dispositionality, or that dispositions manifest themselves as they do only *ceteris paribus*, but that it would be a mistake to set out to characterize dispositionality modally. Rather than explicating dispositionality by reference to necessitation, then, I would prefer to think that claims about possibility

---

[12] Some readers will recognize that the problem here parallels the problem associated with attempts to craft counterfactual analyses of dispositions.

and necessity, modal claims, are made true by the dispositional structure of the universe (an exception being claims as to the modal status of the universe itself). Here is one way it might go.

Spontaneity aside, the manifesting of a disposition with its reciprocal partners is fully deterministic: if you have the right dispositions standing in the right relations, you have the manifestations. The universe unfolds continuously, gaplessly. The appearance of gaps and diversions results from the interrelatedness of dispositions. We expect sugar to dissolve in tea, but its doing so requires extensive cooperation on the part of the surrounding atmosphere, the gravitational field, and the like. Manipulate these, mix in a new element, and you change the manifestation.

Although manifestings involve continuous, simultaneous interactions of dispositions, they can be temporally extended. A dynamic process unfolds over time. Such a process might be relatively uninteresting, as for instance, the body of your automobile's retaining its strength and rigidity over the years, or a comet's orbiting the sun, or more exciting, as in the heating of a kettle of hot water, or the collapse of a star. You could think of processes as comprising sequences of manifestings, each member of the sequence being a manifesting of previous members.

6. Antidotes, Blockers, Finks, and Absences

Return to those cases in which a particular manifestation is 'blocked' or 'diverted'. On the view I am recommending, talk of 'blockers', 'antidotes', and 'finks' is perspectival. Such terms introduce what Descartes called 'extrinsic denominations'. Reflect again on attempts to distinguish causes from 'background conditions'. If a 'background condition' is required for a given occurrence, it is part of the cause of that occurrence. Conditions are relegated to the 'background' only because everyday talk about causation is bound up with talk of responsibility and with pragmatic constraints on explanation. We say that the lit match, not the oxygen, caused the fire, but this is only because the oxygen is presumed present anyway; it would be pedantic to include it in an explanation of the occurrence of a fire.

What occurs when a 'blocker' or 'antidote' is on the scene is not the prevention of a manifestation, but the occurrence of a *different* kind of manifestation. You swallow a poison pill and the poison, in concert with your digestive juices, issues in a particularly unwelcome kind of manifestation. If you take an antidote immediately after swallowing the pill, the antidote 'blocks' the operation of the poison. In this case, 'blocking' amounts to the facilitation of a different kind of manifestation. Details depend on how the antidote works. The antidote might alter the pill's chemistry so as to render it harmless in your system; or it might modify your digestive tract so that the mutual manifestation of its features with features of the pill is physiologically benign. In both cases, the upshot is an ensemble if dispositions issuing in a particular kind of manifestation.

The same point applies to absences and privations. An absence of iron causes anemia. This does not mean that an absence, a privation, a nothing, exerts itself in a way that diminishes red cell counts. Rather, diminished red cell counts are what you get when you have a dispositional makeup that does not include iron. *That* makeup issues in the production of blood with fewer red cells by volume of blood than would a dispositional makeup that included iron.[13]

When you have the dispositions appropriately related, you have their manifestations. Particular manifestations can be blocked, or prevented or diverted, but that is just to say that they can be blocked or prevented or diverted from manifesting themselves in a particular way owing to the presence of whatever disposition partners are on hand. In such cases, what occurs is not *no* manifestation but a different *kind* of manifestation.

Before saying what exactly any of this might have to do with modality, let me summarize.

Something's behavior is a matter of the mutual manifestation of dispositions possessed by the object and dispositions possessed by other somethings with which it interacts. Such manifestations are fully reciprocal, fully symmetrical. When one billiard ball strikes another, *both* balls are affected in a manner shaped by their various characteristics, characteristics of the surface on which they roll about, characteristics of the atmosphere, the gravitational field. These manifestings are straightforwardly deterministic: *inevitable*. If you have the dispositions suitably related, you have the manifestings. To the extent that some dispositions manifest themselves spontaneously, however, the causal system—the dispositional matrix—will be nondeterministic.

7. Modal Truthmakers

We now have the makings of a picture of a nondeterministic universe in which every manifesting, every instance of causation, is perfectly deterministic. Start with a conception of the universe as a dispositional matrix, a vast network of interrelated manifestings of dispositions. This is a conception of a *locked-in* universe, an Aristotelian cosmos of the sort that the Church came to regard as incompatible with an omnipotent creator. Now sprinkle in occasional spontaneous occurrences. Although these occurrences are uncaused, they can and do have perfectly deterministic repercussions. If you think of the universe as a closed system, spontaneous occurrences resemble interventions from the 'outside.' But, if you accept a nondeterministic universe, such occurrences are not *results* of anything, they are spontaneous manifestings, spontaneous unmoved movers.

---

[13] Lactase enzymes naturally 'block' certain manifestations of lactose in the digestive systems of mammals. The lactase enzyme breaks down lactose molecules so they can be absorbed into the bloodstream. The *absence* of lactase results in 'lactose intolerance,' a condition in which the presence of lactose—most often in dairy products—in concert with digestive bacteria is manifested in fermentation and the production of gas.

Spontaneity breeds contingency. Any occurrence, any manifesting of dispositions, that has in its ancestry a spontaneous occurrence, is thereby contingent: *it* might not have occurred. Given massive interconnectivities, it is going to be difficult, perhaps impossible, to find *any* occurrence insulated from spontaneity, a manifestation that is flatly necessary. If the Big Bang was itself spontaneous, a live option, then the universe as a whole is contingent. The universe, this very universe, might not have existed.[14]

The universe would be contingent were the Big Bang spontaneous, but this is not something for which it would be appropriate to seek an explanation. The same holds for local contingencies. To the extent that these are traceable to spontaneous occurrences, they resist the kind of explanation that would discharge shallower contingencies.

So much for contingencies, what of necessities? Necessities are reflected in the deterministic character of dispositionality. The character of the dispositional matrix enables us to predict, manipulate, and accommodate vagaries of the universe as we find it. Necessities, not contingencies, are the ontological defaults, the norm. Unless this were so, in the absence of a benevolent creator and sustainer, chaos would reign.

8. Counterfactual and Subjunctive Conditionals, and Other Loose Ends

Counterfactual and subjunctive conditional judgments make up an important species of modal discourse. Were this radium atom to decay, the result would be a radon atom and an alpha particle that would trigger a detector. Were you to stir a spoonful of sugar into your tea, it would dissolve. Had you failed to remove the crumpets you had for breakfast from the oven, they would have burned. When a counterfactual or subjunctive conditional assertion is true, however, what *makes* it true? What might the truthmakers be for counterfactual and subjunctive conditional truths?

Discussions of such matters nowadays invariably invoke Lewis's alternative worlds. In the most similar or 'nearest' world in which the radium atom (or its counterpart) decays, it issues in an alpha particle and a radon atom. In the nearest world in which you (or a counterpart you) stir a spoonful of sugar into the tea, it dissolves. In the nearest world in which you (or your counterpart) neglect the crumpets in the oven, they burn.

This suggests that truthmakers for such claims are goings-on in alternative universes. The prospect seems odd on the face of it. Why should truthmakers for assertions concerning what transpires or could transpire in *this* universe reside in *other* universes?

Lewis's own view is that truthmakers for counterfactual and subjunctive conditionals *are* goings-on in our universe. These can serve as truthmakers by virtue of bearing

---

[14] The assumption here is that distinct Big Bangs yield distinct universes. If time begins with the Big Bang, then you could think of the Big Bang occurring in proto-time, a temporal analogue of early medieval conceptions of the void taken to lie outside the finite created universe; see Grant (1981).

the right sorts of similarity relation to features of those other universes (see Lewis 1986, 22). This is a slight improvement, but it remains hard to see what a local something's similarity to something somewhere else could have to do with its being true that the local something would dissolve, would issue in an alpha particle and a radon atom, would burn.[15]

Some philosophers seem to doubt that counterfactual and subjunctive conditional truths require truthmakers. This is one way to interpret the suggestion that counter-factuals might be made true by rat-baggish contrary-to-the-fact facts. I myself doubt that every truth requires a truthmaker, but it seems to me that counterfactual and subjunctive conditional truths can be seen to have perfectly upstanding truthmakers.

Return to the three examples mentioned earlier. A radium atom is disposed to decay spontaneously resolving itself into a radon atom and an alpha particle. Sugar and tea include reciprocal dispositions that manifest themselves in the sugar's dissolving. Heated ovens and crumpets are reciprocally disposed, over time, to issue in charred crumpets. These dispositional features of the universe are apt truthmakers for familiar counterfactual and subjunctive conditional truths.

Although I think this is exactly right, matters are more complicated than these brief remarks suggest. Counterfactual and subjunctive conditionals can have distinct kinds of deployment. The examples appealed to thus far might all be thought to subserve broadly action-guiding goals. We want to know what is likely to happen if we leave radium atoms to themselves, if we stir sugar into hot tea, if we leave crumpets unattended in the oven. In most cases, what actually happens is going to depend on endless factors concerning which the counterfactual or subjunctive conditionals are silent. Were you to hold a burning match to a piece of paper, the paper would catch fire—but not if the match's heat would set off the sprinkler system.

The situation is analogous to the scientific deployment of laws of nature. This is hardly surprising given the close association between laws and counterfactuals said to be 'supported' by the laws. I have suggested that you could see causal laws as teasing out contributions made by particular kinds of disposition. Electromagnetic laws, for instance, could be seen as providing an account of how electrically charged particles would behave *qua* charged. Laws can be both explanatory, providing an accounting of the dispositional nature of the universe, and action guiding. Successful interaction with the environment requires that we comprehend, if only in a rudimentary way, its dispositional character.

Imagine that you are a member of a group seated around a dinner table. Someone observes, 'Each of you *could* have been seated in the seat to your immediate left.' This seems correct. It seems contingent that you and your companions are sitting precisely where you are. But is that so? The truth of the original assertion depends on the world's being a particular complex way, one, namely, in which the circumstances responsible

---

[15] Lewis is chiefly interested in giving a conceptual analysis of counterfactual and subjunctive condi-tionals. I am inclined to think that his analysis could well be right, or as close to right as an analysis could be. Nevertheless this leaves open the question as to the truthmakers for counterfactual and subjunctive conditional claims.

for your sitting where you happen to be sitting now are traceable to one or more instances of spontaneity. That would ensure contingency. But it is much more difficult to ascertain what could make it true that, had you not sat where you did, you would have elected to sit one seat to the left (and so for each of your dinner companions). If there is a truthmaker here, our epistemic access to it is going to be highly speculative.

It seems likely that we are bound to understand assertions such as 'Each of you could have been seated in the seat to your immediate left,' not as straightforward expressions of putative truths about the universe, but on the model invoked earlier. Thus the assertion might be meant to express an observation about the dispositional character of the circumstances, including the respective powers of you and your dinner companions. Regarded in that light, it could be seen as expressing a truth without any attendant commitment to contingency.

9. Concluding Remarks

In ontology one thing inevitably leads to another. It is a mistake of an especially pernicious sort to imagine that you can assemble a coherent metaphysical position as you might a radio or a desktop computer: by bolting together generic off-the-shelf components. Part of what I have sought to show is that, if you are attracted to an ontology of powers or dispositions, you are going to want to think very hard about how you might assess a host of related positions, including—even *especially*—widely accepted, 'default' positions.

It would be a mistake, for instance, to bolt the received conception of causality onto an ontology of dispositions, or to plug in a familiar conception of laws. These conceptions developed in large part as responses to the removal of dispositionality from the universe. Dispositions provide resources that make the conceptions super-fluous. To graft laws or law-backed causation onto a universe of dispositions would be analogous to bolting a carburetor onto a modern fuel-injected automobile engine. The result would be something unlikely to run at all.

I do not expect you to agree with everything I have said here. My hope, rather, is that I will have at least convinced you to look more critically at what has become conventional philosophical wisdom. An old adage counsels us never to look a gift horse in the mouth. But when philosophers come bearing gifts, you are well advised to examine those gifts most diligently.

Acknowledgments

Versions of this chapter were read at a workshop (Powerful Qualities: A Workshop with John Heil) at Corpus Christi College, Oxford, at the Tercer Coloquio de Metafínsica Analítica, Buenos Aires, and at a workshop on 'Dispositions and Mind,' Kyung Hee University, Seoul. The author is grateful for comments offered by co-presenters and members of the audience on those occasions.

8

Nine Problems (and Even More Solutions) for Powers Accounts of Possibility

Timothy Pawl

1. Introduction

One way of putting powers to work is to use them to ground (at least some) modal truths. One might hold that truths of possibility are true because of the powers of objects. For instance, *that it is possible that one more person be in this room* is true because of the ambulatory powers of the people in the adjoining rooms. *That it is possible that Slow Steve run a fifteen-minute mile* is true because of the locomotive powers that Steve has (perhaps along with other powers, such as his respiratory powers).[1] Call the family of stronger or weaker views which hold that possibility claims are true because of powers the 'Powers Accounts of Possibility,' or 'Powers Accounts' for short. Call a proponent of a Powers Account a 'Powers Accountant.'

On Powers Accounts, the truthmaker for *that it is possible that Jon storm out of this room* is not some counterpart of his (cf. Lewis 1986, see especially section 1.8). It isn't some man, a lot like Jon, who does, in fact, storm out of this room (or a room a lot like this room). And the truthmaker isn't some necessarily existing abstracta, either, on Powers Accounts (cf. Plantinga 1974). Rather, the truthmaker is as we might expect it to be: it is something about Jon. Namely, the truthmaker is the power or powers that he has that makes him able to storm out of a room; for instance, his ambulatory powers, along with, perhaps, his irascibility (can one calmly and peacefully *storm* out of a room?). Likewise for other truths of possibility: they are true because of the powers of actual things.

---

[1] In this chapter I write of powers such as 'locomotive powers.' One needn't think that there are such things as locomotive powers, though. There might be, instead, a bunch of fundamental powers that, together, are that in virtue of which someone moves. If the reader thinks this, then the reader can take the talk of 'locomotive powers' or 'respiratory powers' as shorthand for referring to the group or groups of fundamental powers in virtue of which Steve locomotes or breathes.

In this chapter I present nine objections to Powers Accounts of Possibility. I start by providing an exceedingly strong Powers Account and offering three objections to it. The objections will prove useful for forming a more moderate Powers Account. I then subject the more moderate Powers Account to six further objections.

2. The Far Too Strong Powers Account and Its Problems

There are many ways to be a Powers Accountant.[2] For illustrative purposes, consider a view we might call the 'Far Too Strong Powers Account' ('Far Too Strong' modifying the whole phrase 'Powers Account' and not merely the word 'Powers,' as if other accounts only make use of weak, or perhaps just regular strength, powers):

> Far Too Strong Powers Account: Necessarily, for every time at which $\Diamond p$ is true, there exists, at that time, some (one or more) objects with some (one or more) powers that are able to bring it about that p is true. Each grouping of objects and powers that can bring it about that p is true is a truthmaker for $\Diamond p$.[3]

Depending on one's view of possibility, one might think that $\Diamond p$ is true at some times and false at others. We might think that *that it is possible that McCain win the 2008 presidential election* was true in October of 2007, but now, years after he has lost, it is no longer possible. This understanding of the term 'possible' is reasonable and useful, but it isn't the use I have in mind for this chapter. Rather, I'll assume, with very many people in the contemporary debate, that the truth-values of possibility claims do not change, and in fact, cannot change.

Given this assumption, we can rephrase the Far Too Strong Powers Account as follows:

> Far Too Strong Powers Account: Necessarily, $\Diamond p$ is true if and only if there exists, at every time, some (one or more) objects with some (one or more) powers that are able to bring it about that p is true. Each grouping of objects and powers that can bring it about that p is true is a truthmaker for $\Diamond p$.

As stated, the Far Too Strong Powers Account is false, for no fewer than three reasons. Seeing the ways in which the Far Too Strong Powers Account fails will provide tests for other Powers Accounts.

One way to see the falsity of the Far Too Strong Powers Account is to focus on truths of possibility about the distant past or future; call this objection the *objection from*

---

[2] For examples of Powers Accountants, see Borghini and Williams (2008); Pruss (2002, 2011); Jacobs (2010). Thomas Aquinas, it can be argued, was also a Powers Accountant. For discussion of this point, see Brower (2005); Leftow (2005a, b); Pawl (2008).

[3] I write of propositions being true at times. Some philosophers reject that propositions are true at times. If one holds that view, the reader is free to change the language of the chapter from that of propositions to utterances or thoughts.

distant times. For instance, it is true *that, possibly, Troy doesn't fall.* However, there is nothing existing now that has the power to bring it about that Troy didn't fall. Likewise for truths about the distant future. For instance, it is true *that, possibly, a peregrine falcon eats a dove on New Year's Day in the year 2500.* However, nothing exists now with the power to bring that about, since nothing now existing has the power to bring it about *that a peregrine falcon eats a dove on New Year's Day in the year 2500.*[4] Thus in both cases the left side of the biconditional is true and the right side is false, and so the Far Too Strong Powers Account is false.

A second way to see the falsity of the Far Too Strong Powers Account is to focus on cases about the present where the only viable powers to stand as a truthmaker for the possibility claim have ceased existing; call this the *objection from presently existing things.* For instance, consider a truth about an existing orphan named Anne: *that Anne exists* is true. Now consider the truth *that, possibly, Anne exists.* By the Far Too Strong Powers Account, the truth of that proposition requires something in existence right now with the power to bring it about that Anne exists. Is there something existing right now with a power to bring that truth about?

Well, there *was* a time when there were some things with the power to bring it about that *that Anne exists* is true. But now her parents are deceased, as sad as that is. Furthermore, the sperm and the egg from which Anne came are also long gone. And Anne alone cannot be the truthmaker, since the Far Too Strong Powers Account requires an existing thing with a power to bring it about that the proposition in question is true, and Anne has no power that is a power to bring it about that *that Anne exists* is true. So it seems that anything that is a candidate truthmaker for the proposition *that, possibly, Anne exists* has ceased existing (unless there is a supernatural being with the power to create her, but we're leaving such beings to the side at the moment). And yet it is still true *that, possibly, Anne exists.* So again, the left side of the biconditional is true, whereas the right side is false. And so the Far Too Strong Powers Account is false.

A third and final way to see the falsity of the Far Too Strong Powers Account comes from considering truths of possibility about non-contingent matters; call this the *objection from non-contingent content.* A truth of possibility, say, $\Diamond p$, is 'about contingent matters' or 'has contingent content' if and only if p is contingent. That is, if and only if it is both possible that p is true, and also possible that p is false (not at the same time, of course). All propositions of the form $\Diamond p$, where p is either necessary or impossible, are propositions about non-contingent matters.

---

[4] One might think that, if determinism were true, then there would be a truthmaker available for truths about the distant future, based on powers of things existing now. But I don't think this is right, at least not without the Iteration principle I give later in the chapter. It isn't that, say, some doves and peregrine falcons now existing would have the power to bring about *that a peregrine falcon eats a dove on New Year's Day in the year 2500,* were determinism true. Rather, they would have the power to bring about something with the power to bring about something with the power to bring about . . . something that has a power to make it true *that a peregrine falcon eats a dove on New Year's Day in the year 2500.*

Consider some truth about non-contingent matters. For instance, it is true *that, possibly, 2+2=4*. By the Far Too Strong Powers Account, if ◊2+2=4 is true, then there is something with a power or powers that makes it true *that 2+2=4*. So, given the Far Too Strong Powers Account, there is something with a power to make it true *that 2+2=4*. But nothing has a power to make it true *that 2+2=4* (*pace* Descartes).[5] So the Far Too Strong Powers Account, as stated, yields a contradiction when dealing with truths of possibility about non-contingent matters.

For no fewer than three reasons, then, the Far Too Strong Powers Account is far too strong. The requirement of an existing power at every time at which the possibility proposition is true is too strong because it fails to yield truthmakers for truths about distant times, it fails in some cases to yield truthmakers for modal truths about currently existing things, and it fails to yield truthmakers for truths about non-contingent matters. Any viable Powers Account, then, will have to avoid these three pitfalls. I present one such Powers Account in the following section.

3. The Moderate Powers Account and Its Response to the Previous Three Problems

One way of modifying the Far Too Strong Powers Account to avoid these three problems would be to affirm what we might call the Moderate Powers Account:

> Moderate Powers Account: Necessarily, (if □*p* is false, then (◊*p* is true if and only if there was, is, or will be, at at least one time, some (one or more) objects with some (one or more) powers that are able to bring it about that *p* is true)). Each grouping of objects and powers that can bring it about that *p* is true is a truthmaker for ◊*p*.

The Moderate Powers Account avoids all three of the problems I raised for the Far Too Strong Powers Account.

The Moderate Powers Account avoids the first problem, the objection from the distant past or future, by not requiring truthmaking powers to exist at each of the times at which the proposition is true. *That, possibly, Troy does not fall* is true because of the powers of the defenders of Troy, or perhaps the powers of the gods watching

---

[5] Someone might object here that perhaps, were there a God, he would have the power to bring it about *that 2+2=4*, and so God would be a truthmaker for non-contingent truths of possibility. This power might be necessarily manifesting, so that even though God has a power to make it such *that 2+2=4*, that truth is still non-contingent. This view, that God has one or more necessarily manifesting powers to make it such that each non-contingent truth is true, does not have the voluntaristic entailments that a Cartesian view is so often criticized for having, since it would not be up to God's will to determine whether or not 2+2=4, or whether or not a triangle's angles add up to 180 degrees. In response, I grant the claim. Were there such a being with such necessarily manifesting powers, then its powers (together with that thing) would be a truthmaker for non-contingent truths of possibility. I will note again that I am leaving such beings to one side for now. It is surprising to see, though, that were there an essentially omnipotent being that necessarily exists, then such a being would provide a response to each of the three objections I have leveled at the Far Too Strong Powers Account. I thank Robert Hartman and Jonathan Jacobs for raising this objection.

over them. *That, possibly, a peregrine falcon eats a dove on New Year's Day in the year 2500* is true because of the powers of the peregrine falcon and dove populations that will exist on New Year's Day in the year 2500.

Note that, on the Moderate Powers Account, whether or not there exists some thing as a truthmaker for $\Diamond p$ depends on one's theory of time. For a presentist, nothing now exists with a power relevant to either example, and so nothing exists *full stop* with such a power.[6] An eternalist will have an existing (though not *now* existing) truthmaker for both the Troy and the falcon example, since those things that I have pointed to as truthmakers for these claims exist. The growing block theorist (i.e. the person who believes that the past and present exist, but the future does not exist) will have an existing truthmaker for the Troy example but not the falcon example. The presentist can say that the truth about Troy *had* a truthmaker, though it doesn't *have* one now (but see Cameron 2010). The presentist and the growing block theorist can both say that the truth about the peregrine falcon *will have* a truthmaker, though it doesn't *have* one now.[7] For some Powers Accountants, having a truthmaker at at least one time is sufficient for grounding a possibility claim in reality.

The Moderate Powers Account avoids the second problem, the objection from presently existing things, in the same way it avoided the first problem, by not requiring truthmaking powers to exist at all times at which the proposition is true. To reconsider the example I gave earlier for this problem, the Moderate Powers Accountant will say that *that, possibly, Anne exists* is true because there once existed some things that had powers able to bring it about *that Anne exists*. Again, whether or not there is an *existing* truthmaker for this modal proposition will depend upon one's theory of time. On eternalism or the growing block theory, Anne's parents (or the sperm and egg in question) exist, and they have the power to bring it about *that Anne exists*, and so they are a truthmaker for *that, possibly, Anne exists*. On presentism, there is nothing existing with a power that can bring it about *that Anne exists*. Nevertheless, again, some might think it sufficient for truth's depending on reality that at some time or other the proposition had a truthmaker.

An additional way to answer this objection from presently existing things is to allow for some possibility claims to be made true by things besides powers. One might think that, for any actually existing thing, it itself is the truthmaker for the proposition, *that, possibly, that thing exists*. Given this, some Powers Accountants might reason as follows: *That Anne exists* is made true by Anne. *That Anne exists* relevantly entails *that it is possible that Anne exist*. And so, Anne is a truthmaker for *that it is possible that Anne exist*.[8] This sort of view is not in tension with Powers Accounts, generally

---

[6] Let's leave supernatural beings to one side for now. If God exists, then there exists something with the power.

[7] The Iteration principle that I introduce later allows a way for the presentist and growing block theorist to posit a present truthmaker for future truths.

[8] This reasoning is an instance of Armstrong's Entailment principle, which says that if T makes p true, and p relevantly entails q, then T is a truthmaker for q as well. See Armstrong (2004, 10).

speaking, though the Moderate Account, as worded, would still require some power or powers to act as a truthmaker for *that it is possible that Anne exist*.

The Moderate Powers Account avoids the third problem, the objection from non-contingent content, by ruling out propositions about non-contingent matters in the newly added antecedent to the biconditional. The Moderate Powers Account only ranges over truths of possibility about contingent matters, and so examples, such as *that, possibly, 2+2=4*, are not included under its jurisdiction. Put another way, the antecedent of the Moderate Powers Account is false on this and all examples of truths of possibility about non-contingent matters. So the Moderate Powers Account is trivially true when applied to truths of possibility about non-contingent matters.

What should one say about the grounding in reality for truths of possibility about non-contingent matters? For instance, if *that, possibly, 2+2=4* does not have its truth-value set by the powers of objects, what does set its truth-value? On my view, truths of possibility about non-contingent matters will have their truth-value set in the same way that necessary truths have their truth-values set. Necessary truths, again, on my view, do not require truthmakers. Rather, necessary truths are true in virtue of their complements' lacking truthmakers. For instance, it is true *that □2+2=4*. On my view, this is true because there is nothing that is a truthmaker for its complement. The complement of □2+2=4 is ~□2+2=4, or, put otherwise, ◇~2+2=4. The truthmakers for possibility claims, given the Powers Account, are powers. So, given the Powers Account, a truthmaker for ◇~2+2=4 would be something which has the power to bring it about that ~2+2=4. Nothing has, had, or will have such a power. So, the complement of □2+2=4 lacks a truthmaker. And because of that, □2+2=4 is true.

Likewise, ◇2+2=4, a truth of possibility about non-contingent matters, is true because there neither was, is, nor will be something that can bring it about that ~2+2=4. This is an application of an entailment principle that says that if *p* has its truth-value set in virtue of something, and *p* relevantly entails *q*, then *q* has its truth-value set in virtue of that same thing.[9] □2+2=4 has its truth-value set in virtue of its complement lacking a truthmaker (i.e. because nothing had, has, or will have a power to bring it about that ~2+2=4). □2+2=4 relevantly entails *that 2+2=4*. Thus *that 2+2=4* has its truth-value set because nothing can bring it about *that ~2+2=4*.[10] I will not try my hand at spelling out relevance. I will say, though, that on my view, an object, *O*, can be relevant to a truth, *p*, even though *p* is not about *O*.[11] Any truthmaker theorist will tacitly assume some understanding of relevance to a proposition in ontological

---

[9] By 'something' in this sentence, I do not mean some [space] *thing*. On the view I put forward, some truths are true in virtue of their complement's lacking truthmakers. But this lacking of truthmakers is not a thing.

[10] One should not generalize this claim that necessary truths are true in virtue of their complements lacking a truthmaker to the claim that any proposition, or even any necessary proposition, whose complement lacks a truthmaker is true. Nothing has a power to bring it about *that 2+2=4*, but also, nothing has a power to bring it about that ~2+2=4. So both ◇2+2=4 and ◇~2+2=4 lack truthmakers, but that doesn't entail that both their complements—□2+2=4 and □~2+2=4—are true.

[11] Here I separate relevance from aboutness, unlike Trenton Merricks (2009, 33–4).

matters. That's what keeps us from considering the contents of our refrigerator when wondering what makes it true *that possibly, Jon storms out of this room*—the contents of our refrigerator are not relevant to this truth (unless Jon is in our fridge).

A second way to answer the objection from non-contingent content is to claim that something or other has the power to make such propositions true. To continue with the mathematical example, *that, possibly, 2+2=4* is true because something or other has a power that makes this true. Something can bring it about *that 2+2=4*. One route is to affirm that some special thing or class of things has the relevant truthmaking powers for non-contingent truths. For instance, one could affirm, along with a minority of theists, that God has the power to bring it about *that 2+2=4* is true. Another route would be to affirm that everything has a power to make it true *that 2+2=4*. If one does employ this response to the objection from non-contingent content, then one needn't add the antecedent to the Moderate Powers Account. One answers the objection from non-contingent content by adding additional powers to the world, not by reining in the principle.

The Moderate Powers Account, then, does not fall prey to any of the three problems I raised for the Far Too Strong Powers Account. Nevertheless, there is a difficulty which it faces that poses a serious problem. For there are truths of possibility concerning contingent matters which did not have, do not have, and will not have prima facie relevant candidate powers as their truthmakers. To such cases I now turn.

4. Powers to Bring about Powers: the Iteration Principle

The following is true: *that it is possible that Slow Steve run an eight-minute mile*. This is true, though he doesn't, in fact, have the power to run an eight-minute mile. (Steve's adjectival moniker is not ironic, unlike most men who have 'Tiny' appended to their name.) But, if he doesn't have the power, something else has to have it, given (i) that powers are truthmakers for truths of possibility about contingent matters and (ii) that the following is a truth of possibility about contingent matters: *that it is possible that Slow Steve run an eight-minute mile*.

On the Moderate Powers Account, so long as he eventually has the power to run an eight-minute mile, that future power will be that because of which the proposition *that it is possible that Slow Steve run an eight-minute mile* is true. However, suppose Slow Steve dies before he ever acquires such a power. And suppose he never had it in adolescence either. Suppose he never, throughout the course of his entire life, had the power to run an eight-minute mile. What could be the power in virtue of which *that it is possible that Slow Steve run an eight-minute mile* is true? Call this objection the *objection from Slow Steve*.

It does not seem to me that any powers that you or I have are relevant here. I have no power to make it true *that Slow Steve runs an eight-minute mile*. If you and I are both very fast and very strong, we might be able to pick him up and run an eight-minute mile. We could even tie his legs to our own, making his footfalls coincide with ours so that his bodily movements somehow approximate running. (Picture a three-legged race extended by one more person into a four-legged race.) Nevertheless, he wouldn't really be running in this case.[12] Perhaps we could have made Slow Steve a Six Million Dollar man, in which case he would have had the powers. Or perhaps we could have set up a science-fiction scenario in which we stimulate his muscle fibers so that he runs quickly. But we didn't. He died without any of this happening. So Steve had no power to run an eight-minute mile, and, it seems to me, none of us had any power to make him do so either.

We could resort to God being the truthmaker for *that it is possible that Slow Steve run an eight-minute mile*, since God could cause Steve to run an eight-minute mile. If there were an omnipotent being, it could provide a truthmaker for every truth of possibility. And were that omnipotent being essentially necessarily existing, then the same thing could do the work of providing truthmakers for all truths of possibility in all worlds.[13] So, one way to answer the questions raised here is to posit a necessarily existing omnipotent being. In fact, the existence of a necessary, omnipotent God would be sufficient to answer all three problems for the Far Too Strong Powers Account as well as the Moderate Powers Account.[14]

But must one get religion to get the Powers Accountant out of the red? It would be better if we could provide a non-divine truthmaker for this truth, since, all things being equal, it is better to have a truthmaker theory that requires less ontological commitment than more. This is especially true when the commitment is to something as ontologically impressive as a necessarily existing essentially omnipotent entity. Isn't there a more naturalistic way for it to be such that neither Steve nor anything else has a power to cause Steve to run an eight-minute mile, but it is true *that it is possible that Slow Steve run an eight-minute mile*?

There is a better way. We should note that we have powers to bring about powers. While Steve did not, does not, and will not have the power to run an eight-minute mile, he did, while he was alive, have the power to bring it about that he has a power to run an eight-minute mile. He could have trained, for instance, and acquired the power to run an eight-minute mile. Then we needn't go through God to get the truthmaker for this truth of possibility. Rather, all we need for cases such as this one are powers to acquire powers. Then we can say that the truthmaker for the truth *that it is possible that Slow Steve run an eight-minute mile* is his power to bring it about that something, namely, Steve, has a power to bring it about that he runs an eight-minute mile.

[12] If you think this would be genuine running, change the example to one where the power of the agent must be employed for it to be a genuine case of so acting.

[13] For some discussions of this possibility, see Pruss (2002, 2011); Brower (2005), Leftow (2005a, b); Pawl (2008).

[14] See footnote 5 for a discussion of how this might work for the third problem, the objection from non-contingent content.

This Steve example, I think, motivates the view that a power to bring it about that there is something that has a power to bring it about *that p* is a power sufficient for being the truthmaker for $\Diamond p$. Steve's having the power to bring it about that something has a power to make Steve run an eight-minute mile is a truthmaker for the truth, *that it is possible that Slow Steve run an eight-minute mile*. That is, I think this example provides reason to believe the following Iteration principle:

> The Iteration principle: If *R* is a power (or group of powers) to bring it about that there is a distinct power (or group of powers), *Q*, and *Q* would be a truthmaker for the truth of possibility, $\Diamond p$, then *R* is a truthmaker for $\Diamond p$.[15]

If Steve's power to train and so forth is a power to bring it about that Steve has the power to run an eight-minute mile, and that power to run an eight-minute mile is a truthmaker for *that it is possible that Slow Steve run an eight-minute mile*, then Steve's power to train and so forth is a truthmaker for the truth *that it is possible that Slow Steve run an eight-minute mile*. Note that the Iteration principle does not say that *R* is a truthmaker for *any* proposition that *Q* would be a truthmaker for. For instance, *Q* makes it true *that Q exists*, but *R* is not a truthmaker for that truth.

We can—and should—also understand the Iteration principle as allowing more power links in the power chain. Steve might never have had a power that, if manifested, would have resulted in a power to run an eight-minute mile. He might have died in a state where he could roll a mile faster than he could run it. Nevertheless, he has powers to acquire powers to acquire still other powers to acquire . . . the running powers to make it true that he could run an eight-minute mile.

The Iteration principle helps to solve another objection, which we can call the objection from *temporally indexed possibilities*. To have a truthmaker for *that it is possible that Slow Steve run an eight-minute mile*, all one needs is either something existing at some time or other with a power to make Steve run an eight-minute mile, or something existing at some time or other with the power to bring about a power to make Steve run an eight-minute mile (or something existing at some time or other with a power to bring about a power to bring about a power to . . . make Steve run an eight-minute mile; henceforth I will assume this iteration without stating it explicitly). However, what should one say about truths of possibility that are temporally indexed? What if the truth isn't merely *that it is possible that Slow Steve run an eight-minute mile*, but is instead, *that it is possible that Slow Steve run an eight-minute mile beginning at T1*? In that case, does the truthmaking power have to exist at or before *T1*? Can the same thing serve as a truthmaker for the proposition *that it is possible that Slow Steve*

---

[15] This principle is closely related to Armstrong's Entailment principle. It is also similar to Borghini and Williams's (2008) P3, which is a statement about when something is possible, not about what the truthmaker is for that possibility (2008, 31). Note that the usage of the term 'Iteration' here is different from one standard usage of the term, wherein a modal claim is iterated if a modal operator appears under the scope of another modal operator (e.g. $\Box\Diamond p$). For such a use of the term, see McMichael (1983, 53).

run an eight-minute mile beginning at T1 and also for the proposition *that it is possible that Slow Steve run an eight-minute mile beginning at T2*? What should one say here?[16]

The Iteration principle provides an answer to the temporally indexed possibilities objection. One needn't have a truthmaking power at or near *T1* to make it true *that it is possible that Slow Steve run an eight-minute mile beginning at T1*. Rather, anything that could have brought about powers to make it true *that Slow Steve run an eight-minute mile starting at T1* can count as the truthmaker for the proposition in question. The same power can serve as a truthmaker for both *that it is possible that Slow Steve run an eight-minute mile beginning at T1* and *that it is possible that Slow Steve run an eight-minute mile beginning at T2*, provided that the power could, via the Iteration principle, bring it about that there are powers to bring about powers to . . . cause Slow Steve to run an eight-minute mile beginning at either time.

On my view, the Powers Accountant who affirms the Moderate Powers Account, along with the Iteration principle, will have an answer to all the difficulties and objections I have discussed in this chapter.[17] However, one might have some objections to the Iteration principle. In the remainder of this section I will consider and reply to one objection to the Iteration principle itself. In the next section I will consider three objections to the conjunction of the Iteration principle with the Moderate Powers Account.

One may worry that the Iteration principle allows for irrelevant truthmakers. For, according to the Iteration principle, anything that has a power, R, to bring about another power, Q, counts as a truthmaker for all the truths of possibility that Q makes true. So if the procreative powers of Bob and Sue are such that they can bring about Tom and Tom's powers, and Tom's powers are such that he can break a world record in fencing this century, then Bob and Sue's procreative powers are, together, a truthmaker for the truth *that it is possible that Tom break a world record in fencing this century*. But, one might think, if anything is irrelevant to world records in fencing, it is Bob and Sue's procreative powers. Thus, Bob and Sue's procreative powers are not a viable truthmaker for the truth *that it is possible that Tom break a world record in fencing this century*. We don't check the fridge for the truthmaker for *that it is possible that Jon storm out of this room*, and we don't check Bob and Sue's marital bed for truthmakers for *that it is possible that Tom break a world record in fencing this century*. But the situation becomes even worse for the proponent of the Iteration principle.

---

[16] I owe this set of objections to Irem Kurstal Steen.

[17] One thinker with such a view, or one very similar to the Moderate Powers Account conjoined to the Iteration principle, is Jonathan Jacobs, who writes:

> Let us say, then, that on the Aristotelian theory, some proposition or truth T is possible just in case there is some actually instantiated property (or property complex) that is a power for some other property (or property complex) that would be a truthmaker for T. (Alternatively, T is possible if there is some property that is a power to bring about a property that is a power to bring about a property . . . , that would be a truthmaker for T). (Jacobs 2010, 236)

One can trace the purportedly irrelevant truthmakers farther back in the causal chain. If A has the power to bring about p, then A's power is a truthmaker for $\Diamond p$. And if B has a power to bring about A and A's powers, then, by the Iteration principle, B's power is a truthmaker for $\Diamond p$. Likewise, if C can bring about B and B's powers, and D bring about C and C's powers, and so on down the line, then we get a backwards regress.

Suppose that there was a beginning to the physical world, and for ease of explanation, suppose it was a singularity. Suppose also that nothing in the physical world (aside from the singularity) just 'pops' into existence, but that everything physical is brought to be by something else physical. (I'm not claiming the singularity *did* pop into existence; I'm just stating that the principle we're working with here doesn't preclude that it did.) Now, it follows by the Iteration principle that the singularity will be a truthmaker for every truth of possibility about contingent, physical matters. For consider any physical thing that isn't the singularity. It was caused by some other physical thing or things. And that something else was caused to be, again, by some other physical thing or things. And so on, until we reach the singularity.

The singularity had the power to bring about the following thing or things in this chain, and that thing with its powers brought about the next thing or things and their powers, and so on down to Tom and his powers. So, by the Iteration principle, the singularity is a truthmaker for the truth of possibility *that it is possible that Tom break a world record in fencing this century*, along with every other truth of possibility about contingent physical matters. But that's ridiculous, says the objector. So the Iteration principle entails that something is a truthmaker for a truth of possibility which can't, in fact, be a truthmaker for that truth. And so the Iteration principle is false. Call this objection the *objection from irrelevant truthmakers*.

One initial thing to note about this objection is that it is too simplistically stated. It wouldn't be Bob and Sue's procreative powers *alone* that make it true *that it is possible that Tom break a world record in fencing this century*. Rather, using the variable names from the Iteration principle, the R-power—the power to bring about the power to bring it about *that Tom breaks a world record in fencing this century*—here must include a bunch of other things, too. Tom isn't just born with amazing fencing skills. He needs a trainer. He also needs sparring partners, proper diet and exercise, etc. The R-power has to include all of these other powers. In doing so, it sounds, at least to my ear, less incredible. It sounds less incredible because it isn't merely Bob and Sue's procreative powers that are the powers to bring about the powers relevant to causing the truth of *that Tom breaks a world record in fencing this century*, as the objection initially had it. Rather, the R-power needs to include all sorts of other, relevant powers.

In response to the objection that the Iteration principle allows for irrelevant truthmakers, I reject that the truthmakers are really irrelevant. The R-powers are relevant insofar as they are relevant to the Q-powers, and the Q-*powers* can bring about p. This is not to say that relevance is transitive. Rather, it is to say that in these cases, cases of being able to bring things about, being able to bring about the about-bringers is relevant, whatever the means by which those about-bringers are brought about.

5. Three Objections to the Conjunction of the Moderate Powers Account with the Iteration Principle

Another method of objection does not focus on the Iteration principle alone, but rather on truths of possibility about contingent matters which it seems the Iteration principle along with the Moderate Powers Account cannot handle well. We can call three such objections the objection from *alien properties*, the objection from *meager worlds*, and the objection from *superlatives*.

Consider the objection from aliens.[18] Armstrong defines aliens as "*non-actual* particulars or properties or relations which, furthermore and very importantly, are not 'combinatorially constructible' from actual particulars, properties and relations" (2004, 86).[19] On this definition, there will be aliens that, nevertheless, are producible given the Iteration principle. This is because there may be powers that, while unmanifested, could be manifested, and, were they manifested, they would produce something with a further power to produce the so-called alien. The so-called alien would not be combinatorially constructible out of any existing thing (since the thing with the power to produce the alien never actually exists), though something has a power to bring it about (via the Iteration principle).[20] Aside from these so-called aliens, though, some people claim that it is possible that there be what we might call 'genuine aliens'—things that can neither be combinatorially constructed from actual things *nor* from the potential products of actual things (say, via the Iteration principle).

Suppose that it is possible that there exist, say, a sort of fundamental particle not able to be caused by anything in the actual world (whether directly or via the Iteration principle). It is possible, but not producible by anything that is or that can come about from what is. Perhaps the energy levels required for it are too high for anything actual to produce. Or maybe the laws of nature that are actual don't allow for it to exist, but some possible sets of laws of nature do allow for it. Suppose such particles would have essential properties, such as, say, schmarge. Then it is true *that*

---

[18] To see more work on aliens, see Armstrong (2000, 3.1.1), Armstrong (2004, 86–9), Borghini and Williams (2008, 38–40); Cameron (2008, 265–8); Fitch (1996, 58–63); Lewis (1986, 159–65). Note that this is a different sense of 'alien' than the sense, employed in another debate concerning truthmakers, that Simons gives the term. See Simons and Melia (2000, 67).

[19] Armstrong answers the problem of aliens with his Possibility principle: "given a contingent truth, its truthmakers, whatever they may be, will also be truthmakers for the modal truth that the contradictory of the contingent truth is (metaphysically) possible" (2004, 86). The Possibility principle, however, is false (Pawl 2010). Andrea Borghini and Neil Williams define aliens properties as follows: "alien properties are the ones that are not possessed by any actual (i.e. past, present, or future) entities, and are not obtainable by means of a conjunction, interpolation, or extrapolation, of some actual properties" (2008, 38, footnote 39). Gabriele Contessa defines aliens as "contingent beings whose existence is completely unrelated to that of any actual being" (2008, 345).

[20] Jacobs also points this out (2010, 4.2.1.1).

it is possible that something have schmarge, though nothing exists with schmarge, and nothing exists that could bring about something with schmarge.[21] As such, this possibility provides a counterexample to the Moderate Powers Account conjoined with the Iteration principle.

In general, a Powers Accountant has three responses available when responding to a problematic purported truth of possibility about contingent content: affirm the possibility claim, deny it, or remain agnostic about it. First, she can affirm that the purported truth of possibility about contingent content is in fact true, and thus that it stands in need of a truthmaker at some time or other. In this case, she has reason to provide such a truthmaker, or at least argue that the existence of such a truthmaker isn't implausible.

Second, she can deny that the purported truth is in fact true, and thus deny the need to provide a truthmaker for the alleged truth of possibility. In such a case, she may well have to motivate the claim that the proposition is not, in fact, possible. This will be a cost for a Powers Account if the proposition in question is intuitively true.

Finally, she may remain agnostic about the truth of the possibility proposition in question.[22] If the Powers Accountant is agnostic about the truth of a possibility proposition with contingent content, then, for consistency's sake, she would have to be agnostic about the existence or non-existence of something with the power to bring it about. For, given that she affirms the biconditional Moderate Powers Account, her agnosticism about one side of the biconditional would be inconsistent with an affirmation or denial of the other side. One cannot reasonably affirm *A* if and only if *B*, be agnostic about *B*, and affirm (or deny) *A*. Rather, precisely because she is agnostic about these possibilities *and* affirms a Powers Account, she must be agnostic about the past, present, or future existence of beings with such powers (or powers to bring about such powers, or powers to bring about powers to bring about . . .).[23]

These three responses each provide a method of responding to the objection from alien properties. The Powers Accountant who affirms *that it is possible that something have schmarge* must either provide something as a truthmaker, or give reason to think

---

[21] I owe this formulation of the objection to Meghan Sullivan. Lewis offers a similar formation of this objection in terms of a world where protons are indivisible (1986, 159). In the world he imagines, no quarks exist, and so nothing with the fundamental properties of flavor or color exist. Van Inwagen offers a similar example (2001, 200–1).

[22] For some attempts to argue that possibility, and our modal knowledge, is much more circumscribed than we philosophers normally take it to be; see Seddon (1972), van Inwagen (1998); van Inwagen (2010). The main strategy in these papers is to argue that genuine possibility requires that the possibility in question be able to be embedded into a systematic totality. Likewise, for genuine modal knowledge, it isn't enough that no contradiction be found in, say, iron's being transparent (to use an example from both van Inwagen articles), or being able to imagine something one can describe as transparent iron. Rather, for modal knowledge, one must have reason to think that the possibility in question can be embedded into a coherent whole. As such, we will have reason to remain skeptical about (or even doubt) some modal claims, even if it appears to us that the terms do not entail a contradiction.

[23] The preceding argument is similar to the argument given by John Divers, arguing that someone who affirms Lewisian semantics for modal operators but is agnostic about whether there are Lewis-worlds besides the actual world must be an agnostic about the truth-value of many modal truths (2004, 673–4).

that it is not implausible to think that there is at least one thing with a power to bring it about that something has schmarge. If there is a cause of the universe (whether something personal, such as a God, or impersonal, such as a world generator) then that thing might well have a power to create something with schmarge. It could have the power directly, as God would, or indirectly through the Iteration principle, as a universe generator may.

The Powers Accountant who denies *that it is possible that something have schmarge* will stop the objection at its first move. It really isn't possible that there exist these other fundamental particles that nothing at all could bring about. As such, there is no reason to affirm the existence of such a thing to bring it about. Since intuitions don't (or, the Powers Accountant might claim, *shouldn't*) run deep here, denying this alleged possibility is not an expensive cost for the Powers Accountant.

The Powers Accountant who remains agnostic about *that it is possible that something have schmarge* can combine these two answers into a hypothetical proof by cases.[24] Either *that it is possible that something have schmarge* is true or it is false. If true, then the answer given by the Powers Accountant who affirms the possibility will be the correct answer. If false, then the answer given by the Powers Accountant who denies the possibility will be the correct answer. So, either the affirming answer is the correct answer or the denying answer is the correct answer. Either way, the agnostic may claim, a Powers Accountant can respond adequately to this objection.

Another objection is the objection from meager worlds. Consider this proposition: *that it is possible that all that ever exists are two electrons.* That seems possible. And it also seems true *that it is possible that all that ever exists is one electron.* However, in that two-electron world, nothing would have the power to make it true *that it is possible that all that ever exists is one electron.* For one thing, neither electron has the power to destroy the other or itself, so neither of the two things which exist in the two-electron world has the power to bring it about that it is true *that it is possible that all that ever exists is one electron.* And for another, even if one electron did have that power, by the time it could use it, it would be too late: there would already be two things existing.[25] If the numbers are suspicious due to their small size, one can increase them so long as the first world contains at least one more electron than the second. In the world with all and only one trillion electrons, it is true *that it is possible that there exist one trillion minus one electrons.* But nothing in the first world—the one trillion electrons world—has a power to bring it about *that there exist one trillion minus one electrons.*[26]

---

[24] Agnosticism about the possibility of aliens is the first response of Borghini and Williams (2008, 38).

[25] I owe this objection to Lauren Ashwell.

[26] Another sort of meager world is the empty world. Such a world, it appears to me, is not possible on a powers account of possibility. For, nothing has the power to bring it about that there never has been anything. By the time it can employ such a power, it is too late: there has already been something—it! For more on meager worlds, see Pruss (2002); Armstrong (2004, section 7.4); Efird and Stoneham (2006, 272–5); and Cameron's response to Pruss's argument (2008).

And, of course, there is no reason to focus exclusively on truths concerning electrons. Given the S5 modal system, a truth of possibility that is true in one world is true in all worlds. And it is true *that, possibly, some human dances the electric slide* in this, our actual world. So in the two-electron world it is true *that, possibly, some human dances the electric slide.* But no mere electron (or pair of electrons) has the power to bring it about that *that some human dances the electric slide* is true. Likewise for very many other truths of possibility. No electron (or pair of electrons) can cause it to be true *that there are some dodo birds* or *that some species have been domesticated or that the earth is composed, in part, of carbon* or . . . , though if one were to affix a possibility operator to each of these disjuncts, each resulting possibility claim would be true in a two-electron world.[27]

A first response to this sort of possibility claim is to question whether it really expresses something possible. Could there be electrons without other fundamental particles, or without fields? Without evidence to support the claim that electrons could exist without anything else at all existing, there is little cost in remaining agnostic about the possibility of the two-electron world.

But set aside agnosticism for the moment. A Powers Accountant will wonder: in the two-electron world, what caused those two electrons to come into being? The potential answers seem to be: nothing at all, something extraworldly (e.g. a universe generator), or something interworldly (i.e. the electrons). Consider the cases.

Suppose nothing at all caused their existence. They are contingent, uncaused, and they exist alone. According to Powers Accounts, no contingent entity is possible without there being some actual thing at some time which could have brought about, either directly, or indirectly via the Iteration principle, the purportedly possible entity. Hence, if this objection requires one to claim that a contingent entity is possible without there being anything at any time which could have caused it directly or indirectly, the objection will be, from the very outset, something no Powers Accountant will find moving. Even aside from the Powers Accounts, if one is pulled toward a causal principle on which nothing contingent comes to be without some cause of its existence, one will deny the possibility of this scenario, and thus deny the adequacy of the objection. If one is unsure of the causal principle just mentioned, but sees it as epistemically possible, that alone can give one further grounds for agnosticism about the possibility of this scenario.

Suppose something extraworldly causes the electrons to exist. Suppose that the electrons are the lone inhabitants of one of the many universes generated in some way by something extraworldly. In that case, while the two electrons are the only things that exist *in that universe*, there are other things that exist *full stop*, one of them being whatever it is that does the universe generating. Thus it would be false that all and only those two electrons ever exist, though it would be true that all and only those two

---

[27] For more discussion of meager worlds and the consequences of their existence on truthmaker theory, see Armstrong (2007); Pawl (2010, sections 3 and 4).

electrons exist in that particular universe. It would be false, then, strictly speaking, *that it is possible that all that ever exists are two electrons.*

If something interworldly causes the electrons, then either that thing is one (or more) of the electrons or it is not. If it is not one of the electrons, then we have reached a contradiction. For, we have reached the claim that in a world where all that ever exists are two electrons, something besides those two electrons exists (e.g. a field, a wave, a god, etc.). Thus, if something interworldly caused the electrons to exist, it is one or more of the electrons that caused them.

Causing other electrons is not a power normally attributed to electrons. But even allowing that, unbeknownst to us, electrons can cause other electrons, there are still problems with claiming both that only two electrons ever exist and that something caused them to exist.

For A to cause B, A has to be prior, in some sense, to B. But nothing is prior to itself in any sense. Thus an electron cannot cause itself. Therefore, given the assumption that something interworldly caused the electrons to exist, one electron caused the other.

Now, either each electron was caused by the other, or one electron caused the other, but that causing electron was itself uncaused. If the causing electron was itself uncaused, then we have a contingent thing just popping into existence, which we gave some motivations for rejecting earlier in the 'nothing at all' disjunct of the proof by cases. If the electrons caused each other, then we reach another priority problem.

The priority problem is as follows. One electron, call it $e1$, caused the other, call it $e2$. And so $e1$ is prior in some way to $e2$. But $e2$ also caused $e1$. And so $e2$ is prior in some way to $e1$. The way that $e1$ is prior to $e2$ is the same way that $e2$ is prior to $e1$ (they are both prior in whatever way that a cause is prior to an effect). But if $e1$ is prior to $e2$, and $e2$ is prior to $e1$, then, by transitivity of priority, $e1$ is prior to itself. And, as I said above, nothing is prior to itself. So it can't be that each electron caused the other.

In summary, if the electrons are caused to exist, then something caused them to exist. And that something is either something else or the electrons. Not something else, given that this would contradict the possibility claim in question, *that it is possible that all that ever exists are two electrons.* And so, if the electrons are caused, they are caused, in some way, by the electrons themselves. But an electron cannot cause itself, and a pair of electrons can't cause one another to exist. And so there will be at least one electron whose existence is not caused. This is something that anyone who finds the causal principle I mentioned above epistemically possible will have reason to reject.

The final objection I will consider in this chapter can be called the objection from superlatives.[28] Consider the following claims: *it is possible that Bob write the most important philosophy article in the history of the world; it is possible that Bob be the fastest person to have ever existed; it is possible that Bob write the most beautiful sonnet*

---

[28] I thank David Robb and Dan Ryder for helpful conversation about this objection.

ever penned. In general, it seems that, for most, if not all, superlatives true of one person, those superlatives could be true of another.[29] In fact, if it weren't the case for some superlative true of you that it could be true of someone else, it would hardly be impressive for you to have it.[30] One might think that it is true of any human now alive *that, possibly, this person is the fastest person who ever lived.* This is even true of people without legs. But what makes such claims true?

One might have worries about applying the Iteration principle to these superlative truths. I certainly do not have any powers to directly bring it about that I am the fastest, smartest, most musically inclined, most poetically inclined, etc. person who has ever lived. Do I have powers to bring about such powers? Well, it seems prideful to think that I do. It seems like a real possibility that I could have trained since birth, diligently and in the most favorable scenarios imaginable, and yet still not attain the swimming prowess of Michael Phelps, eight-time swimming gold medalist in the 2008 Summer Olympics.

It might well be, one might think, that while it is true *that it is possible that Michael Phelps have the same impressive swimming powers he has in the actual world and yet I beat him in a fair 100-m butterfly,* there is nothing that ever did or will exist that has the power to bring it about that I have the power to beat him in such a race.[31] And the same for any of the other superlative claims. It might well be that, try as Bob might, and with others trying as they might, Bob could never have musical powers exceeding those of Bach, or literary powers exceeding those of Shakespeare. Thus, it looks as if there are truths of possibility that have no actual power to make them true, and which the Iteration principle fails to provide truthmakers for. What should a Powers Accountant say to this objection?

Again, the Powers Accountant has the same three choices available to her: deny the possibility claim, agreeing with the objector that there really is not an actual power that can serve as a truthmaker for at least some superlative truths of possibility; remain agnostic about the possibility claim, thus remaining agnostic about the existence of some power to serve as the truthmaker; or affirm the possibility claim, thus affirming that there is something or other (God, a world generator, the best trainer ever) that,

---

[29] There may be exceptions. For instance, if there is an Anselmian divine being, then only that being could be most powerful.

[30] Some superlatives are not available to everyone. For instance, 'being the fastest woman' is unavailable to me.

[31] One might object: Phelps and everyone else has the power to lounge around on the couch and never enter a pool, and I have the power to train eight hours a day. In a world where everyone lounges and I train for eight hours a day, I could be the best swimmer. And so there is no problem with thinking up a situation where the superlative, 'is the fastest swimmer,' is apt of me. In reply, this is not the problem I am raising. The problem under discussion here is that it seems possible that Phelps be just as fast as he is in the actual world, and I still be faster (that's why I talk of Phelps having the same impressive swimming powers he has in the actual world). It seems possible that I have more impressive swimming powers than Phelps, in fact, has, and yet it seems that neither I nor anything else has the power to initiate a causal chain which eventuates in my having such impressive powers.

were it to work upon me, could bring it about that I swim faster than Phelps swims in the actual world.[32]

The Powers Accountant who either denies or is agnostic about the possibility claims in question has some resources available. She can note that while there might well be flukes in races (e.g. Phelps pulls a muscle mid-race), the fact is (or may well be) that our bodies are such that his maximum swimming speed, given his powers, is faster than mine. In fact, it might just be that in any world where he's built like he is and I'm built like I am, his maximum speed will be faster than mine. If such were true (or seemed as if it might well be true), then we have reason to deny (or at least be agnostic) about the possibility that I could outswim Phelps in a fair race, with each of us doing his best. The same goes for the other possibility claims as well. Someone with the intellectual prowess of Bob might just not be able to compete literarily with the likes of Shakespeare.

If the Powers Accountant affirms the possibilities in question, then she will have to provide something as a truthmaker for them, or at least give reason to think that the existence of a truthmaker is not implausible. Supernatural aids allow one way to provide a power to acquire superlatives. Perhaps one could make a Faustian deal with the devil. Another way is to claim that all people really have powers, either directly or indirectly via the Iteration principle, to be the fastest, strongest, smartest, etc. Earlier I mentioned a charge of pride against thinking one has the power to be the best at everything and anything (via the Iteration principle). Leveling such a charge against the Powers Accountant is unjust, for she thinks that *everyone* has these powers. It would be different if she thought that such superlative propositions were true of her— that it is possible that she be the fastest, smartest, etc.—but not true of all others. In that case, the charge of pride might well stick, but not in virtue of her being a Powers Accountant.

6. Conclusion

In this chapter, I have presented a way of putting powers to work as the ontological grounding for truths of possibility. First I presented the Far Too Strong Powers Account as a means of showing three objections that a Powers Account of possibility must face: the objection from distant times, the objection from presently existing things, and the objection from non-contingent content. I then presented the Moderate Powers Account which avoids these three objections. Afterwards, I presented a difficult problem for the Moderate Powers Account, the problem of truths of possibility where the obvious candidate truthmaker or grounding never exists, which I called the Slow Steve objection. To answer this difficulty, I presented the Iteration principle. The

---

[32] Phelps himself appears to have a theory about this. He claimed in an interview with CNN: "Records are always made to be broken no matter what they are. . . . Anybody can do anything that they set their mind to." http://edition.cnn.com/2008/SPORT/08/17/phelps.history.eight.golds/ retrieved May 4, 2011.

Iteration principle, I noted, answers the objection from temporally indexed possibilities. Next I presented the objection from irrelevant truthmakers against the Iteration principle. Finally, I presented three objections to the conjunction of the Moderate Powers Account with the Iteration principle. These were the objection from alien properties, the objection from meager worlds, and the objection from superlatives. I have argued that the Powers Accountant has one or more options available to answer each of these nine objections.

Acknowledgments

I thank Lauren Ashwell, Scott Berman, Matthews Grant, Robert Hartman, Jonathan D. Jacobs, Tim O'Connor, Faith Pawl, Alexander Pruss, David Robb, Michael Rota, Dan Ryder, Joseph Salerno, Irem Kurstal Steen, Eleonore Stump, Meghan Sullivan, Barbara Vetter, Neil Williams, and the participants of the Putting Powers to Work Conference held at Saint Louis University in April, 2011, for helpful comments on this chapter.

PART III

Space, Time, and Persistence

9

Manifesting Time and Space
Background-Free Physical Theories

Alexander Bird

1.

A natural conception of space and time is to regard them as a (possibly infinite) container or stage for the events that make up the history of the universe. They are not part of the contents of the container nor are they actors or props in the action on the stage. They are an inert but necessary background. If space and time are inert, then spatial and temporal relations cannot be considered as true causes, nor can they be considered as dispositional in nature. Consequently, we should not regard such properties as essentially dispositional, but instead take them to be categorical in nature.

I regard the above argument, even if not explicitly articulated as such, to be a powerful source of the widespread view that temporal and spatial relations cannot be essentially dispositional and so are counterexamples to monistic dispositional essentialism—the view that the fundamental natural properties are essentially dispositional in nature. In this chapter, I consider this argument in detail and the grounds for rejecting the conception of space and time that it depends upon.

2.

Brian Ellis (2001, 127, 135, 217–18) takes the view that some fundamental natural properties are essentially dispositional whereas others are not; the latter are essentially categorical. The essentially dispositional properties are those whose essential natures are to be understood in terms of the dispositions they confer on the objects possessing them.[1] For example, it might be that charge is such a property. If so, the property of

---

[1] Why do I talk of properties 'conferring a disposition'? Are not the properties themselves dispositions on this view? I do so because I am using 'property' here in a sparse, ontologically robust sense, whereas 'disposition' is very often used in an abundant, ontologically weak way. To say that a fundamental natural property is a disposition is to run the risk of eliding the sparse and the abundant. Furthermore, it is a claim that Humeans and other anti-essentialists can in fact agree to—they do not deny the existence

possessing a charge of value q_1 confers on any object with that charge a disposition to exert a force on other charged objects and to experience a force, in accordance with Coulomb's law:

$$\mathbf{F} = -\epsilon_0 \frac{q_1 q_2}{r^2} \qquad (1)$$

and to generate a magnetic field when in motion according to the Biot–Savart law:

$$d\mathbf{B} = \frac{\mu_0}{4\pi} \frac{(J dV) \times \hat{\mathbf{r}}}{r^2} \qquad (2)$$

While there are many questions to be asked of such a view, let us assume that it is correct, for current purposes. What is interesting is that Ellis does not think that what goes, in this example, for charge, goes for all fundamental properties and relations. He does not think that anything like this is true of spatial and temporal relations. Thus there is no disposition that reflects the essential nature of a spatial distance nor of a temporal duration nor even of a relativistic space–time interval.

Why should Ellis deny this? Stephen Mumford (2004, 188) suggests what might seem an obvious riposte. Transposing Mumford's response to our example, we may observe that spatial separation, r, is a factor in Coulomb's law just as charge is; it likewise occurs in the Biot–Savart law. Mumford's suggestion is in effect that we can see these equations as reflecting a dispositional consequence of the nature of spatial separation, just as we see them reflecting the dispositional nature of charge.

A parallel riposte for time may be less obvious, but is available nonetheless. In the Biot–Savart law, charge is hidden in the quantity J, which is the current density (i.e. the density of charge flowing *per unit time*). Likewise time is of course implicated in many laws, such as Newton's second law:

$$\mathbf{F} = ma \qquad (3)$$

The contribution of time may be more directly perceptible in derived laws such as:

$$\mathbf{F}t = \Delta m\mathbf{v} \qquad (4)$$

which tells us that the change in momentum due to a constant force is equal to that force times the duration for which it is applied, and:

$$\mathbf{s} = \frac{\mathbf{F}t^2}{2m} \qquad (5)$$

which tells us how far a mass m will be displaced, from stationary, by a force F applied for a duration t.

So there is no lack of laws that refer to temporal intervals as crucial determinants of various outcomes. Thus Mumford's response looks entirely feasible: these laws show

---

of dispositions; they deny that any property is *essentially* dispositional in character. So the dispositional essentialist view of (sparse) property P is that, for some disposition (abundantly understood) D, in virtue of possessing P an object will have D (P confers D on the object); and this connection between P and D is essential to P. That said, I shall relax my usage henceforward: the dispositions I talk of will be natural properties with dispositional essences.

that certain quantities are nomically dependent on time. We can regard these laws as reflecting the dispositional nature of temporal relations.

3.

While I agree that Mumford's response is basically correct, it does also seem to me that there is an intuitive asymmetry between the contribution of charge and the contribution of distance in Coulomb's law; likewise there is an asymmetry between charge and time in the Biot–Savart law and between time and force or mass in Newton's third law and its derived laws. Considering Coulomb's law, it is natural to think of the force as being generated by the charge, and the role of the distance as secondary, as moderating the effect of the charge. It is thus plausible to think of the charge as the disposition, but not the distance. Likewise, in (4) it is tempting to think of the force as the causal power here, and the duration as playing a lesser role. If one thinks that a turned-on tap is disposed to fill the sink, that quantity of water in the sink is determined by how much the tap is on and how long it is on for. The disposition here concerns the tap and rate of flow of water; the duration of the flow is the junior partner in this arrangement. And in (5) the distance moved by the mass is a manifestation of the force and of the mass, which resists the force. The time t in a sense measures how much the force disposition is applied but is not itself a cause, and so cannot be attributed a disposition.

In the last paragraph, I have tried to express the reluctance we might feel towards endorsing Mumford's proposal. I am very far from suggesting that we should allow this reluctance to move us to reject the proposal—on the contrary, I support the proposal. However, I do suggest that this reluctance explains Ellis's view that certain properties and relations are not to be regarded as essentially dispositional, and that these include spatial and temporal relations.

If that is correct, then in order to assess Mumford's proposal we need to identify the source of the intuitive reluctance we feed towards it and then we can come to a view as to whether this intuition may or may not be justified. I suggest that the following reasons might occur to one, prima facie at least, as explanations for this intuition:

(i) Very many laws refer to temporal intervals; they cannot all be regarded as manifestations of a temporal disposition.

(ii) Durations are relations and so cannot be dispositions.

(iii) Where some other nomically relevant property is clearly dispositional, we readily identify that property as the active disposition and so can exclude the temporal relation.

(iv) Time is a metaphysical background and so is non-causal; as such it cannot be dispositional.

I shall now consider these in turn.

(i)

It is true that temporal relations occur in many laws of nature, and so if they are dispositions, they are multi-track dispositions. I myself am reluctant to think of fundamental properties as multi-track dispositions. To do so is to hide a mystery. For example, in classical physics at least, it is I think misleading to think of there being a single multi-track property mass, which manifests itself both in Newton's second law and also in the law of gravitation. Rather, it seems to me as to others, more perspicuous to think of there being two single-track properties, inertial mass and gravitational mass, which as a matter of nomic fact are perfectly proportional. That nomic proportionality is of course a fact that needs explanation, presumably in dispositional essentialist terms. In my view, it is correct that multi-trackness might be a reason for denying fundamental dispositionality, unless it can be explained away. I doubt, however, that this thought is responsible for the intuitive reluctance we have identified. The view just sketched, that multi-track dispositions are not fundamental, is a highly contentious one. Its truth, if it is true, is unlikely to have much of an influence on our intuitions and so does not explain the target phenomenon, our intuitive reluctance to regard temporal relations as dispositional. And if concern about multi-trackness were intuitive, it would target intuitions concerning fundamentality, not dispositionality. After all, charge is involved in several laws of nature—above we have mentioned two, Coulomb's law and the Biot–Savart law, but that does not significantly dampen the intuitive plausibility of the idea that charge is dispositional in nature.

(ii)

One might think that dispositions have to be unary properties, intrinsic properties in particular, and so temporal relations cannot be dispositions. This might be a source of the target intuition. But if so, it is a poor basis for that intuition. Dispositions can certainly be extrinsic, as Jennifer McKitrick (2003) shows. For example, this key is disposed to open my front door, but that disposition depends on the lock with which that door is fitted. The weight of some object is the force it experiences in its local gravitational field and as such implies various dispositions, such as the disposition to depress a spring balance to a certain degree, that are not intrinsic. Correspondingly, there are relations that confer dispositions: key x matches lock y implies that y is disposed to be opened by x. x is heavier than y implies that x is disposed to displace y in a pair of scales. Abelard loves Héloise implies that Abelard is disposed to behave in certain ways towards Héloise. It *may* be that our intuitions that relations cannot be dispositional is stronger when it comes to fundamental properties—these should all be intrinsic, monadic properties. Nonetheless, I am not sure that such an intuition is either that strong or correct. Whether it is correct or not rather depends on what advances in physics reveal to us, but it is entirely plausible that mass, which is dispositional, will turn out to be a relation between a particle and the Higgs field

(Bauer 2011). If so, we might look for an intrinsic property underlying mass, but that would not make us think that mass is not dispositional.

(iii)

The third response suggests that we have a strong intuition that an effect can be the outcome of one disposition only, and so where two properties appear to be involved, only one of them can be regarded as the disposition whose manifestation is this outcome. If some force is the result of a charge at some distance, then since the charge is clearly a causally efficacious disposition, the distance cannot be. Likewise, if an object changes its momentum as a result of some force being applied for a time, since the force is clearly dispositional, the time cannot be. Again, I doubt that our intuitions are especially strong in this regard; furthermore if this were the source of the target intuition, it would be a poor ground for it. Typically a disposition will require a stimulus in order to be manifested. This stimulus will itself typically be the instantiation of some disposition. So one would expect many cases of the manifestation of one disposition to involve a second disposition. Consider a fragile glass that breaks because a hand squeezes it too hard. The squeezing hand can plausibly be thought of having a second disposition, a disposition to deform the object it squeezes. The breaking is therefore the outcome of the interaction of the two dispositions, fragility and the disposition to deform. Whether or not that is correct, I do not think it is ruled out by any intuition of the form 'since one disposition, fragility, is involved, there cannot be a second disposition.' Consider an air-filled rubber balloon that is in a deep water bath. By controlling the depth of the balloon (and hence the pressure on the balloon) and the temperature of the water (and hence the temperature of the air in the balloon), we can use the ideal gas law to calculate the volume of the balloon:

$$V = \frac{nRT}{p} \qquad (6)$$

It seems correct to think of the volume of the balloon as the result of the interaction of two dispositions, the pressure on the balloon p and its temperature T. There seems no inclination to regard one as not being dispositional just because the other is. C. B. Martin develops the notion of 'reciprocal disposition partners' that depends on the idea of dispositions interacting that does not seem intuitively implausible on that ground in particular (Armstrong et al. 1996, 136).

(iv)

The last suggestion is that our intuition that temporal intervals are not dispositions arises from the fact that we naturally think of time as a background and so not as a causal property and so not a disposition. In the next section I shall develop the case for this proposal; I shall argue that if we think of time as a background (and likewise space) then we should deny that temporal (and spatial) intervals have a dispositional character. The Newtonian picture of the world we naturally adopt does indeed characterize time and space as backgrounds. And so this is a plausible source of the intuition we are discussing. That will allow me, in section 6, to undermine that intuition by pointing out that physicists have been developing the idea that an ideal physical theory should be background-free; in particular, time and space are not a background in general relativity.

4.

In suggesting that we have an intuition that temporal relations cannot be proper causes, I am not suggesting either that we do not think of such relations as explanatory or that we never refer to temporal relations in causal contexts. Clearly the fact that temporal relations appear in equations such as (4) and (5) means that they will figure in explanations. Nonetheless, when attributing causation we do tend to think of time as subsidiary in such contexts, as a modifier of the cause rather than as a cause itself. It is as if time is thought of adverbially. It is true that we may refer to time in causal contexts: 'We missed the train because Humphrey took so long polishing his shoes.' Even so, I think that we tend to regard time in a similar light to absences. We talk as if absences are causes, but we are also inclined not to regard them as real, bona fide causes; the real cause is something else (my failure to water the plant is not the 'real' cause of its withering; that was the heat which dried it up). Likewise, we may think of temporal relations as figuring in causal explanations in a secondary, derivative, or partial way.

As mentioned, one hypothesis for explaining this is that we intuitively regard space and time as backgrounds and as such playing only a shadow causal role. This intuition is reflected in many of our theories and infects our metaphysics.

What is a background? According to John Baez (2009), a background structure is "any sort of structure appearing in a mathematical model of a physical system that is *fixed* rather than *dynamical*—i.e., which does not depend on the state of the physical system in question." Baez goes on to give a heuristic characterization, "we can think of a background structure as something which affects the dynamics of the system while remaining unaffected by it." Baez then points out that this violates the reciprocity of cause and effect, a relationship that Anandan and Brown (1995, 351) call the "action–reaction principle" and which they characterize thus:

We shall say that two physical entities satisfy the action–reaction (AR) principle, if they interact in such a manner that each entity both acts on and is acted on by the other entity. . . . [A] physical theory is dynamically complete if all the entities postulated in the theory pairwise satisfy the AR principle. Space-time structure in general relativity is affected, if not wholly determined, by the distribution of matter, as well as itself determining the privileged motion of free bodies. General relativity is thus dynamically complete.   (Anandan and Brown 1995, 351)

Baez gives a simple illustration, the problem of a bead on a wire. In solving this problem, one will treat the wire as a background. The curve of the wire is fixed and does not change and this allows, depending on the equation of the curve, a relatively

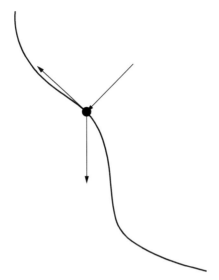

Figure 9.1. The forces acting on a bead on a wire. The wire is treated as a background if no account is taken of the corresponding forces on the wire

straightforward means of calculating the equation of motion of the bead, via the forces of gravity and friction. However, this ignores the fact that the bead is exerting corresponding forces on the wire, which would thus deform or move. Our treatment therefore ignores the AR principle (although the wire is held to exert a force on the bead, no force is taken to be exerted on the wire) and is not dynamically complete. If one did take the forces on the wire into account, then the position of the wire would no longer be a background, because it would not only affect the dynamics of the bead but is also affected by the dynamics. (We would probably then treat the endpoints of the wire as a background.)

Newtonian mechanics is not dynamically complete: time and space are treated as a background. The temporal and spatial metrical structure (i.e. the relationships among space–time points) are fixed. In this case, not *everything* that is part of or a consequence of the structure affects the dynamics of physical objects without being affected by them. For Newtonian space–time determines an absolute position and velocity for objects, but these play no part in affecting the dynamics of those objects. They are nonetheless part of the background structure. In this sense, redundant structure is also background—we might distinguish between active and redundant background. A redundant component of a dynamical theory is one that is surplus to what is required for the theory's dynamical explanations.[2] Absolute time in Newtonian

---

[2] Here is another example to illustrate the notion of redundant structure. A theory uses real numbers to describe position in space and time. However, if space and time are quantized, so that there is no physical sense to positions in space and time between those permitted by the quanta, then we might strictly need

mechanics is redundant because it is irrelevant to the explanation of forces, motions, and so forth—relative time (temporal interval) is sufficient for such explanations. Strictly, redundant background is not in conflict with the AR principle because it doesn't interact at all, although it would conflict with the Eleatic principle, that only what is causally (or nomically) efficacious exists. Active background does play a part in determining dynamics, and so is in conflict with the AR principle. Moving from classical Newtonian space–time to neo-Newtonian space–time eliminates its redundant background. On the other hand, it does not eliminate its active background (i.e. those elements of the classical picture that violate the AR principle).

One might wonder, from the perspective of a dispositional essentialist view of all properties, why the action–reaction principle is important. After all, if the properties and relations in question can be part of an 'action,' why does the lack of a 'reaction' matter? My view is that the AR principle plays a powerful role in our understanding of causation. Basic causal action is always interaction. Interestingly this is a point that Ellis and others (e.g. C. B. Martin, cited in section 3) emphasize very strongly. If that is right, then the fact that time is treated as a background implies that time and temporal relations are not *real* causes. Or if they do exist they are pseudo-causes or modifiers to the real causes but not real causes themselves. Thus in a realistic physics, time as a background structure occupies an uncomfortable and unstable position. It is part of the structure, playing a role in nomological explanation; but also not truly real, not a full cause. So in summary:

time is a background structure ∧ the action–reaction principle is true ⇒ time is non-causal (non-dispositional)

In which case, Ellis is right about time (and likewise about space): temporal properties and relations are not essentially dispositional in nature.

5.

One possible response to the uncomfortable position of time as a background structure is to deny that time really exists at all. The idealist interpretation of Leibniz suggests that this is his solution (Leibniz and Clarke 1965). Of course, such a response does nothing to rehabilitate time as causal or dispositional. But it does eliminate the problem by denying that temporal properties are genuinely natural properties. In which case they are not counterexamples to the claim that fundamental natural properties are dispositional in nature.

only the natural numbers in our theory, not all the structure of the reals. We might continue to use the reals for convenience (we can then use differential equations to provide good approximations), but strictly the additional structure provided by the reals over the natural numbers is redundant.

The alternative is to seek a physics which eschews background structures. One might wonder whether this is to be achieved by adopting relationalism abut time and space. Indeed relationalism of the kind Leibniz promoted and the elimination of background structure are related. They are, however, not the same; and so, I argue, relationalism is not sufficient to resolve the problem facing the monistic dispositional essentialist.

I take relationalism to be the claim:

(R) the existence of space and time are dependent on the existence of material objects and relations among them.

Note that Leibniz's arguments against Newton's absolutism are directed against the *redundant* background structure, not against background structure per se. Thus his arguments from the principle of sufficient reason are effective (if effective at all) only against classical Newtonian space–time with its absolute times, positions, and velocities, but not against neo-Newtonian space–time, even though the latter has plenty of (active) background structure.

Still there is a slightly different, more general, sense of 'absolute' as used by Einstein:

If Newton called the space of physics 'absolute,' he was thinking of yet another property of that which we call 'ether'. Each physical object influences and in general is influenced in turn by others. The latter, however, is not true of the ether of Newtonian mechanics. The inertia-producing property of this ether, in accordance with classical mechanics, is precisely not to be influenced, either by the configuration of matter, or by anything else. For this reason, one may call it 'absolute'.   (Einstein 1999, 15)

All background structures, being immutable, are absolute in this sense.

The debate between absolutism and relationalism and that between substantivalism and relationalism are typically taken to be more or less the same debate. Part of the problem here is that even once we distinguish between philosophical uses of 'substance' and everyday uses, the philosophical uses are still varied. Principal among the features attributed to substances are the following:

(A) Substances are genuine particulars. This is the Aristotelian idea that substances are the subjects of predication but cannot be predicated of other things. This makes them particulars in modern parlance. I think it is implicit in most Aristotle-inspired discussions that substances are normal 'things,' but not gerrymandered combinations of them: Julius Caesar, Brutus's knife, the Temple of Jupiter, are all substances, but their mereological sum is not.

(B) Substances are substrates. This is the notion of substance we find in Locke, and relates closely to the Aristotelian notion: substances are what support or bear properties.

(C) Substances are unchanging. This conception we find in Hume (1978, 220), when he denies that there really is any substance in normal cases, since it is an illusion bred by the smooth changes we perceive in things, that we infer that there is some unchanging thing that "continue[s] the same under all these variations."

(D) Substances are independent fundamental entities, on which others depend (a) for their existence and/or (b) for their properties.

Let as assume that time and space (or space–time) are objects. Then they are genuine, non-gerrymandered particulars, and so are substances according to (A). This is not the sense in which relationalism denies that space and time are substances. Whether they are substrates, (B), depends on the precise relationship between space, time, and matter. For Boscovich, matter is composed of extensionless point particles; what appears to be extended matter is just the spheres of attraction and repulsion around the point particles. However, in the elaboration of Boscovich's view by Michell and Priestley, the point particles are themselves eliminated—we have just space and time and modifications thereof. According to the latter view, it is space–time points that bear properties and so are the substrate in the sense of (B); they are also fundamental, (D). By making matter dependent on the properties of space and time, this is clearly antithetical to relationalism, which claims that the dependency is the other way around. It seems difficult to see how something could be a substrate if it were not fundamental, and so (B) implies (D). If relationalism is true, then the existence of space–time is dependent on matter, and so (D) is false of space–time, and therefore (B) is false also. And so for Leibniz, space and time are not substances in the sense of (B) nor of (D)—for Leibniz the substrate role, (B), and the independent fundamental entity role, (D), are reserved for monads.

Must (C) also be false of space–time if relationalism is true? I presume that Leibniz thought that although time and space were dependent on relations between objects, he did not think that the structure of space and time change as objects move and accelerate. A successful Leibnizian program would recover the unchanging Euclidean mathematical structure of Newton's space and time without their implication of absolute time, position, and velocity. So space and time might be dependent but unchanging.

How does the rejection of absolutism and background structures fit into this picture? The key feature of a background structure is its immutability. And so if we eliminate background structures while retaining the existence of space and time, then space and time cannot have the feature (C). But as just argued, relationalism does not directly imply the negation of (C), only of (D) and (B). The adoption of relationalism per se does not suffice to ensure background-freedom. Whether some proposal for relationalism in fact secures background-freedom depends on the details of that proposal. So relationalism in a Newtonian context does not give us background-freedom. If the General Theory of Relativity (GTR) can be accommodated by a relationalism that denies (C), then that will be because of the particular demands made by GTR. So relationalism in itself is not an answer to the problem facing the monistic dispositional essentialist.

6.

A number of philosophically-minded physicists have argued that a satisfactory theory of quantum gravity must be background-free (Smolin 1991; Rovelli 1997). If they are correct, then that provides welcome if indirect empirical support for the application of dispositional essentialism to spatiotemporal properties. If space and time are not backgrounds, then that removes the motivation for regarding them as sufficiently acausal to be not essentially dispositional.

I shall not review the arguments for background-independence arising from consideration of the prospects for quantum gravity. Rather, I shall remark on the consequences for the issues I have been addressing of the well-known fact that Einstein's general theory of relativity is a major advance in the direction of background-independence, since that advance is sufficient for our purposes. The important development is that the space–time metric in general relativity is dynamical. That is, it is determined by the specific solutions to the equations of the theory and as a consequence its structure is determined by, for example, the matter field.

With this in mind, we can see not only that the structure of space–time is changeable as a consequence of the distribution of matter, but also that this structure can indeed be a genuine cause and can be conceived of in dispositional terms. The well-known rubber-sheet illustration of general relativity emphasizes this point. Not only does a massive object cause space–time to change its structure, but also that structure influences the behavior of matter, for example, the motion of a test particle. It is thus plausible to see the structure of space–time in dispositional terms. One way to see this is to consider that in Newtonian physics, gravitational mass is a simple disposition: a mass exerts a force directly on another. However, in general relativity, this disposition is no longer a simple disposition but a compound one. The gravitational effects of a mass on a test particle are mediated by the distortion of space–time. That is, the gravitational disposition is made up of a disposition to distort space–time *plus* what must be a second disposition, the disposition of space–time to influence the motion of the test particle. The point can be made in more detail by considering the fact that I can distort space–time by subjecting some elastic material object to a stress. That action will also have the effect of creating gravitational waves, which may in turn bring about stresses in some distant object (Nerlich 1994, 183).

To some extent we have moved away from our original question, which was how to characterize temporal duration and spatial displacement in dispositional terms. Instead it looks as if we are attributing dispositions to regions of space–time. Are we now answering a different question from the one we started with? If the question is different, then that is what one would expect as a consequence of the change in the science. The dispositional essentialist view is concerned with natural properties and relations, and in particular with fundamental ones. And so, if our preferred current theory tells us that local space–time metric is what is explanatorily fundamental rather than point to point spatial and temporal intervals, then we need to shift our focus from the (essential) dispositionality of the latter to the (essential) dispositionality of the former.

7.

To conclude: temporal relations and spatial relations present the monistic dispositional essentialist with a problem, because it is difficult to see how these relations can be conceived of as dispositional at all. While pointing to their roles in laws might seem to offer a route to understanding them as dispositional, it remains the case that our intuitions do not endorse a conception of space and time as causal, and that fact is a block on our seeing them as dispositional. The view that space–time is explanatory but not causal in classical physics is one endorsed by other writers on this topic, such as Graham Nerlich (1994). My own diagnosis of this is that the classical view violates the action–reaction principle, and consequently it is implausible to regard space–time as causal. Thus in order to regard space–time as causal and hence potentially dispositional, we need to remove that feature of the classical view that violates the action–reaction principle. That feature is the fact that classical space and time are background structures. And, thankfully (from the point of view of dispositional essentialism) we are not obliged to maintain that feature. Indeed general relativity removes it for us, showing how the variable geometry of space–time is both disposed to undergo changes and is disposed to bring about changes. We are thus entitled not to regard space–time and its properties as purely categorical, but can treat them as we do other fundamental natural features of the world.

Acknowledgments

Research on this chapter was funded by the Australian Research Council Discovery Grant, Neglected Problems of Time.

10

Powerful Perdurance

Linking Parts with Powers

Neil E. Williams

1. Introduction

For the most part, debates over the nature of persistence have been conducted on neo-Humean turf. Though debate rages over the existence of temporal parts, both sides seem content to keep powers—properties with dispositional essences whose nature is to be directed at potential future states of affairs—out of the debate. When talk of properties arises, one can safely assume that it is categorical properties (non-power properties whose causal profiles are contingent) that are being discussed; few in the debate take powers seriously enough to bother wasting their breath on them. Any mention of causation by those who think that causation is central to persistence is similarly neo-Humean. Talk of powers *and* persistence is almost non-existent.

   In the rare instances that the two have been considered together, the conclusion has been that powers are far better matched with *endurantism*, the account of persistence that denies that temporal parts are central to persistence.[1] The suggestion is that *perdurantism*—according to which objects persist by having temporal parts—is a neo-Humean account of persistence, and so powers do not belong there. Stephen Mumford denies that introducing powers to the persistence debate conclusively decides the debate one way or the other, but does claim that "a powers ontologist nevertheless has some reason to favor endurantism as sitting most comfortably with their ontology" (2009b, 226). I do not agree; I think that powers are just as comfortable in a perdurantist framework. In fact, not only are both accounts of persistence open to a powers ontology, both can benefit from its addition. Perdurantists can employ powers as the non-supervenient link between object stages, and endurantists can use powers to explain how it is that objects move along the temporal dimension.

---

[1] So claim Mumford (2009b) and Wahlberg (2009); the only exceptions are my own Williams (2005a,b). I consider Mumford's argument in section 6. Due to commitments he has that I do not share, I do not deal with Wahlberg's concerns directly; nonetheless the argument of section 6 could be used to respond to his concerns.

Despite all the good work I believe powers can do for thinking about persistence, my present aim is modest. It is to lay a foundation for a powers-based account of perdurance by clearing away some initial problems arising from how we conceptualize powers. For the most part my presentation of the positive account will be brief and underdeveloped. It will contain the basic picture, but no more. That is because there is so much implied opposition to this sort of view that there is far more benefit in answering objections first, before working out the details. Most of the opposition does not concern powers and perdurance per se, but comes from a general conception of powers which makes them look ill-fitted for this role. By considering the problems that arise when mixing powers with perdurance, I will show that this is not the case: powers are perfectly at home with perdurance. In considering these objections, we will learn as much about the nature of powers as we do about how they might serve as the glue that links temporal parts. This may seem backwards, but then again you would hardly take a suit to the tailors to get a precise fit if you had not yet decided it was a suit you were going to buy. Hence my aim is to argue that powers are up to the task of linking together temporal parts as part of a perdurantist account of persistence, but I will not yet put them to work. To be clear, it is not my aim to defend the powers ontology, nor perdurance. My aim is to show that the two make a fine match, that is all.

My discussion of the problems with combining powers and perdurance focuses on three worries. The first (section 4) is that powers are not typically thought of as being for manifestations of powers that are of the same type as the power producing the manifestation. But if powers are going to link temporal parts, then given that any perduring object will typically be composed of more than two temporal parts, the manifestations must be for the very same powers as those that produce them. Second (section 5) is that the manifestation of powers is generally understood as a mutual affair arising from the interaction of reciprocal power partners. That is, the 'stimulus' that triggers most powers is nothing more than the presence of other power properties. But as persistence does not look to be interactive, the causal process must involve powers that operate in some other way. The third problem (section 6) is that manifestations are often interpreted as dynamic continuous processes, and therefore unfit to be combined with a metaphysic that takes objects to be composed of short-lived, static, temporal parts. I begin with a brief introduction to perdurance (section 2) and how an ontology of causal powers can be put to use within that account of persistence (section 3).

2. Parts, Perdurance, and Persistence

Two positions dominate the persistence landscape. They are 'perdurantism' and 'endurantism.' Perdurantists hold that objects persist by 'perduring'; that is, by being composed of temporal parts.[2] A 'temporal part' is a short-lived part of an object,

---

[2] For present purposes, I have lumped the stage theory in with perdurantism, as their views differ semantically but not ontologically. Perdurantists claim that subject terms—such as 'chair', 'person', and

considered along the temporal dimension. Just as objects can be divided into spatial parts (the top half of the table; my left foot), by analogy they can be divided into segments of their lifetimes (the first two minutes of your life; the second year of the twenty-first century). The thought is that objects have these parts just like they do the spatial ones and that to persist is to be made up of many such temporal parts.

More often than not, perdurantism is combined with an eternalist account of the ontology of time, resulting in what is known as 'four-dimensionalism.'[3] According to the eternalist, all times (past, present, and future) are on equal ontological footing. There is nothing special about the present: the times before and after are just as real. Just like 'here' points to where we are spatially, 'now' is a term for the present moment of utterance—an indexical that points to one time, but not to a special time qua ontological status. Combining eternalism with perdurance gives us the picture of perduring entities as 'spatiotemporal worms,' which explains why perdurantism is sometimes called 'worm-theory.' One gets worms by circling groups of temporal parts that combine to form persisting entities, much like you might circle the letters in a word search puzzle to pick out a word.

Endurantism is the rejection of perdurantism. Endurantists claim that objects persist by 'enduring,' which on many versions is described as an object's being 'wholly present at every moment that it exists.' What exactly this phrase is supposed to mean I cannot say, but in those cases where endurantism is combined with presentism (the account of time according to which only the present exists), it makes sense that all of a persisting object is located right there in the present. The combination is the most popular version of endurantism, resulting in 'three-dimensionalism.' As part of the presentist/endurantist package, we get a picture of continuants as *moving through time*. Unlike perdurantism, where persisting objects are temporally extended worms, the endurantist picture of persistence is one of flow—with every passing moment the persisting object progresses in its entirety, leaving nothing behind. Other versions understand endurantism as the denial of temporal parts. I find this somewhat odd, as 'temporal part' has a neutral reading that is amenable to all accounts of persistence. I thus prefer to characterize endurantism as the view that persistence *does not depend on* temporal parts. I think endurantists have them, but they supervene on persisting objects, not the reverse.

Another way of presenting the distinction between perdurance and endurance is in terms of a disagreement concerning how 'identity' should be understood when applied diachronically. If we consider the relationship between a-at-t_1 and a-at-t_2 (understood neutrally), endurantism is the view that a is identical in each case—what connects

---

'molecule'—refer to persisting entities (collections of object stages), not the singular stages. Stage-theorists take our object terms to pick out temporal parts—the 'stages.' I use the terms 'temporal part' and 'stage' interchangeably—they are neutral between these two views.

[3] Perdurantism does not commit one to eternalism, but they make for a more comfortable pairing than perdurance does with any other view. The same holds for endurantism and presentism.

the parts of an object's career is nothing less than identity. Perdurantists claim that something less than identity—often called 'gen-identity'—is what connects the various parts of a. In other words, perdurantism is the view that a-at-t_1 and a-at-t_2 are not strictly speaking the same object, but that some connection (weaker than identity) holds between them such that each makes up a moment in a persisting object's career. The primary motivation for perdurance comes from a specific version of the problem of change, known as the 'problem of temporary intrinsics' (Lewis 1986, 202). The problem of change is that persisting objects instantiate different intrinsic properties over their lifetimes, but this is in violation of Leibniz's Law. Nothing can be both bent and straight, yet persons seem to do this all the time and survive. This can be resolved if the having of different intrinsic properties is indexed to specific times. The problem of temporary intrinsics goes on to consider how the time-indexing might be carried out. Three options present themselves. The first is that intrinsic properties are not intrinsic at all, but are instead disguised relations that objects bear to times (bent-at-t_1; straight-at-t_2). The second option tenses the copula: there is no being bent or straight, one is-at-t_1 bent and is-at-t_2 straight. The third is that the different properties are had by temporal parts of persisting objects: the temporal part of x-at-t_1 is bent, the temporal part of x-at-t_2 is straight. Lewis claims that the last is to be preferred, because only it can allow for properties to be instantiated *simpliciter*.

Whether this argument is compelling can be put aside; what matters to us is the account of persistence that emerges. According to it, objects persist through time by having temporal parts, and those parts instantiate the problematic properties. It follows that persisting objects have at least as many temporal parts as needed to accommodate all the intrinsic changes they undergo during their lifespans. But the numbers do not end there. In order to accommodate changes that *could* have occurred during some changeless span of time, even if they did not, we need sufficiently many temporal parts to support any possible intrinsic changes. Persisting objects will be composed of a great many temporal parts indeed. Just how many, and just how long (or short) these parts turn out to be is a matter I consider in section 6 below.

3. Immanent Causation and Powers

None of the benefits one might gain from cutting up objects into temporal parts can be enjoyed without also providing a means of sticking them back together. Objects may persist by having temporal parts, but no perdurantist account is complete unless it offers some criteria for linking them; that is to say, perdurantism is incomplete without an account of diachronic composition.[4] Typical solutions fall into three broad categories: nihilism, universalism, and restricted composition.

---

[4] Accounts of diachronic composition need not be translatable into an account of synchronic composition; there is no requirement that what binds objects over time must also apply *mutatis mutandis* at a time.

As we are dealing with versions of perdurantism, the *nihilist* response (according to which composition never occurs, or only occurs if the parts form a life) is off the table. Common sense dictates that objects persist, not just persons and dogs. That leaves open *universalism*—the view that any combination of parts (spatial or temporal) composes an object, however gruesome or monstrous it happens to be, or some version of *restricted composition*, which limits objects to a subset of those just considered by bringing in more stringent conditions that composed objects must satisfy. These conditions are often referred to as 'unity conditions.' For present purposes, we have no need to decide between the universal and restricted forms of composition. By applying unity conditions, the universalist is able to pick out just those persisting objects that the defender of restricted composition is partial to. Whereas the restricted view takes these to be the only persisting objects, the universalist can treat them as a privileged class.

The unity criterion I defend is a causal one. To my mind, the glue that holds object stages together is causal, as only a causal account is strong enough to give us the right persisting objects. Popular alternatives include spatiotemporal continuity and sortal continuity, but both are subject to counterexamples that causal accounts evade.[5] What the counterexamples show is that these criteria are at best necessary criteria of persistence. For instance, imagine a strange machine capable of annihilating any object, and another with the complementary power to create objects *ex nihilo*.[6] Now bring out a test subject, and put the machines to work. At t_1 we shall imagine our test subject, a cat, is sat quietly in an otherwise empty room. At t_2 we decide to put the first machine to work, and the cat is annihilated. Then, at t_3 we put the second machine to work, and a cat—qualitatively identical to the first—appears exactly where the first had been. At t_4 we leave the cat up to its own business. A standard description of the scenario is that we have destroyed one cat and created a qualitatively identical but numerically distinct *second* cat where the first had been. The second cat is spatiotemporally continuous with the first, and satisfies the same sortal. Hence neither condition is sufficient for persistence.

A common fix, as I have suggested, is to claim that what is required of persistence is the *right sort of causal connection* between the temporal parts of the persisting object (see Hawley 2001, ch. 3 and Armstrong 1997, 74). (It must be of the 'right sort' because the actions of the machines are causal.) To be the right sort of causation it needs to come from *within* the object itself, such that each temporal part is the cause of the next. This right sort of causation is known as 'immanent causation.'

W. E. Johnson defines immanent causation as "the causality in which the cause occurrence and the effect occurrence are attributed to the same continuant," which he contrasts with *transeunt* causation, wherein "the cause occurrence and the effect

---

[5] See Hirsch (1982) to see the spatiotemporal continuity criterion applied; Wiggins (2001) for the sortal criterion.

[6] The basic idea here is borrowed from Armstrong (1980) and Shoemaker (1979). For those who doubt the possibility of such machines, think of them as Gods instead.

occurrence are referred to different continuants" (1964, 128).[7] Similarly, Hermann Lotze speaks of the immanent causal process by which "state a^1 of a thing a begins to bring about a consequent state, a^2, in the same thing," contrasted with the process where by "the same a^1 sets about producing the consequence b^1 in another being b" (1884, 88).

The basics of immanent causation are easy to grasp. Whereas transeunt causal relations involve causal interaction between distinct objects, immanent causation is a form of causation that involves just one object. A single object stage, environment allowing, will produce a successor object stage, 'in its own image.' The cause of the production is the original object stage itself—grounded in its ability to create the latter stage, which is the resultant effect. In this manner, object stage after object stage will be created. The result is a series of object stages that stretch over some period of time. The largest possible chain of object stages created by the immanent causal process will constitute a persisting object. Therefore, two object stages count as part of the same object just in case they are two object stages within a maximally causally connected series of object stages, where that series of object stages are pairwise connected by way of immanent causation.

We have seen that persistence through immanent causation is understood roughly as follows:

> Two object stages constitute object stages of a single persisting object iff they are members in a maximal series of pairwise immanently causally connected object stages.

Whether the arguments in defense of this account are successful is not something we need to consider. What matters is whether we can bring in powers to play the causal role.

Power properties, recall, are intrinsic properties with dispositional essences—unlike categorical properties, their causal profiles are necessary.[8] According to the powers ontology, power properties carry their causal potential inside them. They are not reducible to inert qualities acting in accord with the laws of nature, nor are they mere second-order properties that owe their existence to some other property whose nature is not similarly causal. On this view, powers are genuine first-order properties, and they are the basis of all causation. If there are laws of nature in the powers theorist's world, these laws supervene on either the powers or the ways in which the powers have been exercised. But these laws are not the *doers* of the world: that job falls to the powers.

The typical power terminology has it that the effect brought about by a power when it is exercised is its 'manifestation.' More often than not powers are individuated by

---

[7] Johnson's definition of immanent causation makes reference to 'continuants' (his term for persisting entities) so could not be applied to persistence without some modification.

[8] I prefer to speak of powers, but as the literature uses 'power' and 'disposition' interchangeably, at times I am forced to do the same.

the type of manifestations that they are capable of producing; a power is a power *for* some manifestation-type. That manifestation is produced by the power's state when the power is stimulated in the right sort of way. This stimulation typically involves the presence or absence of other powers, and the particular arrangement they are in. However, it is no part of the powers metaphysic that a power *needs* to be stimulated at any point in its existence; whether or not an object has the power in question is a matter of its having that property, not whether the conditions required for its exercising ever happen to obtain. Nor need it be the case that any single type of power property be *for* just a single manifestation-type: some favor an account according to which each power has a single manifestation-type (powers are 'single track'), whereas others take powers to be capable of responding differently for different types of simulation (powers are 'multi-track') (see Williams 2011b).

What can properties like this do for perdurance? The short answer is that powers (more correctly, the exercising of the right sorts of powers) can be the mechanism by which persistence occurs. The immanent causal connections that link temporal parts of perduring objects can be constituted by powers, instantiated by temporal parts, whose manifestations are the later temporal parts of that same object. Each temporal part of a perduring entity is the manifestation of a specific power of its immediate predecessor: those powers are powers *for* the existence of further temporal parts.

This would mean that two object stages would constitute object stages of a single persisting object just in case they are members in a maximal series of object stage pairs wherein for each pair the latter object stage is the manifestation of some power that has been exercised by the first. Were a pair of fantastical machines to destroy the first of any of these object stage pairs, and create in its place a new object stage exactly like the second would have been, the case would not be one of persistence, because the latter stage was not brought about by the former in the right way. We might have a hard time recognizing that this was the case, but the facts would be in order regardless.

This, I imagine, would be the powers-based immanent causal case for fundamental entities. For the larger composite entities the story would be more complex, as it would involve first the persistence of the spatial parts that compose it, but then various powers concerning the continued arrangement and organization of the composite spatial parts. How exactly this story might go is far from clear, but one might expect to gain greater perspective on the issue by tracking the development of biological entities, as they appear to represent the hardest sort of case.

By this point, many readers are bound to think that these powers are very odd powers indeed. They are certainly not the sort of powers that are generally referenced in a powers ontology and do not resemble those that a mature science might commit us to. But do not take their unusual nature to mean that there cannot be such things, nor that they cannot play an important role. This is, after all, speculative metaphysics we are engaged in, and we should not lose sight of the fact that a causal criterion is arguably the most popular response to the question of what links temporal parts. Hence the powers view is merely a suggested way in which that causal role might be filled. On the powers metaphysic, all causation (both for change and for maintaining the status quo) is due to the exercising of powers. If temporal parts are causally linked, then causal powers can do the heavy lifting of perdurantism. Moreover, for those who are suspicious of this sort of speculative metaphysics, common sense tells us that objects persist, and they must do this *somehow*. Many perdurantists avoid the really hard questions of persistence by assuming that all the temporal parts are present in the world and are neatly arranged—then say little about what the causal criterion they support might be. And endurantists are no better off: they beg the same question when they simply assume that objects can move through time without explanation. Powers for persistence are odd indeed, but they are no stranger than the problem of persistence demands they be, and they come from a positive attempt to answer a question that critics have refused to answer.

Beyond this very brief sketch, I will say no more about how powers can serve to link temporal parts. As I have indicated, it is not my aim to make such an account plausible; I have, after all, done nothing to defend the existence of powers, perdurantism, or a causal account of the unity criterion for persistence. My aim is to show that powers are up to the task. The way in which many folk depict powers would render powers unsuitable for the task I would have them perform. But as we shall see, those are rarely the product of careful consideration. Thinking through these worries will teach us a great deal about powers.[9]

4. Powers as Identical with their Manifestations

The central feature of the perdurantist model under consideration is that temporal parts of persisting objects are linked by exercising powers. For any object whose existence spans more than two temporal parts, it is reasonable to think that the power of the first stage that connects it to the second is type-identical with that which connects the second to the third, and so on. It would be quite surprising to discover that things were otherwise and highly uneconomical to suggest a framework of type-distinct powers accounting for the persistence of each new object-stage. Hence a more economical version of power-based perdurantism has it that all the relevant powers are type-identical, at least across the lifespan of a single object.

However, a number of prominent power theorists claim that powers cannot be like this. For instance, Shoemaker writes that it "is agreed on all sides that the possession and acquisition of powers produces changes in what properties are instantiated in the world" (2011, 8).[10] Yet the actions of the powers we are here considering do not have changes as their manifestations—power-based perdurance requires that the relevant

---

[9] A full defense of this view would take a great deal more discussion from the persistence side of the issue, but I will put those matters to one side, focusing only on what powers need to be like to fit the bill.

[10] On a reading that is more charitable to my own ends, this quotation indicates that changes are due to the actions of powers, not that powers are restricted to producing changes, but plenty of readers will not favor the charitable reading.

powers will *not* be for changes. That is, as any power of type P whose manifestation is also a power of type P involves no change (here I follow Geach (1969) in understanding changes as requiring that for any object x and property F, a change has taken place just in case $F(x)$ is true at some time t_1, but false at some distinct time t_2), power-based perdurance is committed to powers that are not for changes, and many will interpret this as a problem for the view.

This widely held belief—despite capturing many cases—is nevertheless false. Virtually any example of simultaneous causation can be offered as a counterexample to the claim that all powers are for change. To wit, two playing cards leaned against one another are the cause of each other's continued standing, as a result of their being appropriately powered to do so. Likewise for the book resting on the table and the stable bridge under the heavy traffic. Not all causation results in a change, and not all powers need to have different powers as their manifestations.[11]

A more specific version of this worry complains that not only are the relevant powers not for changes, they will be for manifestations that are the self-same power. This runs directly counter to claims like the following, provided by E. J. Lowe:

> A power, P, is never identical with its manifestation-type, M. This is obviously true of *token* powers, since types cannot be identical with tokens. But it is also true of power-*types*. Clearly, even though a power can be a power to acquire *another power*, a power cannot be a power to acquire *itself*: it cannot *be* its own manifestation-type.[12]   (Lowe 2010, 12)

We might capture the general claim that powers cannot be identical with their manifestations as follows:

PP: A power P cannot have as its manifestation the power P.

Lowe obviously thinks that PP is not just plausible, but true. So much so that he is willing to expand on its interpretation slightly but not willing to offer any argument in support of it. I do not share Lowe's opinion.

As Lowe indicates, PP is ambiguous between type and token readings. As no token power can be strictly identical with a power-type, we can dismiss any version of PP that would fill in the first occurrence of P with a token power, and the second with a power-type. That leaves us with two types of disambiguation of PP: those that are token–token, and those that are type–type. Here is one of the token–token disambiguations:

---

[11] Williams (2005b) offers a sustained defense of this point, in addition to the claim that there are other 'static' dispositions whose manifestations are not changes. On some treatments of powers (Mumford 2009a and Molnar 2003), a power is for the same manifestation regardless of the circumstances. According to those views, the two cards have the power to fall (a change, if only a minimal one), and they jointly manifest those powers by collectively staying stood. I am not partial to thinking of powers in this way; after all, does each card not exercise its power to stand when met with the right sort of stimulus, and is this not just another way its power to move is capable of being manifested? As such, are we not right in thinking that the power is *also* the power to be stood?

[12] What ontological category manifestations belong to is an open question. I prefer to treat them as states of affairs, in which case this worry would not arise (see the end of this section), but this view is not widely held. Rather than dismiss the issue out of hand, it is worth considering the objection in case it turns out that manifestations are properties.

PP.1 Token–Token: a token instance of a power P_1, instantiated by object a at t_1 at location l_1, cannot have as its manifestation the existence of that same token instance P_1 by a at t_1 and l_1.

Here the sense of identity is a strict one. PP.1 claims that no power token can have as its manifestation *the exact power token that it itself is*. PP.1 is true, and for an obvious reason: PP.1 is nothing more than a corollary of the claim that (strictly speaking) nothing can be the cause of itself. No token power can be such that it can be the cause of itself; hence, it cannot be the case that a token power has itself as its potential manifestation, so we should have no problem accepting the truth of PP.1.

PP.1 looks to be true, but it is only one reading of PP. Dropping the problematic part of PP.1—that which restricts the manifestation to the identical token—would allow for a more sensible manifestation of the power. As noted, no token power can be strictly identical with a power type, so we cannot have a token-type version of PP. But any token instance of a power can be identical with another instance of that same power-type, to the extent that both power tokens are instances of the same power-type. That is to say, two token powers can be type-identical, which is nothing more than we should expect of two token instances of the same type. Hence we get:

PP.2 Token–Token: a token instance of a power P_1, instantiated by object a at t_1 at location l_1, cannot have as its manifestation the existence of some token instance P_2 (where P_1 is type-identical with P_2) by some object b at t_2 and l_2.

Unlike PP.1, PP.2 is not trivially true, if it is true at all. Barring the case where P_2 is strictly identical with P_1 (the case covered in PP.1), the only reason I can see to endorse PP.2 is that such fine-grained manifestation-types are unlikely. While it is not impossible that a power is for such a highly circumscribed manifestation, I maintain my skepticism. It would be quite surprising to learn that there were token powers that had as their potential manifestations not instances of powers that *just happen* to be had by some object at some time and place, but were *necessarily* for the having of that power by a specified object at a similarly specified time and place. What PP.2 claims is that no instance of a power can be the cause of that same type of power having an instance at some other time and place (where that time and place are specified as part of the identity of the instantiated power) and this is false, even if unlikely.

Once it is appreciated that any token power can have as its manifestation a token power of the same type, there should be no reason for thinking that a power-type cannot be such that its manifestation is that very same power-type. It cannot hold for every such case, as evinced in PP.1, but many other cases are admissible (and not at all suspicious like PP.2). Hence we have no reason to endorse PP.3:

PP.3 Type–Type: a power type P cannot have as its manifestation the power type P.

Consider the case of viral infection. The concern over viral infections is precisely that viruses exhibit the repetition of power-types highlighted in PP.3: a virus v_1's token power to duplicate itself d_1 (an instance of the power-type D) is a power-type shared by all those duplicates it produces, and so on for any further duplicates they might produce. This is how viruses spread within a host. The same is true of the passing of energy: when a billiard ball strikes another it passes on that power of motion to the latter, which it too can do for the next. The passing of type-identical powers, it would seem, is quite common.

Hence, with the exception of cases like PP.1, PP is false. We have no reason to worry that—*as a matter of principle*—powers cannot be identical with their manifestations. But can we avoid the PP.1 cases? After all, power-based perdurance involves the exercising of powers whose manifestations are the same powers had by the same particular. Are the relevant cases perhaps too close to PP.1?

They are close, but they are not the same. There are a number of ways in which they could differ, and at least one in which they always do. First of all, the temporal part of the object a that has the first power token is not strictly identical with the part that has the second. Second, we might reasonably claim that the token power had by the first temporal part is a distinct token from that had by the second temporal part. And finally, even if we concede that a names the whole worm (all of a's parts), and not just this or that part, and also that the token power had by the first part is the same token had by the second, it is still the case that the temporal parts of a are the standard property-bearers, and they are temporally distinct. This gives us a version of PP that differs minimally from PP.1, but does so in a way that avoids the objection.

> **PP.4 Token–Token:** a token instance of a power P_1, instantiated by object a at t_1 at location l_1, cannot have as its manifestation the existence of that same token instance P_1 by a at t_2 and l_1.

Whereas PP.1 relies on our intuition that nothing can be the cause of itself, we have no similar intuition regarding properties of one temporal part being the cause of that same property's being instantiated by some later temporal part of that same object. (Not, that is, unless those intuitions are had by someone in the grip of a theory.) There is nothing odd about saying that some object has the shape it does now *because* it had that shape immediately prior to now. This is, after all, the core of Newton's first law of motion, namely that an object at rest stays at rest, and an object in motion stays in motion, unless acted upon by an unbalanced force.

At this point we should have no problem agreeing that there is no support for the *general* claim that powers cannot have themselves as manifestations. But before leaving the issue there is another reason why we might find this objection unsatisfactory. It concerns the question of whether *any* power has a power as its manifestation at all. If that is not the case, then the objection was never really an objection at all.

Ignoring the purportedly troublesome case of a power's having a power of the same type as its manifestation, consider just the claim that powers have powers as manifestations. Plenty of dispositional essentialists talk this way, especially pandispositionalists (who claim that all properties are powers), but is it really the case that any power is like this? Let me concede that this kind of talk might merely be shorthand, and not intended to be taken at face value, but at face value it is not something we are forced to endorse.

My concern is that this sort of speak, taken at face value, indicates that powers have as their manifestations *properties* (whether they are powers or not), and that strikes me the wrong category for manifestations. Properties—powers most likely— are *constituents* of manifestations. And though they are undoubtedly the most salient constituent of any manifestation, they are not manifestations onto themselves. Much more sensible is that manifestations are *the havings of properties*. This might be understood in terms of events or perhaps processes, but my own preference is to think of manifestations as states of affairs. The potential manifestation of a power is some state of affairs, typically that of an object's having some power property or other.

As I say, this might be what was intended all along. But if it was not, then it offers us a way out of the objection. If it was, then the response above should suffice, and what follows helps us make more sense of how to think of manifestations.

The model I have in mind is adapted from one suggested by David Armstrong concerning the laws of nature. On Armstrong's view, laws play much the same role that powers do for the essentialist, and the similarities are great enough that we can borrow from him without much confusion. According to his early account, a law is a second-order universal—a relation—that holds between two first-order universals. Using the language which is common when speaking of laws, Armstrong tells us that if it is a law that 'All F's are G's,' that is because there is a contingent relation between F's and G's such that something's being an F necessitates its being a G. He symbolizes this law as $N(F, G)$. What causes Armstrong to restate, or better yet refine, his view are laws like Newton's first law, mentioned above.[13]

Using his typical notation, Armstrong would be forced to say there are laws of the form $N(F, F)$, whereby something's being an F (in motion) causes it to be an F (in motion). We have—on the early view—a universal that bears a nomic relation to itself. It is far from clear how such things could be the case. Armstrong's fix is to change the thinking behind the relata. No longer is it the case that laws are relations between mere universals, now they are relations between *states of affairs types*. Though it sounds odd to say that being in motion causes being in motion, there is nothing odd about saying that *something's* being in motion is the cause of *something's* being in motion, even when the 'something' refers to the same object in both cases. Armstrong goes on to suggest a reformed symbolization, but we can skip that here. All that matters for present purposes is the shift from relations between universals *simpliciter* to universals understood as states of affairs types.

---

[13] The core of the early view was first presented in Armstrong (1978) and later refined in Armstrong (1983). The new view appears in Armstrong (1997, 2010).

Returning to powers and their manifestations, I propose we follow suit. A manifestation will tend to be *something's having some property or other*.[14] It might even be the case that a manifestation is that of something's having many properties, or even in some cases *not* having some property or other. And as noted, many or all of the properties will be powers. But they will not exhaust the manifestation. Looking at a simple case will show how natural this is to our thinking. What is the manifestation of solubility? It is *the salt's* going into solution. And of fragility? None other than *the vase's* shattering. And when micro-entities act in virtue of their masses and energies, it is the *particle* that is attracted or repelled.

Owing to Armstrong's influence, it is possible that when folk speak of powers having powers as manifestations, they intend to be interpreted at face value. If so, this is an alternative to that sort of view. If not, then we have seen what that view really points to and why having the same power-type serve as (a constituent of) its own manifestation is not a concern.

5. Reciprocity and Unilateral Powers

The standard form of manifestation for powers is that of *mutual* manifestation of *reciprocal* dispositions. The salt and solution combine for the manifestation that is their joint effect. Likewise for the striking of the match: it is a coordinated effort that takes the appropriate powers and cooperation of the match, the surface, and the enfolding oxygen. This was Martin's lesson for us all, and it is an important one. Not only does it allow us to get past outdated models of powers wherein one power is 'active' and the other 'passive' (where the passive power is bent to the will of the active as if it was not involved, or at least not willingly), it gets us past the anthropomorphic model that sees powers as either 'agent' or 'patient.' Martin's causal picture is egalitarian: powers act together for whatever they jointly produce.

But Martin's picture comes at a cost. It leaves out a class of cases that look, at first blush, to be just as causal as the others, but that are distinct in that they involve just *one* object. Reciprocity and mutual manifestation cannot apply to them, because there are not multiple entities at work. For example, consider Newton's first law of motion or the β-decay of a radium atom. Both are examples of immanent causation: the cause and effect are attributed to the same particular. In some cases—but not those just mentioned—the story involving the same particular might be retold as an interaction of its parts. The crystalline structure of the glass, for example, might be seen as resulting from the mutual interaction of the molecules that constitute it. But decay is not like this, nor motion it would seem. They form a special kind of case, outside the region covered by Martin's causal model.

---

[14] They will not always be like this. Some manifestations will be nothing at all, such as when the power is one of annihilation. Though never mentioned, the same applies to Armstrong's view.

Maybe these just are not causes at all. Ellis and Lierse (1994, 40) label them 'propensities,' because they deny that causation is involved. They argue that the cases lack the interaction required of causation. Such cases are not causal, it would seem, precisely because Martin's model does not apply. But they *do* look like causes, despite the model not fitting. And if they are not causal, then what are they? Dubbing them 'propensities' as opposed to powers is of no use at all. When powers are the mechanism of change within the universe, how can one allow that change takes place if powers are not involved? If such cases fall outside the scope of powers, then we have changes in the universe that just *are*. If Ellis and Lierse can tolerate that, then why not make all change similarly mysterious and align with the neo-Humeans?[15] I cannot believe that powers would account for most, but not all, of the world's changes. I am therefore forced to think that all changes are the result of powers, and so that powers are at work in these 'propensity' cases. And once one begins treating those cases as causal, it is natural to extend the causal story even to cases of non-change too, in order to keep the picture straight.

If it cannot be the case that these cases are causal—to wit, if there cannot be powers that operate non-mutually—then there is no hope for a powers-based account of persistence. Armstrong writes that

from Martin's point of view, it might be good to replace talk of cause and effect by 'reciprocal disposition partners for mutual manifestations.' That fits in nicely with Newton's Third Law. But what does he do about something—an electron, perhaps—continuing to exist? With Russell, Armstrong is inclined to see this as a case of causality. A continuing thing is a certain sort of causal line. One might speak of immanent causality here. But reciprocity is lacking.
(Armstrong, Martin, and Place 1996, 150–1)

Martin's mutual manifestation model is fine for Newton's third law, but what of Newton's first, where the reciprocal partners are missing? Can this be causal?

I suggest it can. In his response to Armstrong, Martin indicates that the 'partners' of the reciprocal dispositional partnerships that produce the mutual manifestations are the dispositional *properties*, and need not be instantiated by distinct particulars. That is, though the typical examples of dispositional partnerships involve dispositional properties of two or more objects, nothing prevents the partners from being two properties of one and the same particular.

Armstrong's case of the previous state of a thing causing its own successive state without having any reciprocal disposition partners is a case of an entity that exists in and for itself, absolutely independently of everything else (including electromagnetic and gravity fields of force, etc.). Even so, it is not an example of a total lack of reciprocal disposition partners. A previous state x of a thing a at t_1 has *innumerable* reciprocal dispositional partners in *other* states of a at t_1 for the continuance of state x of a at t_2.   (Martin 2008, 91)

[15] According to Humean supervenience, the world is just a vast mosaic of qualities, distributed about space and time. Change in those worlds just *is*. Facts, rules even, about changes supervene on what changes just happen to exist, but the changes themselves are unanalyzable.

He goes on to say that the only case where this would not apply would be that of a perfectly simple and irreducible single state, which he bitingly suggests only God could exhibit.

In the absence of a better response, Martin's would suffice. After all, I know of no natural concrete particular that has only one power, nor any reason to deny that the many powers of a given particular could not serve as reciprocal disposition partners. There are two things to be said in favor of this response. First of all, there is no denying that the powers of an object work collaboratively in the manifestations they (and therefore the object) produce and contribute to. There is mutuality in even the simplest of particulars. In fact, the powers by which we characterize particulars, perhaps even those by which we classify them into kinds, are really just the ones we observe the object as having. But who is to say that those powers are not the result of a great deal of masking and swamping and similar 'internal struggles' before we see any result? Things could be much more complex than we appreciate, and so the answer Martin provides is entirely plausible. Second, we are talking about a very unusual class of powers indeed. Not just the ones within a particular, but powers *for the very persistence of particulars*. These are not your mother's powers! Science does not touch them—they are not the stuff of empirical study. But something is at work here, and whatever it happens to be, it is unlikely to resemble anything else familiar. With that in mind, they might well be the product of mutually interacting powers within a particular. So odd are these powers, who is to say that the electron's mass and energy and spin are not what it takes to manifest persistence?

Martin's response is adequate, but it is not the one I prefer. For the most part I do not think Armstrong's objection is a serious one, beyond pointing to a *gap* in the theory. It is only a problem if we assume reciprocity is intended to cover every case of causation. Instead I prefer to respond by augmenting the theory. Some powers—most even—are *reciprocal* powers, and these powers operate cooperatively for mutual manifestations. But the others—the problematic cases—are powers whose manifestations come about without partners; they are the *unilateral* powers. Hence causation should *not* be replaced by talk of 'reciprocal disposition partners for mutual manifestations,' but with talk of *either* 'reciprocal disposition partners for mutual manifestations' *or* 'unilateral dispositions for solitary manifestations.' The model was not mistaken, just incomplete. Talk of causation as if it *always* involved mutuality was mistaken in the first place.

The natural question at this point is this: what serves as the stimulus for the unilateral powers? Powers are such that they need *triggers* in order for them to exercise their manifestations. For mutual powers, the conditions under which they are stimulated involve the presence (and absence) of other powers, along with their arrangements. But what plays this role for the unilateral powers, if they are not stimulated by other powers. Could it be that time itself is somehow the trigger? Or that a temporal part has a built in sensitivity to its own duration, resulting in manifestation when its tenure is up?[16] But now we have converted time into a powered partner. It is an object (albeit a strange one) with powers that interact with the unilateral powers; the unilateral powers no longer seem unilateral at all.

Can a more charitable reading rescue the response? The account on offer says that unilateral powers are powers that do not require reciprocal powers, but that may have been too hasty. Perhaps reciprocal powers are those that work with other powers, but not time. Time—though object-like—might be such a strange kind of object that it can be excluded, in which case unilateral powers are those that act in accord with time, but nothing else. Dare I say, time is so mysterious, and our intuitions about it so limited, that it might play some role in triggering powers like this or in some other way we have yet to imagine. If nothing else, I would have a hard time making sense of someone who claimed to have such firm intuitions about time that they were convinced this was not the case.

We know so little about time that—for all we know—it could be up to the task. Could anything else serve as the stimulus? Nothing better comes to mind; time might win by default. But it is such a hollow victory, and the prospects of finding an at all plausible trigger seem so bleak, that it suggests we need a different approach altogether. Perhaps nothing presents itself as a plausible trigger because we should never have been looking for a trigger in the first place. To wit, when it comes to unilateral powers, talk of triggers and stimulus conditions may not be appropriate at all. In a recent effort to demonstrate that analyzing powers in terms of conditionals distorts the notion of power, E. J. Lowe indicates that some powers *do not have triggers*. He writes:

Not every physical state that is apt to be described as a 'disposition' can plausibly be assigned a 'stimulus.' Consider, for example, the disposition of radium atoms to undergo spontaneous radioactive decay. We know that the 'manifestation' of this disposition—the actual radioactive decay of radium atoms—is perfectly insensitive to external conditions, in the sense that varying those conditions makes no difference to the probability that any given radium atom will undergo radioactive decay within a specified period of time. The decay, when it does occur, is not 'triggered' by any 'stimulus.'   (Lowe 2011, 22)

It is striking how natural Lowe's case is, and consequently how easy it is to agree that our conception of 'power' or 'disposition' does not demand that a stimulus be involved. As Lowe indicates, it is not just that no stimulus can be plausibly assigned to this power, but rather that it makes more sense that it is not the sort of power for which talk of a stimulus is appropriate.

Perhaps the lesson to be learned is that the notion of 'stimulus' is not, as had been thought, part of the basic understanding of what it is to be a power, but confined to those powers that are exercised mutually. To speak of powers then is not always to

[16] 'Dualists' like Ellis (2009, ch. 5) might have different intuitions. According to Ellis, there are power properties and non-power properties, and the latter influence the way the former are manifested. Though I cannot help but think that this renders the non-powers powers after all, I concede that this sort of dualism is (barely) consistent.

conjure up thoughts of what *conditions* must arise for the power to be manifested, but just to think of a causal ability. Where conditions form part of how we grasp a power's nature it is a reciprocal power we have in mind. The reciprocity *just is* the conditionality. Conversely, no conditions are required in those cases where the power is a unilateral power. Given how we think of stimulus conditions—in terms of the presence, absence, and arrangement of other powers—it seems only natural that the notion of stimulation should be tied to powers that require partners to bring about their manifestations. Mutuality and co-stimulation go hand in hand—but unilateral powers have no such restrictions.[17]

My original suggestion was that we divide powers based on whether they operate reciprocally or unilaterally. But that is much too easily misunderstood as suggesting that the difference concerns what sort of stimuli each responds to. Now we can see that a better way to make the distinction between reciprocal and unilateral powers concerns the very notion of stimulation itself. Those that demand stimulation to be exercised are reciprocal; those that do not are unilateral.[18] It is with this distinction that talk of causation should be replaced.

6. Antidotes for Stage-Fright: Static Parts and Dynamic Processes

We have seen that the perdurantist relies on temporal parts to explain how persisting objects can instantiate incompatible intrinsic properties, and that in order to account for *possible* changes an object might have undergone (but did not), the persisting object needs at least as many temporal parts as would permit these possible changes. Consequently, most persisting objects will have very many temporal parts indeed. In fact, they will have to have so many temporal parts that the duration of each must be incredibly short, perhaps even instantaneous.[19] How else could one accommodate all those possible changes but by making the parts momentary? Not only will temporal parts have extremely short durations, but also each is unchanging. Though they accommodate the possibility of incompatible change, the stages themselves are incapable of change; the stages are *static*, so to speak. Change is a matter of different

---

[17] Moreover, talk of 'stimulation' seems to go hand in hand with a picture of as yet manifested powers lying in wait for the right conditions to be exercised, and this makes stimulation sound all the less relevant to powers of persistence. Unlike fragility, for example, these powers are not instantiated by temporal parts prior to being exercised—they arise in a state that produces the next temporal part without delay.

[18] Our sketchy knowledge of such things may force us to admit vague cases (to the extent that our concept of a given power makes it hard to say whether talk of a stimulus is appropriate or not we are similarly hard pressed to categorize it as one or the other), but I take it that the vagueness is confined to our concept, and not the power itself.

[19] More on this at the end of this section.

properties being instantiated by different stages. The temporal parts, therefore, exhibit change collectively, but not individually.[20]

In seeming contrast to the static nature of temporal parts, powers are often understood as giving rise to processes, where a process is a prolonged event that may encompass numerous changes to its constituent particulars. On a number of views of powers, the manifestation of a power just is some process or other: a power is a power *for* one or another process-type. These processes-types may be highly specific, perhaps to the extent that they have their stages essentially, making them amenable to classification as natural kinds.[21]

That powers may have processes as their manifestations is not itself problematic for a powers-based account of perdurance, but it quickly becomes so if we conceive of those same processes as *essentially dynamic*; that is, if we understand those processes as flowing continuous events that are constantly in act and undergoing seamless change. If the manifestations of powers are dynamic and continuous in this way, then they will be a poor fit for the perdurantist's unchanging static temporal parts, if not downright incompatible with them.

If a power-based account of perdurance is to work—never mind made attractive— these two pictures must be brought in line with one another. According to Stephen Mumford, the prospects do not look good:

Change in a particular can be understood as a continuous and constant process in the sense that it contains no proper portion that is not undergoing change. While the whole process involves movement from one state, condition or property to another, each proper portion of that process also involves change. The process should not, therefore, be broken down into its static, instantaneous parts. If one tried to understand the process in that way, one would lose something of its dynamic and developing nature.   (Mumford 2009b, 228)

If, as Mumford claims, powers are tendencies to give rise to processes that are "continuous, dynamic, natural processes," and further that particulars are "*always* acting," then powers look like poor partners for perdurance (2009b, 228). In order to show that powers and perdurance are indeed well matched, we will have to consider some different ways in which processes might be understood.

I will deal with this objection by responding in two parts. There is only one objection here, that temporal parts are too short-lived and static to be partnered with a dynamic powers metaphysic, but we can divide it into two by considering (1) how the view handles powers whose manifestations are protracted processes, and then (2) how the view deals with the duration of temporal parts relative to powers that are exercised very quickly.

---

[20] This has led to the objection that perduring objects do not in fact change (Thomson 1983). Though I recognize that intuitions about these things can differ, I cannot help but treat the no-change objection as anything but an uncharitable understanding of change. The perduring object has different properties at different times—this is change enough.

[21] Ellis (2001) defends such an account.

Temporal parts have a short temporal duration. Just how short they are is a question I will save for the second part of the response, but for now it is safe to say that in order to accommodate potential change, they have to be quite short indeed. And however short that turns out to be, it is much shorter than the time it takes for a fire to consume a building, a large block of ice to melt, or a caterpillar to turn into a butterfly.

The two pictures we have been considering lend themselves to two ways of modeling protracted processes. On the first—the model most amenable to perdurantism—processes are drawn-out events encompassing a great deal of change, but they are dissectible into ever-so-many short-lived events, none of which itself includes change. Let us call this model of processes the 'domino' model, in reference to the art of domino toppling.[22] The second model of processes, the 'adamantine' model, sees them as continuous and impenetrable. To split them up is impossible, as the process would thereby cease to be a member of the same process-type, or cease to be natural in the right sort of way, or fail to be properly understandable. If processes are adamantine, then they are not amenable to the perdurantist's framework.

Both are perfectly good models of processes, but which best fits how we think about powers and their manifestations? Mumford believes it is the latter, and therefore that powers and perdurance are a poor fit. I do not agree. Though I find the treatment of manifestations in terms of processes intuitive and attractive, I nevertheless think that the domino model best captures their ontology. To be clear, my aim here is not to tease out our basic intuitions about processes, nor to argue that the domino model is the right model for thinking about processes, especially where they are the manifestations of powers. My claim is that the domino model, rather than the adamantine model, fits best with how folk working on powers tend to conceive of processes, and in so doing I will thereby remove one obstacle to combining powers and perdurance.

However, before arguing that our thinking about manifestations fits best with the domino model, let me respond to the charge that understanding a given process in terms of the domino model would see us "lose something of its dynamic and developing nature." The response is simple: to understand a process as dissectible into ever-so-many parts does not thereby privilege those parts in terms of how we understand the process. We do not fail to see the forest for the trees when we learn that forests are little more than collections of trees. The fine-grained perspective on the process merely offers a different perspective; our understanding of the process as a whole should not differ in the least. This continues to be the case even if one interprets the domino model as claiming that the short-lived parts are somehow more fundamental, where the processes depend for their existence on 'ontologically

[22] In domino toppling, long stretches of dominos are placed on their ends so that if any one is knocked it will cause those that follow it to fall as well. The result of a 'toppling' is a lengthy process whose individual elements are easily distinguished, and where it is obvious that the larger process is composed of numerous shorter events.

prior' temporal parts.[23] Regardless of the ontological facts, nothing dictates how the processes must be *understood*.[24]

Back to the two models of processes. I think powers folk are thinking of processes, or should be, in terms of the first model. My evidence comes from an observation regarding the debate over the conditional analysis of dispositions. A great deal has been written about the conditional analysis of dispositions (perhaps too much). For those who have somehow managed to avoid this wealth of discussion, the basic issue concerns whether the possession of a disposition can be analyzed in terms of subjunctive conditionals.

According to the 'simple conditional analysis,' an object a has the disposition to m just in case there is some stimulus s such that if a is in s it will m. The simple conditional analysis fails because objects can lose or gain dispositions in just those conditions when they would be manifested (Martin 1994).[25] Dispositions can be, in the standard lingo, 'finkish.' David Lewis (1997) replies to the problem of finkishness by arguing that all dispositions must have some intrinsic property (partly) responsible for the effect we credit the disposition with—a 'base,' and that the analysis should be amended to require that the base property is retained through the manifestation, or at least until the manifestation has begun. Along with a few other changes we can ignore, the result is Lewis's revised conditional analysis, which is safe from finkishness.

But it is not safe from 'antidotes' (Bird 1998). An antidote is something which breaks the causal chain that leads to the manifestation of a disposition without removing the causal base. Dispositions take time to do their thing. Between the time t when the stimulus comes along and the time t_1 when the manifestation is complete there is plenty of time to add something to the scenario that will stop the manifestation from coming about.[26] For example, consider a standard fragile glass that is struck with adequate force to break it. Left to its own means the glass will soon be broken. But now imagine there is a sorcerer, wise in the ways of physics, who

> may be able to administer shock waves to the struck glass which precisely cancel out the shock of the original striking, hence saving the glass from destruction. . . . [T]he causal chain leading to breakage may have started—shock waves have begun to travel though the glass and minute fractures to appear. But before the glass breaks something interrupts the chain.
>
> (Bird 1998, 228)

---

[23] Perdurance carries no such commitment. Lewis writes, "When I say that persons are maximal R-interrelated aggregates of person-stages, I do *not* claim to be reducing 'constructs' to 'more basic entities'" (1983b, 77). Mumford, however, is unnecessarily wary of this sort of priority, claiming that if the static temporal parts are "primarily real," then the powers theorist should eschew them, because "dynamic powers and processes are fundamentally real in the dispositional ontology" (2009b, 230). I do not think what Mumford says about the dispositional ontology is true; at best this expresses his own view, not that of powers theorists more generally.

[24] Sider (2001, 211) makes a similar point.

[25] The simple conditional analysis is also subject to counterexamples involving 'mimicking' and 'masking'; see Johnston (1992).

[26] Antidotes can also be added beforehand and thereby stop the causal chain from ever starting, but it is the late antidotes I am interested in.

The object is (and was) fragile but the counterfactual is false; the revised analysis also fails.

Enough with the history lesson. What emerges from the debate are two features of manifestations relevant to our present concerns. They are that: (i) stimuli work with dispositions of objects to *initiate causal chains*; and (ii) these causal chains are *interruptible*. To my knowledge, no one in the literature finds these features surprising or untenable. (And why would they? This is common sense!) Both features indicate a strong preference for thinking about processes along the domino model, not the adamantine model. First of all, a causal chain is a series of smaller causal events that are 'linked' together in a sequence. The whole that they form might be perfectly continuous, but it is made up of a series of smaller, shorter-lived, causal events, in keeping with the domino model. The 'chain' metaphor is a dead giveaway: chains are larger wholes composed of shorter, self-standing, individual links. This metaphor would be entirely out of place if we took these processes to be seamless, as the adamantine model does. Second, the very idea that these causal chains are *interruptible* relies on a conception of processes that sees them as composed of smaller parts. To be able to stop a process part way through requires that there are natural breaks in that process. The notion of antidotes exploits this feature. It looks like the domino model is the right model for our thinking about processes.

It is this latter feature—interruptibility—that I find most compelling when thinking about the right model for processes. It indicates that not only are we thinking of the processes that dispositions give rise to when stimulated as prolonged, we see them as unfolding stepwise, with natural cleavages into which metaphorical spanners can be inserted. I take it that this settles the debate as far as protracted processes are concerned.

An interesting consequence of thinking about processes in this way is that it no longer seems reasonable to claim that powers have manifestations that are *protracted* processes. Consider once more the notion of a causal chain. A causal chain is a series of steps—each causal—leading from one state of affairs to some other, via a series of intermediate states of affairs. According to the powers metaphysic, each of these causal steps is due to the actions and interactions of causal powers. In other words, every step in a causal chain involves the stimulus and manifestation of a power. It is therefore mistaken to claim, in any strict sense, that this causal chain—*in its entirety*—is the product of a single power being stimulated. A more apt description is that the first power stimulated *initiates* a causal chain; to wit, its manifestation is a state of affairs that contains a power for some further state of affairs, that contains a power for some further state of affairs, that . . . and so on until we have a state of affairs that is the 'typical' manifestation we tend to speak of. In which case the manifestation, properly speaking, of the first 'causal chain initiating' power is not the *final* link in the causal chain at all, but just the *next* link. That next link will be such that it is not only powered in the right sort of way, but also highly prone to being appropriately stimulated, and so on. All else being equal, stimulating the first power in the right way will initiate a causal chain that will 'terminate' in the manifestation we had previously (and clumsily) described the power as being for.[27] But it need not run to completion, and that is precisely because the causal chain is made up of short power/stimulus/manifestation links, any one of which can, in principle, be messed with so as to block the production of its manifestation.[28]

But not all manifestations are like this. Some are not interruptible. Not because they are not initiators of causal chains, but because they are too short. They are, in keeping with the chain metaphor, only one link long. They are not interruptible because they do not have natural breaks. These are the short processes.[29]

Are short-lived manifestations, those that do not have many steps, or just one, best understood under the adamantine or domino model? Here I think the right response is that these manifestations are adamantine. They lack the natural breaks that the protracted processes have, and therefore lack places to be interrupted. But does this not spell trouble for powers-based perdurance? Have I not just conceded that we have impervious changes, ill-suited to a treatment by static temporal parts? I suggest not.

The objection assumes that changes, however brief, are not amenable to a meta-physic of short-lived, static, temporal parts. But given that these parts can accommod-ate change collectively, the question is really one of how big temporal parts are. The assumption behind the objection seems to be that the short process case is just like the protracted process case, only with a shorter duration. That is, the short processes involve continuous—and uninterruptible—change, and must be made up of many short-lived unchanging temporal parts. However, unlike the protracted case, there is no reason to think that the time it takes for a single-link manifestation to arise is any longer than the duration of any temporal part. In other words, as long as temporal parts have a duration that is just as long as the short processes manifestations take to come about, then there is no worry here. A power is stimulated and its very quick manifestation is some new state of affairs with some change in properties. Why think that this involves anything more than two temporal parts—one for the first stimulated state and one for the latter?

---

[27] 'Terminate' is in scare quotes because the causal chain does not really end here; it is only ended to the extent it is salient to the original misclassifying of the power.

[28] This has its own set of interesting consequences. The first is that this makes it look as if—in principle—a power that we name according to the terminus can have antidotes at any link in the causal chain. The second is that antidotes do not appear to offer a unique class of counterexamples to the revised conditional analysis. If an antidote is taken early (before stimulus), it might remove the disposition, and therefore is acting as a fink (Bird 1998, 229 concedes this), or it could hide the fact that the disposition is present by acting like a 'masker,' just as lactase masks the disposition of milk to kill humans (Bird 1998, 231). If the antidotes are 'late' (added to the scenario after the causal chain has been initiated), then it has not really prevented the manifestation of the initial power, whose manifestation was the first link in the chain, not the last, which has been prevented. Hence the counterfactual is no longer false. Can antidotes be added during the manifestation of a single link in the chain? I do not see how—these do not seem to be interruptible, as discussed below.

[29] As the above argument claims, all manifestations are short like this, we just tend to pick out chains of them, rather than the single links.

A natural response is as follows: temporal parts are instantaneous, and the exercising of powers (with non-protracted processes for manifestations) are not. But the natural response is a poor one. I concede that it is common in the perdurance literature to speak of temporal parts as having a zero or near enough duration. They are, as described by many, instantaneous in this sense. Sider (2001, 60) treats temporal parts as instantaneous, as does Hawley (2001, 48). But even on the assumption that they are correct, the response only succeeds if powers take longer than this to be exercised. And that is not something I claim to know, nor anyone else. If anything, when I imagine how long it takes a stimulated power to go the first step in a chain, or the whole way if it is a one-link chain, I find myself imagining that it is instant. If the response is to stand, the onus is on the objector to show us that they take longer than this.

But even if this seemingly impossible demonstration is in the offing, we still have nothing to fear from this objection. That is because perdurantism is not committed to instantaneous temporal parts. Some perdurantists claim that temporal parts are instantaneous, but *not all*. One can be a perdurantist without instantaneous temporal parts.[30]

The present worry arises from an alleged mismatch between the duration of temporal parts and the time it takes a power to be manifested. I have argued that the exercise of powers seems to take less time than the objector assumes, and that temporal parts can have longer durations than the objector assumes, making the possibility of a mismatch more remote. But I think the case can be stated even more strongly than this.

Hawley (2001, 48–53) argues for instantaneous temporal parts on the grounds that temporal parts must be short enough to accommodate possible—not just actual—changes, and that possible changes are as fine-grained as time itself. The first step in her argument is perfectly reasonable: if temporal parts are to be capable of instantiating (*simpliciter*) incompatible properties, then their duration can only be as long as any possible change. But I see no reason to endorse her second step, and therefore no reason to endorse her conclusion. According to Hawley, to exist at different times (as anything longer than an instant would) is to instantiate incompatible properties. But unless these are intrinsic properties (not the relations they appear to be), then there is no problem having temporal parts that span greater-than-instant durations.

Here is what she *should* have said, and also why the potential temporal part/manifestation mismatch is not a concern. Temporal parts need to be short enough to accommodate possible changes. Therefore, they need to be exactly as short as the *mechanism of change* requires them to be. For Hawley (2001, 88), a Humean about causation, that mechanism would allow for instantaneous differences in the state of the

---

[30] See Zimmerman (1996). Zimmerman points out that C. D. Broad and Russell believed that objects persist by having temporal parts, but both rejected that parts could be instantaneous. Lewis (1983b, 77) also endorses non-instantaneous parts, as does Heller (1990, 11). Sider (2001, 60) recognizes this alternative, but *chooses* to treat them as instantaneous. I am sure there are others.

world, so she would end up with the same account.[31] But if the mechanism of change is the exercise of powers, then the temporal parts will be *exactly as long as it takes for power to manifest*. There is no space, on a powers-based account of perdurance, for the exercise of powers to fail to line up with possible changes. They are the source of the possible changes! Fans of Humean supervenience might claim that temporal parts can be as short as zero-duration instants, but their motivation for doing so (the belief that all occupants of time frames—however short—are logically and metaphysically isolated from one another) is not a motivation the powers theorist shares. When it is powers that are responsible for change, *they* will dictate the duration of temporal parts. That could mean, after all is said and done, that temporal parts are instantaneous after all, just as long as that is how fast powers are manifested. But if the powers take a little more time, then the temporal parts will be a little bigger too. As indicated above, my impression is that manifestations are instant, but this is not the finding of a firm intuition, that is just how it seems to me.

On the off-chance that manifestations are not instantaneous, let me deal with one further objection. There is an ontologically innocent sense of a temporal part—as perfectly instantaneous—that is shared by Humean and non-Humean perdurantists alike, and to which the endurantist should be similarly open. It is the snapshot which captures the nature of an object and its properties for any 'instant' (a zero-duration temporal atom). The ontological status of such parts will vary from one view to the next: Humeans will take them to be the basic temporal parts, presentist endurantists will see them as what exists on the knife edge of the present but that are only fictional before and after, and so on. I have claimed that the shortest duration of a temporal part is dictated by the mechanism of change; it is an open question whether *these* temporal parts will be instantaneous. Should they turn out not to be, what should be said about these instantaneous parts that I claim all parties should countenance?

The simple answer is that some parts are causally significant parts, and others are nothing more than mereological abstractions. I do not deny that there are innocuous instantaneous temporal parts, but if they are smaller than the smallest parts given by the mechanism of change, then they are nothing more than ways of speaking about the *actually* smallest temporal parts. They are as innocent on my view as they are for the endurantist: ways of speaking about objects at times, without any serious commitment to their abilities that are not derivative on the larger parts they are abstracted from.

We can compare this innocent notion of temporal part with its spatial analog. There is a perfectly natural sense of (spatial) part that corresponds to the material occupants of any given spatial region, such as the *z*-shaped region within my chest cavity.[32] Anyone ought to admit that such parts exist. Like I am suggesting of the temporal

---

[31] I must concede I find this Humean account mystifying, as the 'causes' come after the fact of states of the world obtaining. Any state of the world can simply appear after any other, without explanation or reason. But Humeans seem fond of it.

[32] The *z*-shaped region was suggested to me by David Hershenov.

case, few would be willing to admit that these parts have properties unique to them, have sortal predicates that apply to them, are causally significant (independently of whatever respectable parts they might overlap), and so on. But these are parts, even if not interestingly so. I treat the instantaneous parts in the same way.

We started out with the worry that unchanging short-lived (or even instantaneous) temporal parts might be a poor match for the processes that powers can give rise to. But it turns out that the typical understanding of manifestations is that they arise step-wise in a manner that is highly amenable to the perdurantist's ontological framework. We might recast the original objection this way: temporal parts can only be as small as the mechanism for change permits, and that mechanism takes an awfully long time. But that is simply false. Recognized powers can have very short time frames needed to manifest—the manifestations of physical micro-entities are either instantaneous or near enough—and the protracted processes that some powers result in are best understood as causal chains (of manifesting powers) that the first power initiates when stimulated.

Despite everything I have argued, I am sure that some readers will remain unconvinced. This is hardly uncommon territory when philosophical intuition is involved. I suspect that at least some of those who remain unconvinced simply refuse to see the dynamic processes that powers produce as fitting with the static temporal parts the perdurantist supports. These might well be the same folk who conclude from Zeno's paradox of the arrow that motion simply cannot be understood in terms of ever-so-many motionless parts occupying different places at different times.[33] We need not concern ourselves with the specific details here, except to point out that for nearly as long as the paradox has been around, there have been solutions offered that embrace the treatment of motion in terms of distinct motionless parts occupying different places at different times.[34] Marc Lange (2005) even argues that the motionless parts are up to the task if they instantiate the appropriate dispositions. As I say, I am not concerned with the details of that debate, only that plenty of folk find getting the dynamic out of the static is a perfectly sensible thing to do, and I am with them. So it may be that some folk continue to be opposed to a powers-based account of perdurance, but they cannot claim that powers and perdurance are an unhealthy mix, or that powers prefer endurantism.[35]

---

[33] See Arntzenius (2000) for a clear presentation of the paradox, and why many of the standard responses do not work.

[34] Perhaps most famous is Russell's (1938) 'at-at' theory of motion.

[35] Mumford (2009b) raises a second argument against a powers-based account of perdurance. He notes that according to Hawley (2001), the relation that sticks temporal parts together is non-supervenient. That is, not determined solely by the parts and their intrinsic properties (a non-supervenient relation is an external one; one that does not hold merely in virtue of its relata existing). He goes on to argue that this would lead to an objectionable account for the powers theorist, as it would make powers contingent (because intrinsic facts about the stages that are causally connected would not determine facts about their being stages of the same persisting object).

I am not convinced that powers are unable to perform the non-supervenient task Hawley asks of them. (Compare two states of the world connected as stimulated power to manifestation, versus those same two

7. Conclusion

I have a preference for systematic metaphysics, and think the final evaluation for any ontology involves scorekeeping across a host of problems. A good ontology wins the decathlon, not the hundred-yard dash. I also have a preference for powers-based ontologies; that is, those that countenance properties with dispositional essences, whose nature is to be directed at potential future states of affairs. To my eye, powers look well suited to serve as the grounds of causes and laws. But my first preference tells me that any success powers might enjoy in serving as truthmakers for the laws of nature is not nearly enough. If a powers-based ontology is to win the day over its neo-Humean opposition, it will have to be judged across a host of metaphysical problems. That was the point of this chapter: to fight the battle on a new front by taking powers into the heretofore largely uncharted waters of diachronic identity.

There is still much to be done before we can say with confidence that powers and perdurance can be paired up in the way I propose, and only then can we start to assess how attractive the combination is. But it can no longer be claimed that powers are not configured in the right sort of way to serve as the glue that links temporal parts into persisting objects. We have learned that: (i) powers can have manifestations that are type-identical with the powers that produce them; (ii) there is a class of powers whose manifestations are produced unilaterally, that are distinguished from their reciprocally responding cousins based on the need for stimulation; and (iii) that powers are process initiators whose manifestations are incredibly brief. Powers and their exercising are now primed to serve as the immanent causal mechanism.

Nor can it be claimed that perdurance is essentially a neo-Humean account of persistence, such that powers theorists ought to be endurantists. Treating metaphysics systematically means that what we say about properties will affect how we think about the laws of nature, and these will push us in a certain direction regarding modality, and so on. Certain sorts of responses to metaphysical problems find their homes more naturally in either the neo-Humean camp or the anti-Humean camp, but rarely in both. In systematic metaphysics views tend to cluster. But not all solutions to all problems are like this. Persistence, I contend, is one metaphysical arena that is neutral—the various accounts can be adopted by proponents of either camp. I have taken a few steps towards showing that this is the case.

---

states arising for some other reason; it would appear that powers-based causation is non-supervenient.) But regardless, there is no cause to worry. As Hawley writes, "we face a dilemma: either there are non-supervenient relations between stages, as I have argued, or else causation is non-Humean" (2001, 87). It is not hard to see which disjunct the powers theorist should opt for.

PART IV
Mind

11

Conflicts of Desire
Dispositions and the Metaphysics of Mind

Lauren Ashwell

Very few of us have a psychology such that all of our desires can be satisfied together. Our everyday experience of desiring is that of competing wants pushing and pulling us in different directions. Such is the stuff of human drama and tension, of movies, novel plot lines, and song lyrics—someone who loves two people, but cannot be with both, or wants to be with someone but is also drawn to another lifestyle that they believe to be incompatible with the requiting of the love. Or someone who wants very much to pursue their own dreams but also wants to live up to a parent's very different dreams for them. However, it is not just pop culture that recognizes conflicts of desire—even the Bible talks about conflicts of desire, about desires *fighting* against each other: "What causes fights and quarrels among you? Don't they come from your desires that battle within you?" (James 4:1). Our ordinary conception of desiring involves thinking of desires as forces which battle against each other, that cause us to feel 'torn,' and that may overpower each other.

But desire conflict is also experienced at a less dramatic level—I may want to have more of the main course, but I also want to leave room for dessert. I want to soak up some beach-front sunshine on my next holiday, but I also want to go skiing. I want to finish the novel I'm reading tonight, but I also want to get my work done. These desires are experienced as *conflicting*—if I have more of the main course, then I can't have dessert, if I go on holiday in the Caribbean, I can't also go to Colorado, and if I finish my novel then, unfortunately, I'm not going to finish my work. Such desire conflicts, I will argue, ought to lead us towards a particular account of the relationship between mental states and behavioral dispositions—one that recognizes that the conflict that we experience when we have conflicting desires is *mirrored* in the conflicting ways that we are disposed to behave.

The idea that desires are closely connected with behavioral dispositions is, of course, a central part of most forms of behaviorism. Desires, on such a view, simply *are* dispositions towards actions aimed at fulfilling their content. But a close connection between desires and dispositions is also central to many kinds of functionalism, and it is so commonly held that Timothy Schroeder has called it "The Standard Theory" of desire (2004, 11–27). Here are two statements of the view: "desires are dispositions to act in certain ways under certain conditions" (Smith 1994, 115); "to desire that P is to be disposed to act in ways that would tend to bring it about that P in a world in which one's beliefs, whatever they are, were true" (Stalnaker 1984, 15).

It seems to follow from a view like Stalnaker's that for everything we desire, we are disposed towards actions aimed at satisfying the desire—so if you aren't disposed to act in ways that aim towards satisfying a particular desire, you simply don't have that desire. Thus, when you have conflicting desires, you also must have conflicting behavioral dispositions. However, dispositional conceptions of desire often come along with a rider that suggests that when you have conflicting desires, you don't have conflicting dispositions. For example, Janet Levin says that for the analytic functionalist, Blanca's desire for coffee isn't just a disposition to order coffee, but the disposition "to order coffee when it is offered, *if* she has no stronger desire to avoid coffee" (2013).[1] This statement of the relationship between desire and behavioral dispositions appears to be motivated by a concern about conflicting behavioral dispositions; if one was not concerned about this, explicit mention of not having any stronger conflicting desire would be unnecessary.

Views on which behavioral dispositions are determined by the whole set of mental states working in concert, such as that expressed by David Braddon-Mitchell and Frank Jackson (1996), also seem to be motivated partially by concerns about conflicts between behavioral dispositions. On Braddon-Mitchell and Jackson's view, our beliefs and desires determine how we are disposed to behave as a *corporate body*, as an entire system, in concert. This suggests that the way any one mental state disposes us in fact depends on the entirety of our mental state system. For example, they claim that the belief that there is a tiger in the vicinity does not dispose you on its own towards any particular behavior, because "[i]t is a whole complex of mental states that points to running in a certain direction, not any one or another individual mental state . . . the behavior which subjects are disposed to manifest depends on the totality of the mental states they are in" (1996, 37). Their view is not simply that what we in fact *do* depends on the totality of our mental states, but that our dispositions depend on our entire set of mental states.

Now, I don't deny that what we in fact *do* depends on our entire mental state system—the behavior that someone in fact manifests depends on the totality of the mental states they are in. What I do deny is that our behavioral *dispositions* are determined in this way—the dispositions that we have in virtue of particular desires *do not* depend on the totality of our mental states. By focusing on cases of desire conflict, I will argue that those who think that desires are essentially related to some kind of

---

[1] Given the direction of Levin's conditional, this is not exactly equivalent to a view that *excludes* conflict in behavioral dispositions, but it is suggestive of it.

disposition ought to adopt the view that when we have conflicting desires, we also have conflicting behavioral dispositions.

1. Desire as Dispositions

Here's a story that we often tell our students in Philosophy of Mind classes: The move from behaviorism to functionalism came in part from the recognition that mental states do not dispose us to act *in solitudo*. The behavioral dispositions that we have in virtue of believing or desiring something are dependent on what *other* mental states we are in. We aren't disposed towards any *particular* behavior, in virtue of some single belief—for example, there is no particular behavioral disposition associated with the belief *that this bus goes to Central Square*; in order to get this belief involved in producing behavior, we need some desire: Do I *want* to go to Central Square?[2]

So, since there is no particular behavior necessarily associated with the belief *that this bus goes to Central Square*, it cannot be that this belief is *identical* to some particular behavioral disposition. Thus, the project of analyzing individual mental states in purely behavioristic terms fails—in order to define what it is to believe something, in terms of particular behavioral dispositions, we will also need to appeal to what *else* you believe and desire.

Desires, too, seem to depend on beliefs in order to dispose you to do particular things. Although desires seem to involve a push towards action, they don't generally push towards *particular* actions without a representation of the world—without beliefs.[3] In order to get started on a plan concerning how to bring about things that I want, I need to have some beliefs about how the world actually is—I need to have some representation of my actual situation. I also need to have some beliefs about how to get *from* the situation represented as being actual *to* a situation in which my desire is satisfied. If I desire that I have a cup of coffee, in order to act on this desire I need to have some beliefs about how I might get one.

Thus, desires don't generally dispose you towards particular action all on their own. What one is disposed to do in virtue of having a desire is determined by one's beliefs. If you desire that p, you are disposed towards doing things that you believe would make it the case that p—things that would satisfy that desire. The beliefs about how to satisfy one's desires are conditions on which particular form our behavioral dispositions take. The belief that ϕ-ing will bring about p determines the form of the particular behavioral disposition that one has in virtue of desiring that p. Desires thus involve

---

[2] I don't here wish to enter into the controversy about whether Humean belief-desire psychology is true. There may be beliefs that motivate without the assistance of a relevant desire—but all that is needed for this point is that *some* beliefs require an accompanying desire to dispose us towards particular actions. If that is the case, then these beliefs—and thus beliefs in general—cannot be identical to particular behavioral dispositions.

[3] Again, we only need for this point the claim that *some* desires require beliefs to dispose us towards particular actions.

second-order dispositions—dispositions to have particular behavioral dispositions.[4] If S desires that *p*, then S has a second-order disposition whose manifestation condition is gaining a first-order disposition to do specific things, where those specific things are determined by S's beliefs about how she can make it the case that *p*, or at least make *p* more likely.

Now, this is all well and good for simple cases. But what happens to your behavioral dispositions when you have conflicting desires? I may be conflicted between ordering the ravioli and ordering the lasagna—both have equally mouth-watering descriptions—I have a desire for each of them, but no desire to order both. But can I be *both* disposed to order the ravioli and furthermore *also* disposed towards *not* ordering the ravioli, but ordering the lasagna instead? If every desire involves a disposition to act in ways you believe will satisfy the desire, it seems that you must be disposed towards two actions, *even though* you are not disposed towards performing both. Is this really possible?

There are reasons one might deny that we can have dispositions that conflict in this way. First, it does sound somewhat strange to say that something or someone is both disposed to ϕ *and* disposed to not-ϕ. If someone is quick to act angry at the slightest provocation, we say that he is disposed to anger upon provocation. We might say he has an irascible disposition. But it is unlikely that we would say that someone is both disposed to get angry in a certain situation and disposed not to get angry in that very same situation. When we ascribe dispositions to people, this is usually to predict and explain behavior. If I'm not likely to order the lasagna *and* also likely to order the ravioli, it seems that we shouldn't say that when I am considering what to order at my favorite Italian restaurant I am both disposed to order the lasagna *and* disposed to order the ravioli, even if I have conflicting desires for these two options.

Now, most metaphysicians don't think that dispositional ascriptions are exactly the same as ascriptions of tendencies—objects may have dispositions despite not tending to manifest them, even when in the appropriate conditions for manifestation of that disposition. The Simple Conditional Analysis of dispositions, that an object *x* has a disposition to *M* in conditions *C* iff *x* would *M* in *C*, is no longer generally accepted. However, the examples given to show that objects can have dispositions that they would not manifest in their appropriate stimulus conditions usually involve something from the *outside* inhibiting the expression of the disposition. For example, an irascible

---

[4] Here I claim only that desires *involve* a second-order disposition toward action; note that I intend that what I have to say will have bearing both on views that *identify* desires with these dispositions, and also on those that claim that such dispositions are merely *part* of what it is to have a desire. The view argued for here can also be easily modified to be compatible with the claim that there might be *some* types of desires that do not motivate towards action (so long as those types are individuated by content rather than by relative strength—that is, if it isn't the view that only one's strongest desires motivate)—for example, desires concerning matters that are impossible to change, such as the desire that 2+2=5. However, I do not think that the kind of dispositional account of desire that I'm considering here requires this modification, as it seems to me that if you do desire that 2+2=5, and came to believe that you could do something to make this true—as irrational as that is—this would dispose you to do that thing.

person may not in fact get angry when provoked, because someone happens to be standing by, ready to inject him with a very quick-acting relaxant whenever he is provoked. He is still disposed to anger even though he will never in fact become angry, and even though he would not get angry if provoked. The fact that he is disposed to anger is part of the explanation for why the relaxant-injector is standing by. But conflicting desires aren't something external, like someone else poised to inject you.

It is controversial whether it is possible to have such interference from intrinsic sources.[5] I will argue that those who think desires are closely associated with dispositions ought to accept that there can be intrinsic dispositional interference—in other words, they should accept that the dispositions involved in desiring can conflict. But before that, a caveat. I will talk about one's stronger desires winning out in cases of conflict. This isn't always correct; it needs some modification. One's *stronger* desires do not always win out in a case of conflict. I have a strong desire to win the lottery; however, my beliefs about how likely I am to win if I purchase a ticket means that I don't in fact buy one (though I might feel tempted). My beliefs about the likelihood of success in desire satisfaction enter into determining whether I follow a particular course of action.[6] There may also be other reasons that a stronger desire doesn't win out in a case of conflict; Randolph Clarke (1994), for example, argues that sometimes other features of the desirer, like perhaps *habits*, may tilt the balance in favor of the weaker desire. I will, for the purposes of this chapter, set this complication aside.

2. Alternative Dispositional Structures

For the purposes of issuing in particular behavioral dispositions, it seems that desires generally depend on which relevant beliefs the desirer has, and beliefs generally depend on what relevant desires the believer has. The question that concerns us here is whether the disposition we have in virtue of having some particular desire *also* depends—and, if so, *how* it depends—on whether we have any other desires that conflict with it.

If we cannot have conflicting behavioral dispositions even though desires are dispositional, the dispositions that desires are associated with will have to have as part of their conditions of manifestation that there is an *absence* of stronger desires. Thus, desires require that there are no stronger conflicting desires in order to be in their appropriate stimulus conditions as the absence of stronger desires is *part* of the stimulus conditions for the second-order desire. Just as desires require means–end beliefs in order to issue in a particular behavioral disposition, desires also require the

---

[5] See Choi (2005), Cohen and Handfield (2007), Handfield (2008), Handfield and Bird (2008) for arguments against the possibility of intrinsic dispositional interference; see Ashwell (2010); Clarke (2008) for arguments for the possibility of intrinsic dispositional interference.

[6] See Mele (2003) for discussion of this.

absence of stronger conflicting desires to dispose you towards behaviors. I will call this view the *Absence of Desire in the Stimulus* model.[7]

An alternative option is that the presence of stronger conflicting desires *frustrates* the manifestation of the second-order disposition, but without the absence of stronger desires being part of its stimulus condition. I'll call this view the *Second-Order Frustration* model.

These two different options are in fact versions of models you might propose to explain putative cases of a kind of dispositional interference called *masking*. As I mentioned in the last section, once upon a time it was widely thought that you could analyze dispositional ascriptions using a simple corresponding conditional statement. However, C. B. Martin (1994) and Alexander Bird (1998)—and others—proposed counterexamples to such an analysis. Masks are one such kind of counterexample; an object's disposition is masked if, were the object to be in the disposition's correct stimulus conditions, the disposition would not manifest due to an interference that interrupts the causal chain from stimulus to manifestation so that the disposition does not manifest, even though the object continues to have that dispositional property.[8] Here's a standard example of a mask from the literature: a glass is fragile, although since it is wrapped in bubble wrap, it would not break when struck or dropped.

There are two ways that you might explain the role of the bubble wrap. One option is to claim that the bubble wrap *masks* the glass's fragility. The bubble wrap interferes with the manifestation of the disposition—despite the glass's being in fragility's appropriate stimulus conditions. This is analogous to the *Second-Order Frustration* model for desire, where the presence of stronger conflicting desires prevents a weaker desire from manifesting in a particular behavioral disposition. The second-order disposition associated with the weaker desire is *masked*.

The second option is to claim that because of the presence of the bubble wrap, the glass isn't actually in the correct stimulus conditions for fragility, because the stimulus conditions for fragility requires the *absence* of things like bubble wrap.[9] So it isn't actually a case of masking. This is what the *Absence of Desire in the Stimulus* model

---

[7] Another way your desire-associated dispositions could be structured to avoid conflicting behavioral dispositions is for desires to be associated with third-order dispositions: dispositions to gain, under the conditions that the desire is your strongest one relevant to the situation at hand, second-order dispositions towards gaining first-order behavioral dispositions. On this view, only our strongest desires out of a conflicting set are associated with second-order dispositions. I won't discuss this third option here, but my arguments below can also be run against this view—note that this view has some important similarities to the *Absence of Desire in the Stimulus* model, as these third-order dispositions will require an absence of stronger desires as part of *their* stimulus conditions.

[8] Sometimes masks are also called *antidotes*—ingestion of an antidote at the same time as a poison may work to prevent the poison harming the one who ingests it, without removing the poison's noxious disposition. See Bird (1998). *Finks* are another type of dispositional interference that also show the simple conditional analysis to be false—finks prevent the disposition from manifesting in its appropriate stimulus conditions *by* removing the disposition before it has time to manifest, thus also preventing the disposition from manifesting. See Martin (1994).

[9] This is the view that David Lewis holds about masking cases. See Lewis (1994).

claims is going on when you have conflicting desires; in order to be in the appropriate stimulus conditions for a desire's associated second-order disposition to manifest—where the manifestation is the gaining of some particular behavioral disposition—a lack of stronger desires is required.

In what follows, I will argue that the *Second-Order Frustration* model is preferable to the *Absence of Desire in the Stimulus* model; after that, I will argue that once we have accepted that the dispositions we have in virtue of desires can frustrate each other at the second-order level, we should also allow that sometimes our first-order behavioral dispositions frustrate each other too.

3. Choosing between Alternative Dispositional Structures

On the *Second-Order Frustration* model, cases of conflicting desires are cases of intrinsic masking at the second-order level. The presence of a stronger conflicting desire prevents other conflicting desires from issuing in first-order behavioral dispositions. Alternatively, on the *Absence of Desire in the Stimulus* view, weaker desires do not issue in behavioral dispositions because the absence of stronger desires is built into the stimulus conditions; thus, they are not cases of masking.

The *Second-Order Frustration* model has several advantages over its rival. First, although on both views which particular actions we are disposed to do depends on what other desires we have, the desires on the *Second-Order Frustration* model interact and prevent first-order dispositions towards action in a way that is quite different from the way that a lack of beliefs about how to achieve our desired ends prevents us from acting. On the *Absence of Desire in the Stimulus* model, both a lack of relevant beliefs and the presence of a stronger conflicting desire stop us from forming first-order dispositions to act in the same way—by making it the case that we are not in the appropriate stimulus conditions for the second-order disposition.

Second, the *Second-Order Frustration* model can distinguish between intuitively different desire profiles. Suppose Amy feels torn between going somewhere remote and peaceful on her next vacation, and going to visit friends and family. Both are appealing, but, in the end, suppose that her desire for a peaceful retreat is stronger. Beth, on the other hand, desires a peaceful retreat for her vacation, and has a second conditional desire to visit friends and family only if she does not desire a peaceful retreat more. Amy has conflicting desires; Beth does not.

Amy and Beth's vacation choices will be similar—they might both, for example, end up renting cabins in the woods somewhere. But the situations with their desires are quite different. On the *Absence of Desire in the Stimulus* model, however, the dispositional profiles that they have in virtue of these desires will be far too similar. Amy's desire to go visit friends and family requires the absence of the stronger desire to have a quiet vacation, as does Beth's. Yet the clear difference between someone with this kind of non-conflicting conditional desire and someone who is experiencing conflict ought to be captured in the dispositions associated with the desires.

An important difference between Amy and Beth is the feeling of conflict. The *Second-Order Frustration* view better accounts for the *tension* that we feel when our desires conflict. The feeling of being pushed and pulled towards different options is the experience of having conflicting dispositions. The *Absence of Desire in the Stimulus* model must find some other way to explain this sort of tension, while the *Second-Order Frustration* view fits more cleanly with the phenomenology.

One might reply that the difference in their dispositional profiles is only to be found in their feelings about different possible actions—Beth is settled in her choice, and Amy is less so—and that this difference in feelings needn't be explained by Amy having conflicting dispositions while Beth does not. But part of the tension that Amy feels is a readiness to act on the weaker desire; this is the pull that she feels towards that option. A better explanation for this is that she is in fact disposed to do things to satisfy this desire, but this disposition is frustrated. So the *Second-Order Frustration* model can more easily differentiate between intuitively different desire profiles, and also fits better with the feelings of conflict.

Even once we are set on a particular course of action—and thus are set on which desire (or desires) we are going to satisfy—we can still feel the pull of a forgone option, because we still want to take that option, even though we don't want it most. This pull requires *effort* to resist. When I still feel the attractiveness of what I in fact want less, I will need to exercise self-control. I may want most of all to finish the work that I'm doing, but be tempted by the lure of surfing the Internet instead. I *want* to check my email, read the news, peruse Facebook—but it is not what I want *most*. Should I in fact resist the temptation, this will require effort on my part. The fact that I need to exert some effort to not take the tempting option, even though it is not my strongest desire, suggests that even where a desire is not our strongest regarding an option, there is still something actively pulling us towards doing things that will satisfy that desire. There is a feeling of having to hold oneself back, to counteract something that draws you towards the tempting option—in this case, the temptation of procrastination.

Now, I think that tendencies towards preferring the *Absence of Desire in the Stimulus* model comes from an uncomfortableness with dispositions that do not manifest in their stimulus conditions—if we do not manifest a disposition that we have, we must not be in the correct stimulus conditions. We very often *hear* dispositional ascriptions as conditionals connecting the stimulus with manifestation. Thus, once we see that dispositions might be masked, and, indeed, *intrinsically* masked, the *Second-Order Frustration* view should look more appealing.

There is no principled reason why we should think that intrinsic masks are impossible, but extrinsic ones are possible. The standard arguments for why we ought to accept extrinsic dispositional interference can be made analogously for intrinsic dispositional interference. For example, we wrap glasses in bubble wrap *because* they are fragile—their fragility is the explanation for why we pack them carefully when moving them. The bubble wrap *prevents* the fragility from manifesting. Bird suggests this type of explanation for why a vase that is (extrinsically) protected by a sorcerer should be considered fragile even though it would not break if struck: "After all it is natural to say that the sorcerer is concerned to protect his vase because it is so fragile"(Bird 2007a, 30). Yet it makes no difference to this sort of explanation whether the protection is intrinsic or extrinsic. The irascible person we considered earlier could have employed someone else to stand near him to inject him with relaxants when he is provoked, or he could have implanted a device inside himself that did the same thing, or he could have learned techniques (counting to ten, breathing exercises, and the like) to prevent himself from acting angry when provoked. In all cases, his irascibility is the explanation for why the preventative measures are taken.[10]

Those who deny the possibility of intrinsic masking of this sort will have to say that while this person is irascible if he only uses extrinsic measures to prevent his angry outbursts, he is not irascible if he has learned preventative techniques. The use of the techniques is simply to prevent him from *becoming* irascible. Yet why does he use these techniques? He feels the beginnings of the process that leads towards the manifestation of his irascibility. This is interrupted by the use of the techniques. The best explanation for this is that he is, in fact, irascible, but this character trait is prevented from manifesting by an intrinsic mask. Similarly, when we feel torn between two things that we desire, we can feel the pull of the weaker desire. We prevent ourselves from acting by exercising self-control; it can be difficult to resist desires even when they are not our strongest.

The kind of model of the metaphysics involved in cases of conflicting desires that I have been considering requires that there are intrinsic masks—the second-order dispositions involved in desiring are prevented from manifesting, but the dispositions masked are still there. But if we also consider the possibility of intrinsic finks, we can account for features of some cases of temptation. Temptation involves my being disposed to act in one way, but in the very situation where that disposition should manifest, my dispositions change.[11] Joe wants most of all to eat healthily, but with the chocolate cake in sight, the relative strengths of his desires shift. His desire to eat healthily should result in his declining the cake, but the sight of the cake strengthens his desire for it, and weakens his desire to resist.

We also need intrinsic finking to account for cases of weakness that aren't quite right to describe as temptation: Suzy might want most of all to do well on her test, and so

[10] See Ashwell (2010) for further arguments that the arguments for the possibility of extrinsic masks carry over to the case of intrinsic masks.

[11] Usually finks are defined as properties that *completely* remove the disposition in question. Successful temptation will usually not involve the total removal of the previously stronger disposition, but a change in the relative strength of two dispositions such that the weaker one now becomes stronger. There will also be cases of *un*successful temptation, where temptation does not result in you acting against your better judgment, but where the presence of the tempting option results in a weakening of the disposition to resist it. Even though these aren't technically cases of finking as it is usually defined, they are structurally similar cases of dispositional interference.

be disposed towards looking over Lucy's shoulder to get the answers. But at the last minute, as she starts to look over Lucy's shoulder to copy, she might be overcome with guilt, and thus no longer desire to look over Lucy's shoulder, and no longer be disposed to do so.[12]

Once we accept that there is intrinsic finking and masking at the second-order level, we ought to think that finking and masking may occur at the first-order level too. Sometimes we may be disposed towards two particular options without *realizing* that they are conflicting, and thus the dispositional interference happens when we resolve this conflict by making a decision about what to do. The feeling of conflict may in some cases be better understood as conflict at the first-order level—we may feel pulled between *particular* options, particular behaviors. Desires involve second-order dispositions to be disposed towards particular behavior given one's particular beliefs; desire conflict may result in conflict at the second-order or first-order level.

4. Conclusion

The experience of conflicting desires involves an experience of being pushed and pulled in different directions. Such a feeling is best understood in terms of *actually* being pushed and pulled in different directions—being disposed towards conflicting actions. The existence of active forces towards a less desired option is shown by the effort it takes to resist desires. If the absence of desire is put into the stimulus conditions instead, we cannot think that we are ever literally torn between two options, and we have no explanation for why we feel we must *hold ourselves back* from things we want less—why self-control can be *hard*.

The picture we are left with is still compatible with many views of the metaphysics of the mind—with both functionalism and dualism, for example. It involves thinking of our behavioral dispositions as conflicting rather than coherent, and thus better accounts for the messiness and incoherence of our desires.

Acknowledgments

Particular thanks to Richard Holton, Rae Langton, and Alex Byrne for many detailed comments on an early draft of this chapter.

---

[12] Though it isn't clear that this is a case of a *desire* finking another desire (guilt may not be best understood in terms of desires), it is still a case of a desire being intrinsically finked. There seems also to be cases of intrinsic finking with other mental capacities too—my disposition to recall people's names on greeting them can be finked by the anxiety of getting it wrong.

12

Colors and Appearances as Powers and Manifestations

Max Kistler

1. Introduction

Humans have only finite discriminatory capacities. This simple fact seems to be incompatible with the existence of appearances. As many authors have noted, the hypothesis that appearances exist seems to be refuted by reductio: Let A, B, C be three uniformly colored surfaces presented to a subject in optimal viewing conditions, such that A, B, and C resemble one another perfectly except with respect to their colors. Their colors differ slightly in the following way: the difference between A and B and the difference between B and C are below the discrimination threshold, but the difference between A and C is above this threshold. According to an intuitive construal of what an appearance is, given that A and B appear (to the subject) identical in color, A and B have the same (color[1]) appearance P_1; likewise, B and C have the same appearance P_2. B's appearance is both P_1 and P_2. This seems to imply that $P_1 = P_2$. But then, A and C also have the same appearance, which contradicts the hypothesis that A and C are discriminable. If A and C are discriminable with respect to their color, they do *not* have the same appearance with respect to color.

The paradox arising from such a series of judgments of sameness or difference between pairs of colored surfaces seems to belong to the class of sorites paradoxes. Here is Armstrong's way of raising the issue.

If A is exactly similar to B in respect X, and B is exactly similar to C in respect X, then it follows of logical necessity, that A is exactly similar to C in respect X. 'Exact similarity in a particular respect' is necessarily a transitive relation. Now suppose that we have three samples of cloth, A, B, and C, which are exactly alike except that they differ very slightly in color. Suppose further, however, that A and B are *perceptually* completely indistinguishable in respect of color, and B

---

[1] If not stated otherwise, it will be tacitly understood in what follows that the appearances I speak of are color appearances.

and C are *perceptually* completely indistinguishable in respect of color. Suppose, however, that A and C can be perceptually distinguished from each other in this respect.

(Armstrong 1968, 218)

Armstrong uses the paradox arising from the non-transitivity of non-discriminability to argue against the existence of sense-data.[2] The concept of sense-data has widely been abandoned for reasons independent from the present problem (cf. Barnes 1945; Fish 2010). However, Armstrong's argument can be reconstructed so as to refute the existence of appearances, or 'looks' (as we will call visual appearances) on any construal, not only in terms of sense-data. When a subject looks at a uniformly colored surface S, the color of S will look to the subject a certain way, so that there seems to be a look, which is part of the content of her perception.[3]

   According to Armstrong's argument, the existence of looks (for him: sense data) is refuted by a reductio. If there were looks, they would have contradictory properties; therefore there are no looks. Here is how he presents the reasoning.

Now consider the situation if we hold a 'sensory item' view of perception. If the pieces of cloth A and B are perceptually indistinguishable in color, it will seem to follow that the two sensory items A_1 and B_1 that we have when we look at the two pieces *actually are identical in color*. For the sensory items are what are supposed to make a perception the perception it is, and here, by hypothesis, the *perceptions* are identical. In the same way B_1 and C_1 will be sensory items that are identical in color. Yet, by hypothesis, sensory items A_1 and C_1 are not identical in color!

(Armstrong 1968, 218)

In what follows, I will show that there is a way to construe colors and their appearances in a way that does not fall prey to the reductio just sketched.

2. An Analysis in Terms of Powers and Manifestations

The concepts of power, disposition, and manifestation may help to describe the situation without any contradiction. Objective colors, as well as other perceived properties, are powers. This is certainly not a new idea. On the contrary, it is, since Locke's analysis in the *Essay* (1689), one of the most influential conceptions of color, which has many followers in the twentieth and twenty-first centuries. To mention only one of them: "I therefore elucidate colors as powers, in Locke's sense, to evoke certain sorts of discriminatory responses in human beings. They are also, of course, powers to cause sensations in human beings (an account still nearer Locke's)" (Smart 1959, 149).

---

[2] In a similar way, Dummett (1975) argues from this paradox to the non-existence of phenomenal qualities. According to Wright (1975), it shows that color predicates are not observational, which means that a subject cannot tell just by observation whether such a predicate correctly applies to a given surface or not.

[3] This can be said independently of the metaphysical interpretation of the situation: in the perspective of adverbialist theories of perception, the way S looks to a subject T is a property of T (or of an event involving T). In the perspective of intentionalist theories, it is part of the content of a representation T forms at the occasion of this experience. Jackson and Pinkerton (1973, 269) are wrong in thinking that the argument can be generalized only "against any act-object, as opposed to adverbial, style of analysis of sensations."

I suggest introducing a new twist in the analysis of colors as powers, which is the key to overcoming the sorites paradox threatening the existence of appearances. Colors are what have traditionally been called 'multi-track' dispositions. I think the best way to understand them is this.[4] Colors as objective properties of the surfaces of objects are powers. Such a power grounds, not a single disposition to manifest itself in one way, but a whole set of dispositions. For each context of observation of a given colored surface, the color grounds a disposition to appear to a given observer.[5] The appearance is a manifestation that is specific to the power, the observer, and the context.

Part of what makes the concept of color puzzling is that a colored surface of an object can, without itself at all changing in any intrinsic respect, vary in the way it looks, due to various changes that are external to the object and the intrinsic properties of its surface: among variations that may make the object look different with respect to its color are changes in lighting, changes in the atmosphere, and changes in the subject perceiving the object, neurophysiological or psychological. The conception of the color of an object as a power makes it belong to the class of objectivist theories of color. According to the power view, the physiology and psychology of the perceiving subject do not determine the *objective* color of perceived objects, but they contribute to determining how the color *appears* to the subject. Such appearances are manifestations of the objective powerful color property. A given determinate objective color can appear differently to different subjects, and to one subject at different times because one objective power grounds many different dispositions to manifest itself. Consider the set of all possible factors that may determine the look of a specific determinate color. Triggering conditions are sets of these factors. In each situation, the power, together with the triggering condition and the laws of nature, determines how the color will manifest itself. For each triggering situation, there is a well determined disposition: If a subject is in triggering situation T_i (composed, among other factors, of lighting conditions as well as neurophysiological and psychological conditions), then color C will manifest itself in color appearance A_i. In the context of sorites arguments, the most important dispositions are those of judging whether one color appears the same or different with respect to a second color. In Armstrong's example considered above, the objective color of item B grounds (together with a great many natural circumstances, such as the presence of light, of a well functioning perceptual apparatus and nervous system) the disposition of a subject to judge that B has the same color as A,[6] in a typical

---

[4] Here I use the account of dispositions and powers suggested in Kistler (2012).

[5] As one anonymous referee has suggested, it might seem simpler to cut out the concept of disposition from this picture, and just say that a power can manifest in different ways. However, the concept of disposition is useful in making explicit the relation between the power and its manifestations, especially with respect to those manifestations that are only possible but not actual. To each *possible* manifestation that the power gives objects possessing it, corresponds one *actual* disposition. Instead of saying that the power *can* manifest (i.e. does *possibly* manifest itself) in different ways, the use of the concept of disposition makes it possible to say that objects that have the power (powerful property) *actually* have a whole range of dispositions to manifest.

[6] This is not exactly the same as judging that A and B are indiscriminable. The terms 'discriminable' and 'indiscriminable' designate themselves *capacities*, which may manifest themselves in the long run, even if

situation ('triggering condition') in which she is shown B next to A. The judgment is the manifestation of the disposition.[7]

Let us now have a closer look at the structure of the 'sorites' argument that seems to refute the existence of appearances on the basis of a contradiction that can be derived from the fact that the indiscriminability of colors is non-transitive. Following Raffman (2000), Fara (2001), and others, I will call this argument 'Non-trans.' Let A, B, and C be objects with very similar colors, as described in the quote from Armstrong at the end of section 1. The argument presupposes three principles.

> **Sameness Principle**[8] **(SP):**   For all objects x, y, for all subjects s of experience of type S, if x looks the same as y with respect to some perceptual dimension R, there is an appearance (or a 'look'[9]) X, such that X is the appearance of x and X is the appearance of y.

> **Difference Principle (DP):**   For all objects w, z, for all subjects s of experience of type S, if w looks different from z with respect to some perceptual dimension R, there is an appearance W, such that W is the appearance of w and there is an appearance Z, such that Z is the appearance of z, and $W \neq Z$.

> **Uniqueness Principle (UP):**   For all objects x, for all subjects s of experience of type S for each respect R in which x can appear to subjects s, there is a unique[10] appearance X, such that: for all times t, if x is presented at t to s in conditions that are normal (or optimal) with respect to the perception of aspect R, then x appears to s as X.

With SP, DP, and UP, one can derive a contradiction from the existence of a situation in which indiscrimability is non-transitive. Such situations have the formal structure described in premises 1–3.

> (1) A looks to be the same color as B.
> (2) B looks to be the same color as C.
> (3) A looks to be a different color from C.

---

they do not in a single trial. Hardin (1988) shows that a scientific experiment may well establish that a subject can discriminate A and B in the long run, in the sense that she will more often than random judge that A is different from B, even if she will judge in many individual occasions that she can see no difference between them. More significant still, an experiment conducted with many subjects may well show that A and B are objectively discriminable even if many subjects judge them equal on many occasions, and maybe also if some individuals always judge them equal, on all occasions. See below, section 5.

[7] I put aside here two further distinctions: (1) the judgment may or may not be expressed. I take the most immediate manifestation to be the mental act (Raffman 2000, Proust 2001, Proust 2010) of judging, whether or not it gives rise to a public expression. (2) I will also neglect the distinction between the mental act of attending to a pair of stimuli and the act of making the judgment itself (Raffman 2000, 158).

[8] Here is how Fara expresses the Sameness Principle: "x looks to be the same color as $y \rightarrow \exists c(x$ looks to have c & y looks to have c)" (2001, 914).

[9] I will use 'appearance' and 'look' interchangeably in this chapter, except when stated otherwise: 'appearance' is more general and can also be applied to sensory modalities other than vision, whereas 'look' applies only to visual perception.

[10] X is meant to be a type, not a token.

(4) There is a look A_1, such that A has look A_1 and B has look A_1. (1, SP)

(5) There is a look C_2, such that B has look C_2 and C has look C_2. (2, SP)

(6) There is a look A_3 and a look C_3, such that: A has A_3 and C has C_3 and $A_3 \neq C_3$. (3, DP)

(7) $A_1 = A_3$. (4, 6, UP)

(8) $A_1 = C_2$. (4, 5, UP)

(9) $C_2 = C_3$. (5, 6, UP)

(10) $A_3 = C_2$. (7, 8)

(11) $A_3 = C_3$. (9, 10)

(12) $A_3 = C_3$ and $A_3 \neq C_3$. (6, 11)

The contradiction in line 12 has been derived from three premises (1–3), together with three principles, SP, DP, and UP. Which of these premises should be abandoned?

It seems impossible to deny the possibility of situations in which premises 1–3 are all true. All three principles (SP, DP, and UP) presuppose the existence of looks. This leaves open several possibilities. One may conclude, following Armstrong, that there are no looks, which implies that SP, DP, and UP are all false. But the argument does certainly not provide by itself a sufficient reason to draw such a radical conclusion. It is worth exploring other less radical options. Of the three principles, DP seems to be the least problematic. If one supposes that there are appearances, and more particularly in this case, looks with respect to color, it seems unavoidable that two things that look different have different looks.[11] However, SP and UP can be questioned and have been questioned.

In what follows, I will examine some analyses of the problem raised by the apparent non-transitivity of indiscriminability that deny either SP or UP. None of them makes essential use of the notions of power and manifestation. My strategy will be to check whether these analyses can accommodate the following intuitions.

Non-transitivity of Indiscriminability (NTI):   There are series of objective colors (or other objective perceivable properties) such that indiscriminability between adjacent pairs of elements of the series is non-transitive.

Existence of Looks (EL):   There are looks: aspects of perceptual experience that are directly accessible to the subject and perfectly known to her (i.e. known completely and infallibly).

It will turn out that none of the analyses in the literature is compatible with both NTI and EL. However, as I will show, if looks are construed as manifestations of powers, NTI and EL can both be accepted.

Armstrong (1968) and Dummett (1975) accept NTI and deny EL. They take Non-trans to be valid, and conclude that it refutes the existence of looks by reductio. Wright

---

[11] To my knowledge, DP has not been questioned (except indirectly, by questioning the existence of appearances as such).

(1975) argues that Non-trans shows that predicates that seem to express looks (observational predicates) are incoherent. I will not explore such radical conclusions any further here. Rather, my aim is to explore whether it is possible to acknowledge NTI and nevertheless save EL (i.e. the existence of looks). I take NTI to be uncontroversial and will not try to justify it here.

3. Denying UP

It is psychologically plausible that UP is wrong. Indeed, the appearance of some object O in a given respect does not only depend on the objective features of the object, on the physiology of the subject and the viewing conditions, but also on the context in which O is seen. In the case of color vision, many experiments show that the appearance of the color of O is influenced by other colored objects which are part of the same visual scene as O. Appearances are "shifty," to use Hellie's (2005, 487) expression. Without UP, the reductio does not go through because a given objective property doesn't give rise to a unique context-independent appearance, which could then be used as the middle term in a sorites argument. Without UP, step 8 in the above argument is blocked:

(8) $A_1 = C_2$. (4, 5, UP)

Thus, one cannot derive the fact that B's look, when seen together with A (A_1 according to step 4) is identical to B's look, when seen together with C (C_2 according to step 5).

To deny UP is to suppose that it is possible that B's appearance in the context of a judgment of comparison with A (which I will call 'B_1 (A_1)') is not identical with B's appearance in the context of a judgment of comparison with C (which I will call 'B_1 (C_1)'). The present hypothesis is that B_1 (C_1) may differ from B_1 (A_1). If B_1 (A_1) $\neq B_1$ (C_1), no paradox can be constructed any more. Therefore, to avoid the paradox, it is not necessary to deny the Sameness principle as well.

Both Robinson (1972) and Jackson and Pinkerton (1973) have shown that (1) (a premise equivalent to) UP is not plausible "in view of the familiar fact of perceptual relativity" (Jackson and Pinkerton 1973, 270), because "the same object can have various sense data" (Robinson 1972, 85), corresponding to its appearance in various circumstances, and (2) without (a premise equivalent to) UP, "the paradox vanishes" (Robinson 1972, 85). However, it is not enough to show that UP is not true in general, in other words, that it is *sometimes* false. It must be shown that UP is false in the particular situation described by the premises of Non-trans.

Premises SP and UP seem especially plausible in that particular situation insofar as it is not made clear whether the two comparisons—of A with B and of B with C—are made (1) simultaneously or (2) in succession. On the one hand, if the two discriminations are made together (at the same time, as it were in one glance), it seems indeed plausible to suppose that B's look is the same when B is seen together with

A as *B*'s look when *B* is seen together with *C*. After all, there is only one glance in which *B* appears. On the other hand, if these two comparisons are made separately, in succession, it appears to be a substantial assumption that *B*'s look is the same in both comparisons.

Colored objects are permanent substances. It is possible, or at least conceivable, that their surfaces do not undergo any change in color during a certain lapse of time. However, the looks of such colored surfaces of objects cannot be assumed to be substances lasting through time, and even if some sense could be made of a look lasting for some while, it would be difficult to justify the hypothesis that some aspect of that look remained constant through time. On the contrary, looks are perceptual events, or aspects of perceptual events, which are in general subject to permanent change. Therefore, if two comparisons (*A–B*) and (*B–C*) necessarily required two successive perceptions (more precisely, two acts of comparison, which are dated mental events), there would necessarily be *two* looks, B_1 (A_1), and B_1 (C_1), corresponding to the look of *B*, when it is seen together with *A* and compared to *A*, and to the look of *B* when it is seen together with *C* and compared to *C*. But then, given the ephemeral character of looks, which is due to their dependence on context, both on what is perceived at the same time in other parts of the visual field and on what has been perceived by the subject earlier, there is no reason to suppose that these two looks, B_1 (A_1), and B_1 (C_1), are identical.

However, this reasoning presupposes that the two comparisons are necessarily made *separately*. If it were possible that the two comparisons be made with respect to *the same* look B_1, one would after all have constructed a situation which leads to a contradiction (and thus refutes the existence of looks).

Both Robinson (1972) and Jackson and Pinkerton (1973)[12] argue that there are necessarily two looks in play, so that no sorites argument can be constructed and no contradiction follows. According to Jackson and Pinkerton, the hypothesis that the same look (of *B*: B_1) is involved in the comparison of *A* and *B* and in the comparison of *B* and *C* is "logically impossible" (1973, 270). "The suggestion that *A* might look to be the same color as *B*, *B* might look to be the same color as *C*, while *A* looks to be a different color from *C*, to one and the same person at one and the same time, is inconsistent," because this "suggestion involves one object, *B*, looking to have two different colors at the same time to the same person, which is impossible" (1973, 271). They agree with Armstrong that this leads to a contradiction, and conclude that the hypothesis of the existence of a unique B_1 must be rejected.[13]

However, it remains to be seen whether Robinson's and Jackson and Pinkerton's defense of the existence of sense-data can be adapted to a conception of color perception that does not make use of sense-data but only of objective colors and color

---

[12] Their strategy is taken up by Raffman (2000) and Fara (2001).

[13] The difference with Armstrong's conclusion is that they conclude only that UP should be abandoned (there can be, in this situation, no unique look involved in two comparisons), where Armstrong takes it that the contradiction justifies the more general conclusion that there are no looks.

appearances. In what follows, I shall propose an analysis that (1) justifies abandoning UP while (2) retaining SP and EL and (3) is compatible with NTI. Being only concerned with appearances (conceived as sense-data), neither Robinson nor Jackson and Pinkerton raise the latter issue with respect to indiscriminability judgments bearing on *objective* colors of surfaces. However, with respect to the appearances of A, B, and C, the question of transitivity cannot even be asked: if UP is false, there is no common look of B, which could be used as a "middle term" in a sorites argument.

Once objective colors are taken into consideration, we can construct an even stronger argument against UP. If UP were true (i.e. if there was a one–one correspondence between the objective colors A, B, C and their looks A_1, B_1, C_1), colors (and the objective properties of the objects of perception in general) would be single-track dispositions, as it is tacitly understood in the traditional Lockean analysis. However, and surprisingly, if colors were single-track dispositions, then, given the one–one correspondence of B and its unique manifestation B_1, Non-trans would refute not only the existence of looks but also the existence of objective colors, which manifest themselves by their looks.

Here we seem to have a place where 'powers may be put to work.' The metaphysical analysis of the relations between powers, dispositions, and manifestations shows how reality must be structured so that (1) UP can be false, whereas both (2) EL and (3) NTI are true. I will make a suggestion along these lines in section 7 below.

4. Denying SP, Supposing that Representations of Colors Are Exact: Goodman/Clark

The most influential strategy to avoid the refutation of looks by Non-trans has been introduced by Goodman (1977) and further developed by Clark (1993). In terms of our analysis of the logical form of Non-trans, this strategy can be interpreted as based on the rejection of the Sameness Principle (see Fara 2001). Goodman and Clark deny that the fact that two objects look the same with respect to color suffices to establish that there is a property, traditionally called appearance or look, that is directly apparent to the subject. Supposing that such a property exists leads to the sorites contradiction. However, contrary to Robinson and Jackson and Pinkerton, Goodman's and Clark's aim is not merely critical. Indeed, Clark provides a positive metaphysical interpretation of colors and looks, which goes beyond finding a way of avoiding the conclusion of Non-trans. Discrimination and difference judgments are made by subjects on the basis of the perception of objects. Although these judgments bear on external objects, they must be made on the basis of some representation which has psychological reality. The challenge is to account for this psychological reality without falling into the trap of the sorites argument. Goodman's and Clark's strategy is to introduce a new kind of entity that is supposed to take over the role of looks, but differs from looks in being immune to sorites arguments. "Qualia," as Goodman and

Clark call them, are psychological entities for which there is no principle equivalent to the Sameness Principle. No sorites argument refutes their existence even if all other premises are kept, including the Uniqueness Principle.

Qualia are defined indirectly, with the help of the concept of matching: x and y match if they look the same.[14] Two qualia x and y are identical if they do not only match each other but if for all other qualia z, either z matches both x and y, or z matches neither x nor y (cf. Goodman 1977, 196). Qualia thus conceived have coherent identity conditions and do not fall prey to any sorites argument. The reason is that they do not obey any principle of the form of the Sameness Principle. It is not the case that for all objects x, y, if x looks the same as y with respect to R ('if x matches y with respect to R'), there is a quale Q such that Q is both part of the content of the representation of x and part of the content of the representation of y. It is crucial for the concept of qualia that matching of two perceived objects with respect to R is not sufficient for the sameness of the qualia caused by the perception of x and y. x and y may well match although the qualia by which an observer represents them are not the same. This happens precisely in the situation described by the premises of Non-trans. The fact that B matches A is not sufficient for their qualia QA and QB to be identical. On the contrary, the fact that there is a third item C which matches B without matching A, establishes that qualia QA and QB are not identical.

The problem with this strategy is that it changes the subject rather than solving the problem. The aim was to understand how there can be looks although their existence seems to be refuted by Non-trans. Goodman and Clark reply that there are no looks, but that their role can be taken over by qualia. Qualia in Goodman's and Clark's sense are the content of representations. They are theoretical properties postulated in order to explain judgments of perceptual similarity and dissimilarity (Shepard 1962; Shepard 1965). Qualia are subjective, because they are the content of representations which are partly determined by constraints imposed by the subject, in particular by its neurophysiology. However, qualia, as defined by Goodman and Clark, are not looks as we use the concept in this chapter[15] because qualia are not known (1) directly nor (2) completely nor (3) infallibly by the subject that has them.

---

[14] Goodman (1977, 197) takes the predicate 'match' to be basic and provides no analysis.

[15] Armstrong considers the possibility of conceiving sense-data in a similar way, and criticizes it for similar reasons. "The upholder of sensory items" says Armstrong, may "abandon the view that we have incorrigible knowledge of the nature of the items at the time of having them" (1968, 219). As Armstrong notes, such a doctrine would be paradoxical, in the sense that it is incompatible with a central tenet of the sense-datum doctrine. Sense-data are defined by the fact that the appearance–reality distinction does not apply to them: They are what they appear to be. Thus it is impossible to say of a sense-datum that the very subject to whom it appears ignores what it is; for this presupposes that the way it appears to her (and which she knows by immediate introspection, or acquaintance) is not what it really is. Broad (1923, 244) seems to take sense-data to be only incompletely known. This seems to be incompatible with the very notion of a sense-datum. We might take this to be a verbal issue: What Broad calls sense-data just are not sense-data, in the sense of what appears necessarily as what it is, and about which the subject cannot be ignorant. Rather, they might be powers to give rise to sense-data: powerful properties of the perceptual experience.

It is part of the concept of a look (or in general, of an appearance) that it is possible for the subject to acquire *direct* knowledge of how things look (or appear) to her. It is essential for looks that knowledge of the sameness or difference of the looks of A and B can be acquired directly: if A_1 and B_1 are looks it is sufficient for the subject to inspect A_1 and B_1 themselves to know whether they are identical or not. However, the subject cannot tell by direct inspection alone whether two items A and B produce the same quale in her psychological quality space. The fact that they look exactly the same ('match') with respect to some dimension of perceivable qualities, such as color, is necessary but not sufficient. If there is a third item C that looks different from one (say A) but looks the same as the other (B), (in Goodman's terminology: if there is C which matches B but not A), the quale QA by which the subject represents the color of A is not identical with the quale QB by which the subject represents the color of B. The crucial point is that there are situations where $QA \neq QB$ but where the subject cannot by introspection directly acquire knowledge that $QA \neq QB$.

Moreover, even if A and B match and if it is in fact true that $QA = QB$, the subject can never *be certain* that $QA = QB$: It is impossible for the subject to check all third items, which might possibly reveal that $QA \neq QB$. The identity $QA = QB$ always remains hypothetical. Depending on what is taken to be sufficient for knowledge, the subject might nevertheless be said to know that $QA = QB$. Even then, however, qualia are not looks because such knowledge is not direct: knowledge that $QA = QB$ requires inspection of items that are different from both A and B.

With the help of the concept of qualia, it is possible both (1) to accept that indiscriminability is non-transitive (NTI), and (2) nevertheless to maintain that there is something, the quale, that has psychological reality and accounts for the way things appear to a subject. However, qualia are not looks. Insofar as the Sameness Principle bears on looks, it is paradoxical to deny it.[16] Denying it means denying that a subject can tell just by looking how things look to her, and denying that a subject can know whether two things that look the same really have the same look. It is not paradoxical if the subject's (partial) ignorance is taken to bear, not on how things look, but on the qualia by which their perceptible qualities are represented. But then, the paradox arises if qualia are supposed to be appearances which do not directly appear to the subject.

The fact that qualia do not satisfy the conditions we have imposed on looks is no reason to deny that they are real. Rather, they can be understood as being real powers. Just as a subject of perception has only incomplete knowledge of the objective

---

[16]   Fara says that it is a "truism" (2001, 909) that "if any two color patches look the same, then if one looks red so does the other" (908). She also says that it would be confused to attribute an observational predicate such as being red to one object and to deny it to a second item if these two items look the same: "I cannot see my way through to the possibility that two color patches might look the same, yet that 'looks red' applies to one but not to the other" (909). Armstrong says that Goodman's strategy, namely "abandon the view that we have incorrigible knowledge of the nature of the items at the time we have them" (1968, 219), while it is not logically absurd, "is nevertheless most implausible." Jackson and Pinkerton agree that "it is not open to the sensory item theorist to argue that in the kind of case described in the above quotation [the non-trans case; MK] the percipient is mistaken about the nature of his sensory items" (1973, 269).

properties she perceives, she has only partial knowledge of her own qualia. Each manifestation gives the subject partial knowledge: looks reveal part of the nature of objective colors, but also part of the nature of her own qualia. The fact that a subject judges that A and B 'match' means that the objective colors are very similar, but also that the qualia QA and QB, by which she represents these objective colors, lie close together in her psychological quality space.

5. Denying SP, Supposing that Representations of Colors Are Inexact: Hardin

According to Hardin (1988) it is an illusion that looks (and apparent colors in particular) fall prey to sorites arguments. It stems from an oversimplified conception of looks, according to which a look can be exhaustively determined and known by one subject at one instant. He shows that this is not the only way to conceive of the psychological basis of perceptual appearance, and furthermore that there is an alternative, scientific way of conceiving that basis. The value of the scientifically measurable properties in this basis, which Hardin misleadingly calls "looks" although, as I shall argue, they are not looks in our sense, can be determined by statistical means. Hardin claims that, understood in this way, "looks" are immune to refutation by sorites arguments. "If we are prepared to count statistical ensembles of observations and observational data—a quite common practice in science—Nontrans . . . must be rejected" (1988, 214). Furthermore, the construal of looks as objective theoretical properties, which can be determined by direct introspection only to a finite degree of precision, paves the way for a coherent "concept of phenomenal color," according to which phenomenal colors "are often indeterminate" (1988, 214).[17]

The statistical treatment of comparisons between colors shows that the judgments subjects make of a given pair of colors are not constant, neither for the same subject over time, nor within a group of different subjects. Rather, such judgments are spread out in a way one would expect from a process in which noise is added to the process of signal treatment.[18] One can assume that the factors producing this 'noise' are "randomly distributed and thus representable by a normal (Gaussian) distribution curve" (Hardin 1988, 215). As a result, the scientific construal of the appearance of a color is not a point in color space (the space corresponding to the contents of perceptual representations) but an imprecise value, spread around a mean value with a distribution that can be characterized by its standard deviation. According to Hardin, this is sufficient to show that "the sorites problem does not arise" (1988, 220). If looks are construed as imprecise theoretical properties, each with its mean value

---

[17] Hardin takes care to distinguish this thesis from the claim that it is "just phenomenal color *predicates . . .* [that] are often indeterminate" (1988, 214, my emphasis).

[18] Discriminating between colors can be represented as the extraction of "a signal which is transmitted over a noisy channel" (Hardin 1988, 215). This idea is taken up by Hellie (2005).

and standard deviation, their distributions can overlap. The sorites paradox arises as long as one identifies represented properties with single looks, on the basis of single comparison judgments of one individual subject at one occasion.

To one individual (to use our own symbols introduced above), B_1 can seem to be the same apparent color as A_1, and also seem to be the same apparent color as C_1. However, statistical sampling of many judgments of one subject, and of many subjects, will show that the look B_1 is neither identical with A_1, nor with C_1. Instead, their characteristic distributions overlap. The points in the overlap zone correspond to judgments according to which the two looks are equal.

In the terms of the premises of Non-trans we have distinguished in the preceding discussion, Hardin denies SP: The observation of a statistically significant sample of comparison judgments of a given pair of items (within the triple A, B, C that gives rise to the sorites paradox), say A and B, will show that the representations $R(A)$ and $R(B)$ are not identical although they may be judged to look equal for many individuals on many occasions.

However, Hardin's account accepts UP not only as a plausible empirical hypothesis. UP is built into the construal of phenomenal properties: the phenomenal property as which a given item A appears to subjects of a given type is defined as the statistical distribution of the individual appearances, as they are manifested in various comparison judgments. All appearances of one item, to the same subject and to different subjects, are integrated in the unique phenomenal property.

Hardin's account does not adequately solve our problem of showing that EL and NTI are compatible, for two reasons.

(1) Hardin's "phenomenal colors" (1988, 214) are not appearances or looks at all. They are theoretical properties, constructed according to a scientific methodology, from a third person perspective, on the basis of a statistical evaluation of many first person appearance judgments. Knowledge of such "phenomenal properties" can only be acquired indirectly. It would be more appropriate to call appearances or looks "phenomenal properties." Hardin's "phenomenal properties" are ill-named: There is no subject to whom they appear at any time and who knows them directly, by how they appear. As Goodman's and Clarke's defense of qualia against the sorites paradox, phenomenal colors as construed by Hardin's are a Pyrrhic victory against the sorites refutation of appearances: Hardin shows that there is a property that does not fall prey to the refutation; but it is not an appearance.

(2) Moreover, Hardin's construal of phenomenal properties as objective measurable quantities with a mean value and standard deviation, obtained from the statistical treatment of many appearance judgments, does not solve the problem in all generality. As Hardin himself admits, "the sorites argument could be resurrected" (1988, 220) with a series of phenomenal colors that are so close together that their difference could not even be detected by statistical means, on the basis of a large set of individual comparison judgments. If the objective difference in the stimuli is so small that it would take a very large number of trials to detect a subjective difference in the ways these stimuli appear to subjects, it seems practically impossible to avoid changes in the

experimental situation. In such cases, "the signal gets buried in the noise" (220). This means that, given the practically limited number of trials, the distribution curves that ground the objective distinctness of different looks are themselves not infinitely sharp. As a consequence, there are "phenomenal colors" (i.e. distribution curves) that are so close together that they cannot be distinguished by statistical means. Sorites arguments can be constructed with respect to such phenomenal colors. A series of very close distribution curves can serve as premises of an argument that has exactly the same structure as Non-trans. There is a series of phenomenal colors, such that they appear equal even in the long run to a large group of observers, although the first and last in the series appear different to them. Therefore, there are no such phenomenal colors, scientifically construed on the basis of the statistical evaluation of a large number of appearance judgments.[19]

Hardin's own reply to this problem is that "it doesn't arise in everyday color-attributing practice" (1988, 221), and that it has "little bearing on a rational reconstruction of the rules governing color predicates in a public language since such predicates are necessarily *much* coarser than the fine grains of just noticeably different colors perceivable by particular individuals" (221). This fact shows that the problem doesn't threaten the meaning of ordinary language predicates;[20] however, it does not save the existence of "phenomenal colors" from refutation by sorites arguments.

6. Denying SP, Supposing that Representations of Colors Are Inexact: Hellie

Both Hellie (2005) and Zeimbekis (2009) argue that the paradox of Non-trans can be avoided by conceiving perceived qualities as determinables, corresponding to regions, not points, in quality space.

Let us suppose that phenomenal qualities, such as colors, sizes, and shapes are representations in a psychological quality space (i.e. a psychological space of the content of the representations of perceived qualities [Shepard 1962; Shepard 1965]). Let us suppose that hues can be represented in a two-dimensional surface in a psychological color space (Shepard 1962). Determinate and determinable predicates and properties can be ordered in a series: colored is a determinable relative to red, and red is a determinable relative to scarlet. Each determinable color corresponds to a part of the color surface. The higher a represented color is in the determinate–determinable hierarchy, the larger is the corresponding surface: the surface corresponding to

---

[19] In a similar vein, Raffman judges that,

> the statistical relation defined by the psychologists seems equally likely to be nontransitive: there are or can be three stimuli A, B, and C such that, for example, A and B are judged different only 40 percent of the time (hence are indiscriminable), and similarly B and C, but A and C are judged different 70 percent of the time (hence are discriminably different).
>
> (Raffman 2000, 157)

[20] Therefore, it can be used as a defense against Wright (1975).

scarlet is a proper part of the surface corresponding to red. "Super-determinates" (Funkhouser 2006) lie at the bottom of the hierarchy: they are perfectly determinate and correspond to points in the psychological quality space.

Zeimbekis argues that the empirical limitations in the discrimination powers of any real cognitive system make it "impossible for any discrimination system to discriminate super-determinate shape and size properties" (2009, 352). He concludes that "phenomenal sizes and shapes are determinable types" (346), in the sense that each phenomenal size corresponds to a whole region of determinate objective sizes. However, Zeimbekis does not conclude that phenomenal appearances are determinables *as appearances* (i.e. in the sense of corresponding to an extended region of representations). For Zeimbekis, appearances are determinables only relative to the objective properties they represent. "Phenomenal sizes . . . stand in a determination relation to objective sizes" (353).

By contrast, Hellie (2005) takes phenomenal properties (i.e. representations of objective properties acquired through perception) to be "inexact" *as appearances*, in the sense that the identity of a phenomenal property corresponds to an extended region in the psychological space of representation. Hellie represents the situation establishing the non-transitivity of indiscriminability in the following way: $R(A, e)$ is the representation of a color A in experience e. It corresponds to a region in psychological quality space that contains A. According to Hellie, the fact that A and B are indiscriminable in experience e means that the representations of the colors of A and B overlap: There can be "indiscriminability without sameness of representation" (2005, 485). This is equivalent to a denial of (SP).

Hellie explicitly makes the hypothesis that the phenomenology of the represented properties has exactly the same structure as the representations. The consequence is that the subject does not perfectly well know the phenomenal properties. His account "allows for indiscriminability without sameness of phenomenology" (2005, 496). In this sense, Hellie's analysis suffers from the same defect as Hardin's: Representations corresponding to extended surfaces in psychological quality space are not looks and should better not be called "phenomenal," because the subject does not know them directly and exhaustively. In particular, the subject who perceives A and B, which look the same, does not know just by looking (in experience e) whether A's and B's phenomenal colors $R(A, e)$ and $R(B, e)$ are identical or just overlapping. I take it to be incompatible with the notion of phenomenology that there are phenomenological facts that are not directly accessible to the subject herself.

7. Looks as Manifestations of Powers

Let us take stock, and answer the question we started with, whether there is a way to account for the phenomena of appearance that is compatible both with

Existence of Looks (EL):   There are looks: aspects of perceptual experience that are directly accessible to the subject and perfectly known to her.

Non-transitivity of Indiscriminability (NTI):   There are series of objective colors (or other objective perceivable properties) such that indiscriminability between adjacent pairs of elements of the series is non-transitive.

We have seen that it is possible to acknowledge the possibility of situations such as those described by the premises of Non-trans, and still avoid the contradiction that Non-trans derives from these premises. This is possible by rejecting at least one of DP, UP, or SP, without rejecting the existence of looks as such. I have argued that DP and SP cannot be rejected without threatening the existence of looks and the intuition that they are directly and completely known by the subject, by the very experience in which they are present to the subject. A subject would not know how things appear to her if it were possible (as it is if SP is denied) that (1) she judges A and B to look the same, but that nevertheless (2) the look of A differs from the look of B. Thus, the existence of looks can only be justified if SP is maintained. The same reasoning shows that the existence of looks requires DP: A subject would not know how things appear to her if it were possible (as it is if DP is denied) that (1) she judges A and B to look different, but that nevertheless (2) the look of A is identical to the look of B. Abandoning SP or DP is equivalent to abandoning the idea of looks as immediately and perfectly known to the subject on the basis of the very experience of having them. In other words, SP and DP are constitutive of the conception of looks as immediately and completely known to the subject. If two things look the same with respect to R, there is a look they share; and if two things look different with respect to R, there are two different looks.

At this point, the only way to save the existence of looks from contradiction is by dropping UP. We have already seen that this fits well with the hypothesis that colors and other perceptible properties are "multi-track" powers. Given that the context contributes to determine how things appear, how an object looks to subject S_1 will in general differ from how it appears to subject S_2, even if viewing conditions are normal, or optimal; and how an object looks to S_1 at t_1 will in general differ from how it looks to S_1 at t_2. For each perspective and each context, there is a different disposition grounded on the relevant properties of the object, to manifest itself in the mind of an observer. This is equivalent to the negation of UP: it means that it is not the case that a given object manifests itself, with respect to a given perceptible aspect, such as color, with a unique look.

There remains an important obstacle on the way to an adequate construal of looks. We have found that extant analyses of appearances, qualia, or 'phenomenal colors' are all incompatible with EL, according to which looks are immediately and completely known to the subjects to which they appear, by the very fact that they appear to the subject. On the other hand, Robinson's and Jackson and Pinkerton's analysis justifies the existence of looks, but only in the framework of the theory of sense-data. In that framework, NTI does not make sense because discrimination judgments are not taken to bear on objective colors, but rather on sense-data.

I can here only sketch how manifestations of powerful objective colors can comply with the intuitive constraints expressed in EL. This is possible if looks are construed as (parts of) the contents of acts of comparison. Let us suppose that these acts are judgments.[21] According to this hypothesis, if a subject judges that A looks the same as B, A's look is constituted by the fact that it is equal to B's look. If the subject judges that A looks similar or different from B with respect to its color, A's look consists in A's similarity or difference with respect to B's look. The only way to comply with EL is to suppose that the content of the judgment exhausts the appearance: there is nothing more about the look of A than how S judges it to be at a given moment. Of course, this hypothesis raises a lot of new questions. One may immediately worry that this account of appearances gives rise to a regress: the look of A can only be constituted by a judgment of its sameness or difference with respect to B if the look of B is already known.

The hypothesis that appearances are constituted by acts of comparison has important consequences. One consequence is that it is incompatible with the thesis of the representational theory of phenomenal consciousness (Dretske 1995) that a subject's representing a property is sufficient for the property to appear to the subject. Our hypothesis leads to the result that representing a property is not sufficient for the property's appearing to the subject. Perceptual judgments require representations because they are mental acts that have representations as objects; but the very existence of the representations does not guarantee that the subject directs her attention to them nor that she will make a judgment bearing on them. Phenomena such as change blindness and inattentional blindness (see Most 2010) seem to be incompatible with a pure representational theory, insofar as they seem to show that a subject can represent many things and events without their appearing to her. Our hypothesis can account for these phenomena. The hypothesis that the appearance results from a perceptual judgment fits with the fact that a subject is 'blind' to objects and events it represents but to which it does not direct its attention. Perceptual judgment requires directing one's attention to a perceived object or fact. Here is a question which calls for further empirical and conceptual work: is perceptual attention in itself sufficient for making things appear, or do they only begin to 'look' a certain way once they have been made objects of perceptual judgments? We cannot explore such questions here; however, they suggest that it is fruitful to conceive appearances as manifestations of powers.

8. Conclusion

Starting with an analysis of a famous apparent paradox arising from a series of judgments of perceptual comparisons with stimuli so similar that their difference

---

[21] Raffman suggests that looks are constituted by judgments. "I shall speak indifferently of patches' *looking red* and *being judged to look red*" (1994, 45; emphasis Raffman's). According to Raffman, looks can arise either from discriminatory judgments, which I am presently considering, or from categorical judgments, when one color is judged to belong to a perceptual category stored in memory. It is controversial whether there is a notion of judgment that can be applied to the comparison judgments I am considering and that does not rely on the use of concepts. If all judgments make use of concepts, the hypothesis remains open that at least some appearances precede such judgments (Zeimbekis 2013).

lies under the discrimination threshold, our aim was to find out whether there is a metaphysical picture of perception and its objects, which allows discrimination between objective colors to be non-transitive, and still makes room for the existence of what I have called 'looks,' or more generally 'appearances.' I have taken looks to be defined by the possibility for the subject to know them immediately, exhaustively, and infallibly. I have suggested that this is possible if colors and other objective properties that are objects of perceptual judgments, are 'multi-track' powers. Each occasion of comparison between two perceptible items is a triggering condition, relative to which the power gives rise to a disposition to appear in a certain way to a given type of cognitive subject. If the subject makes a comparison judgment, the item appears to her in a way constituted by the judgment. The appearance results from a cognitive act of the subject, and is therefore directly and completely knowable by the subject.

All other accounts of appearances we have examined either construe appearances as sense-data (Robinson, Jackson and Pinkerton) or as contents of permanent representations. Such permanent representations as "qualia" (Goodman and Clark) and "phenomenal properties" (Hardin, Hellie) are powers rather than manifestations of powers, in the sense that they are not directly and completely manifest to the subject. The content of representations, whether sharp or "determinate" (Goodman, Clark) or spread out or "determinable" (Hardin, Hellie), can only be explored and completely known with scientific methods. Such representations and their contents are not looks in our sense because they are not immediately accessible to the subject.

If looks are construed as contents of perceptual judgments, they are ephemeral, in the sense that their existence is limited to a particular situation. This is a consequence of the fact that they are manifestations rather than powers. Here lies the main difference between our proposal and the accounts we have considered. Permanent representations, such as Goodman's qualia and determinable qualities in a psychological space, are powerful properties. Just as objective powerful properties (such as the objective colors of perceived objects), the representations a subject forms of the colors she perceives are powerful properties of the subject. Both are only indirectly accessible to the subject. The subject acquires new partial knowledge on both objective and subjective powerful properties each time she makes a perceptual judgment. Each acquisition of such partial knowledge gives rise to an appearance, so that the appearance itself is completely knowable by the subject. However, this knowledge concerns only an ephemeral manifestation, not a power, and is therefore of very limited use.

Acknowledgments

I thank my auditors at St. Louis, Oxford, Paris, and Bergamo, as well as Pascal Ludwig, John Zeimbekis, and two referees for Oxford University Press for very helpful critical remarks.

13

Must Functionalists Be Aristotelians?

Robert C. Koons and Alexander Pruss

Functionalism remains the most promising strategy for 'naturalizing' the mind. We argue that when functions are defined in terms of conditionals, whether indicative, probabilistic, or counterfactual, the resulting version of functionalism is subject to devastating finkish counter-examples. Only functions defined within a powers ontology can provide the right account of normalcy, but the conception of powers must follow classical, Aristotelian lines, since the alternative (an evolutionary account of normativity as proposed by Ruth Garrett Millikan) is inconsistent with a plausible principle of the supervenience of the mind on local conditions.

1. Functionalism

Naturalizing the mind demands that the fundamental vocabulary of psychology must be wholly physical (for description of inputs and outputs), plus the language of causation, dispositions, counterfactuals, or function, as well as the terms of logic and mathematics, achieving as a result a so-called 'topic neutral' language. British philosopher and logician Frank Ramsey (1929) offered the logical tools needed to express mature functionalism, describing a logical process that has come to be known as 'Ramsification.' We start with the true (and at present not fully known) theory of psychology, one including explicitly mental terms and predicates (like 'pain' or 'conscious of'). This theory is supposed to capture the one Pattern of interactions that is definitive of having a mind. We form a single, gigantic conjunction of all of the postulates of the theory and then replace each mental predicate by a second-order variable of the same type (i.e. one-place predicate variable for monadic predicates, two-place predicate variables for binary predicates, etc.). Finally, we append a series of existential quantifiers to the beginning of the formula, one quantifier for each variable-type. The resulting 'Ramsey' sentence is now in a topic-neutral language, since the only predicates that remain are either part of the language of physics and mathematics, or belong to a category of causal or modal language, such as causal predicates, probabilistic connectives, nomological necessity operators, or subjunctive conditional connectives.

Clauses of the Ramsey sentence will have a form something like one of these:

(1) If the system x is in internal state S_n and in input state I_m at time t, then x at the next relevant time $t+1$ is in internal state S_k and output state O_j. (Indicative conditional)

(2) If the system x were in internal state S_n and in input state I_m at time t, then x would at time $t+1$ be in internal state S_k and output state O_j. (Subjunctive conditional)

(3) Whenever the system x is in internal state S_n, x has a disposition to enter immediately into output state O_j and internal state S_k in response to input state I_m. (Dispositional state)

(4) System x's being in internal state S_n confers upon it the power to produce output state O_j and internal state S_k immediately in response to input state I_m. (Causal power)

Here, x is either the whole mind or a subsystem. This could in principle be a very low level subsystem, say a logic gate that takes two truth value inputs and returns their disjunction, or a very high level one, say one that takes desires and beliefs and outputs motor activation signals.

The project of Ramsifying psychology raises a number of questions, including the following:

• What sort of language is involved in the specification of the links between inputs, internal states, and outputs?

• Does the theory make use of material or subjunctive conditionals, or does it make reference to causal powers or intrinsic dispositions?

• If it does make use of causal powers or intrinsic dispositions, how are these to be understood?

  – In a Rylean way, as equivalent to the truth of a subjunctive conditional?

  – In a Dretske–Armstrong–Tooley way, as following from facts about primitive laws of nature?[1]

  – Or in an Aristotelian way, according to which powers are intrinsic properties of substances, definable in terms of their inputs and outputs, and conferred on substances by essential or accidental natures, and dispositions are powers together with a teleological directedness towards their exercise?

First we will argue that the material and subjective conditional views are untenable, and then we will evaluate the dispositional and powers views. We will argue that the

---

[1] See Dretske (1977), Tooley (1977), and Armstrong (1983).

only plausible form of functionalism requires that the connections between inputs, outputs, and mental states be described as causal powers, in accordance with the assumptions of standard Aristotelian metaphysics.

2. Conditional Functionalisms

2.1. Material Conditionals

Functionalisms built on indicative or subjunctive conditionals have little hope of success. The most obviously unsuccessful are *material* conditional accounts, simply because the conditional clauses will be satisfied by any system that never actually receives the inputs. The moon will count as a human-level mind, just one that never actually gets to think about anything because the activation conditions are never satisfied.

2.2. Non-material Conditionals

Standard problems with conditional accounts of dispositions apply just as well to all the non-material conditional forms of the accounts. We can imagine, for instance, that the individual has strapped to her a bomb that explodes if system x is in internal state S_n and receives input I_m at time t, but that in fact this condition does not obtain. Then, the subjunctive conditional (2) is false, and (1) will also be false on plausible non-material readings (e.g. ones based on conditional probabilities). Yet, having such a bomb that never goes off strapped to one, while unfortunate, does not make one not have a mind.

One might try to use context-sensitivity to ward off such worries, for instance by saying that in evaluating conditionals or conditional probabilities we should only consider those causal factors that are internal to the system x. But we can replace the bomb by a fatal disease, and the distinction between 'internal' and 'external' causal factors will become untenable.

What if the antecedents of the conditionals are strengthened to include the claim that the whole system survives until the next relevant time? Here we borrow an idea from Harry Frankfurt (1969): the introduction of a purely hypothetical neural-manipulator. The manipulator wants the subject to follow a certain script. If the subject were to show signs of being about to deviate from the script, then the manipulator would intervene internally, causing the subject to continue to follow the script. Moreover, if by some near-miracle the subject succeeded in deviating from the script for a step, the manipulator would push the subject right back to the script. We are to imagine that the subject spontaneously follows the script, and as a consequence, the manipulator never intervenes.

Frankfurt introduced such a thought experiment to challenge the idea that freedom of the will requires alternative possibilities. We use it to show that the existence of mental states is independent of the truth of counterfactual conditionals linking the states to inputs, outputs, and each other. It is obvious that the presence of an inactive manipulator cannot deprive the subject of his mental states. However, the manipulator's presence is sufficient to falsify all of the usual non-material conditionals and conditional probabilities linking the states. If the manipulator's script says that at time $t+1$ the subject is to be in state S_n, then that would happen no matter what state the subject were in at time t.

Again, it won't do to say that the conditionals need to hold on the assumption of no external interference (see Smith 2007). For we can always replace an external intervener by an internal one—say, an odd disorder of the auditory center of the brain that causes it to monitor the rest of the brain and counterfactually intervene.

Moreover, cognitive malfunctioning is surely possible as a result of injury or illness. The theory to be Ramsified cannot plausibly incorporate the effects of every possible injury or illness, since there are no limits to the complexity of the sort of phenomenon that might constitute an injury or illness. Injury can prevent nearly all behavior—so much so, as to make the remaining behavioral dispositions so non-specific as to fail to distinguish one internal state from another. Consider, for example, locked-in syndrome, as depicted in the movie *The Diving Bell and the Butterfly*. Therefore, the true psychological theory must contain postulates that specify the *normal* connections among states.

Without resorting to Aristotelian or evolutionary teleology (an option we will discuss later), our only account of normalcy will be probabilistic. Thus, a system *normally* enters state S_m from state S_n as a result of input I_m provided it is *likely* to do this. However, serious injury or illness can make a malfunctioning subsystem rarely or never do what it should, yet without challenging the status of the subsystem as, say, a subsystem for visual processing of shapes. And, again, a merely counterfactual intervener, whether external or internal, can change what the system is likely to do without manipulating the system in any way.

Alternately, one might try to define normalcy in terms of what systems *of the same type* are likely to do. Thus, a system *normally* enters state S_m from state S_n as a result of input I_m provided that most of the time systems of *this type* do this. A serious problem here is that we are giving the functional claims in order to characterize the *type* of system. But it is then circular in the functional claims to refer to other systems of the same type. One might try to Ramsify over types to solve this problem, but one will still have problems with one of a kind minds.

Moreover, the probabilities of state transitions in systems of a given kind depend deeply on the environment the systems are in. A plausible account would have to say that a normal transition is one that is likely to occur in systems of the given type *in a normal environment*. But, again, it does not appear possible to specify a normal environment without resorting to something like teleology or proper function.

2.3. Rylean Conception of Dispositions

Rylean dispositions (see Ryle 1949) correspond to the subjunctive conditional: if C were to be realized, then E would result. Hence, Rylean dispositions are also subject to the objections to conditional views when used to formulate functionalism.

2.4. Nomological-deductive Model of Powers

A thing or system of things S has the C-to-E nomological-deductive disposition if and only if there is some description $D(S)$ satisfied by S and laws of nature L such that $L\&C\&D(S)$ entails E (or, perhaps, such that the rational probability of E on $L\&C\&D(S)$ is constrained to be very high). Again, the bomb and fatal disease objections to conditional views rule out nomological-deductive dispositions when these are used to formulate functionalism.

3. Three Theories of Normativity

There are three plausible accounts of the basis of normativity: Aristotelian powers, agential intentions, and evolutionary accounts.

3.1. Aristotelian Normativity

An Aristotelian can give a straightforward account of normativity: a substance is supposed to produce E on occasions of C if and only if its nature includes a C-to-E power (one might also prefer more active terms like 'tendency' or 'striving').

This account may appear insufficient in the light of the possibility of indeterministic powers. Could not a substance have both a C-to-E and a C-to-non-E power, in which case it would neither be supposed to produce E in C nor to produce non-E in C? One might complicate the account by excluding such cases of competition in some way, or positing higher order powers that decide between the competing powers. But there are also two simpler moves. One move is to say that in such cases, the substance is in the 'unhappy' position of being supposed to do incompatible things—it will necessarily fail at one of them.

A more complex move is to say that it cannot happen that a substance has both a C-to-E and a C-to-non-E power. Rather, the substance has a C-to-E and a C'-to-non-E power, and if it happens that both C and C' obtain, then the substance will fail to do one of the things it should do. This move fits with a natural metaphysical interpretation of quantum indeterminacy. Take an electron in the mixed spin state |up>+|down>, and measure the electron's spin, thereby forcing the electron's state to collapse indeterministically to |up> or to |down>. Suppose the electron ends up going to |up>. What explains its going to |up> is not that the electron used to be in state |up>+|down>. Rather, what explains its going to |up> is that the electron used to be in a state that had an |up> component (or had a significant such component). That the state also had a |down> component is true but does not help to explain the electron's transitioning to |up>. Thus, the electron has two powers with incompatible outcomes and different, but potentially co-occurring, activating conditions: (a) being in a measurement situation with a state with an |up> component and (b) being in a measurement situation with a state with a |down> component.

Functionalism can then be put in an Aristotelian mode, referring to the presence of powers to produce outputs and internal states (including other powers). The result would be a non-reductive and non-physicalist version of functionalism, since the form of the theory would rule out the states' realizers being merely physical states of constituent particles (see Bealer 2010).

3.2. Agential Normativity

Normativity of a kind arises from agents' intentionally making and using things:

(5) A thing is supposed to produce E on occasion C if and only if its maker or users intend it so to do.

For example, hammers are supposed to drive in nails, since this is what the makers and users of hammers intend to do with them. There are two problems with incorporating this kind of normativity into our universal psychological theory of the Pattern of mind. First, it would make it a matter of metaphysical necessity that every mindful thing is an artifact, made and intended to be used by other agents. Second, it would generate an infinite regress, since the agents who are using the mindful things must themselves have minds, necessitating that they too are artifacts made and used by still earlier agents. The regress (or circularity) is vicious, since the relevant norms never acquire any content.

A functionalist might instead try to make use of Wittgensteinian norms which arise from communal rather than individual agency:

(6) A thing x is supposed to produce E on occasions C if and only if there is a game G in which x is a participant in role R, and G includes the rule that participants playing role R produce E on occasions C.

Presumably, a game's including such a rule consists in its participants' believing that others will satisfy the rule, and intending to satisfy it themselves, conditional on its satisfaction by others. (See David Lewis's [1969] *Convention.*) This again results in a vicious regress or circularity if all mental activity is supposed to be dependent on the presence of such normativity. In other words, just as we saw for individual agential normativity, while there can be cases of this sort of normativity, it cannot be that this normativity is foundational with respect to the mental life.

Furthermore, surely some solitary animals, such as sharks, have mental properties, even though they do not participate in any Wittgensteinian games.

3.3. Objections to Evolutionary Accounts of Normativity

The third and final potential source of normativity is evolutionary selection. If a system x belongs to a reproductive family F, then x is supposed to produce E under circumstances C if and only if doing so is one of F's adaptations. This seems to be the most promising alternative to the Aristotelian account, since there doesn't seem to be any vicious circularity or regress.

Ruth Garrett Millikan developed such an account in considerable detail (in *Language, Thought, and Other Biological Categories* [1984]). Here is a simplified version of her definition (1984, 28), which will be a paradigm of such accounts of normativity:

> (7) A thing x is supposed to produce E in circumstances I if and only if (i) x belongs to a reproductive family R in which some feature C occurs non-accidentally with nontrivial frequency (i.e. strictly between 0 and 1), (ii) there has been a positive correlation between having feature C in R and producing E in circumstances I, and (iii) this positive correlation has been in part causally responsible for the successful survival and proliferation of family R (including x itself).[2]

Similar proposals have been made by Larry Wright (1973), Karen Neander (1991, 1995), Nicholas Agar (1993), Kim Sterelny (1990), David Papineau (1993), and Fred Dretske (1995). Here, for example, is Neander's definition:

> (8) Some effect (Z) is the proper function of some trait (X) in organism (O) iff the genotype responsible for X was selected for doing Z because Z was adaptive for O's ancestors. (Neander 1995, 111)

Neander distinguishes a range of options for the evolutionary account of function, from what she calls the "High Church" approach of Millikan to her own "Low Church" version (1995, 126–36). The two versions differ by restricting the genuine proper functions to those corresponding to the 'highest' level description meeting definitions (7) or (8) (the "High Church" option) or to the 'lowest' level (the "Low Church" option). Higher-level descriptions refer to more remote effects, such as being able to find suitable nutrition, while lower-level descriptions refer to more proximate effects, such as accurately indicating the presence of an opaque moving body. Our objections apply to both versions as well as to the "Broad Church" option, which would count all levels as containing genuine proper functions.

There is a further distinction between historical or backward-looking accounts (including all of those mentioned above) and the forward-looking account of Bigelow and Pargetter (1987). Forward-looking versions of (7) and (8) are easy to generate: simply replace the past-tense references to causal contributions to the survival and

---

[2] Millikan's actual definition requires that C be a 'Normal' or reproductively established characteristic of R. Instead of requiring that C be positively correlated in R with the function F, she requires only that the positive correlation hold in some set S which includes x's ancestors, together with "other things not having C." Her exact wording of clause (3) is:

> One among the legitimate explanations that can be given of the fact that [x] exists makes reference to the fact that C correlated positively with F [i.e. the function of producing E in circumstances I] over S, either directly causing reproduction of [x] or explaining why R was proliferated and hence why [x] exists.   (Millikan 1984, 28)

None of these variations would make any difference to our objection.

reproduction of ancestors with present-tense references to an increased propensity to survive and reproduce on the part of existing members of the population. Most of our objections will apply with equal force to the forward-looking version. And there is a special objection to forward-looking accounts, based on the following dilemma: either the dispositions to reproduce are defined in relation to the 'normal environment' of the species, or not. If so, the account is viciously circular, since an environment is normal for the species only if members of the species are disposed to reproduce in it. Alternatively, if we define the forward-looking dispositions in relation to the organisms' actual environment (whether normal or not), then we get the absurdity that we can tell a priori—simply by observing that we still have a mental life—that our external environment is still normal.

There are a number of objections to these evolutionary accounts.

Objection 1: Can 'reproduction' be defined naturalistically and without reference to function or teleology? Complex organisms (especially ones that reproduce sexually) never produce exact physical duplicates of themselves. Conversely, since everything is similar to everything else in some respects, every cause could be said to be 'reproducing' itself in each of its effects. Real reproduction involves the successful copying of the essential features of a thing. For living organisms, these essential features consist almost entirely of biological functions. Hence, we cannot identify cases of biological reproduction without first being able to identify the biological functions of things. Yet, Millikan's account requires us to put the reproductive cart before the functional horse.

A Millikanian version of functionalism would have the consequence that a thing has a mind only if it belongs to a reproductive family *R* for which the standard Pattern of dispositions has successfully contributed to the survival of *R*. Thus, whether a thing has a mind depends on the evolutionary history of its kind. This engenders a second problem.

Objection 2: Millikanian functionalism (i.e. the backward-looking version of the evolutionary account) has the implausible consequence that mental functioning is one generation behind neural functioning. For a mutation can never be normal on her account in the generation in which it first occurs—it only becomes normal in their descendants. For instance, on this view, presumably one of our distant vertebrate ancestors, call it Sim, evolved the first form of those neural structures that are responsible for consciousness. But it was Sim's children, not Sim, that were conscious if we use Millikanian functions as the backing for functionalism. For on Millikanian views, the structures as found in Sim did not function normally. It was only once their non-normal functioning helped Sim reproduce that they functioned normally in Sim's descendants and hence made them conscious. Not only is this an implausible claim, but it has an undesirable epiphenomalist consequence. Consciousness as such is useless to us—it does not affect our action or fitness. Assuming Sim's children had no relevant new mutations, their behavior was much like Sim's, but they were conscious while Sim was not.

Objection 3: What does it mean for a particular disposition to 'cause' or to 'contribute' to a particular instance of R-reproduction? There are two possible answers. First, we could say that the disposition contributed to the act of reproduction just in case some exercise of the disposition by the parent occurs in the actual causal history of the creation of the child. Second, we could instead require that the disposition be part of a *contrastive* explanation of the reproduction: part of a minimal explanation of why in this instance reproduction or survival occurred, as opposed to not occurring. (The forward-looking version of Bigelow and Pargetter must rely on contrastive explanations, since that is the only way for a trait to contribute to the present propensity to survive and reproduce.)

The first answer would greatly over-generate adaptations. Any feature of the parent that is both the product of some disposition of the parent and that influences in any way the process of reproduction would count as one of the kind's essential adaptations. For example, suppose that rabbits are disposed to twitch their left rear leg whenever a cosmic ray strikes the spinal cord at a single point, and suppose that this disposition was actually exercised by some rabbit in the past as it was successfully locating a bunch of carrots. Even if the twitch played no role in explaining the rabbit's survival, it would still count as adaptive, so long as it was part of the total cause of this rabbit's survival in this concrete instance.

Thus, we'll need to turn to the second answer, contrastive explanations. The use of contrastive explanation fits standard biological practice, which identifies adaptations with the results of natural selection, and selection is inherently contrastive in nature.

Now to our objection. Say that a region R of spacetime is *impotent* provided that nothing in R can affect what happens in spacetime outside R. Consider first the following principle:

(9) (Almost global supervenience of physical minds.) Suppose worlds w_1 and w_2 are exact physical duplicates, except in an impotent region R of spacetime. Then w_1 contains an instance of mindedness outside of R if and only if w_2 contains an exactly similar instance outside of R.

Imagine a world w_1 which contains a planet much like earth, where history looks pretty much like it looks on earth, and which also contains a Great Grazing Ground (GGG), which is an infinite (we only need: potentially infinite) impotent region. Moreover, by a strange law of nature, or maybe by the activity of some swamp aliens, whenever an organism on earth is about to die, it gets hyperspatially and instantaneously transported to the GGG, and a fake corpse, which is an exact duplicate of what its real corpse would have been, gets instantaneously put in its place on earth. (We will call it 'earth' for convenience but we shan't worry about its numerical identity with our world's earth.) Furthermore, there is no life or intelligence outside of earth and the GGG.[3] Moreover, the organism dies as soon as it arrives in the GGG.

---

[3] Assume that any swamp aliens who created the GGG and the transport system don't count as alive or intelligent.

Our world's earth has organisms with real minds, and the earth in w_1 has a history that is just about the same. The only difference is that in w_1 all the deaths of organisms occur not on earth but in the GGG, because they get transported there before death. But this does not affect any selective facts. Thus, the evolutionary theorist of normativity should say that the situation in w_1's earth is similar enough to that on our earth that we should say that w_1's earth contains organisms with exactly the same minds.

The hard work is now done. For imagine a world that is exactly like w_1 outside of the GGG, but inside the GGG, immortal and ever-reproducing aliens rescue each organism on arrival, fixing it so it doesn't die, and even make the organism capable of reproduction again. Furthermore, they do the same for the organism's descendants in the GGG. The GGG is a place of infinite (at least potentially) resources, with everybody having immortality and reproduction, with the aliens shifting organisms further and further out to ensure their survival.

Now in w_2, there is no selection: Nobody ever dies or ceases to reproduce. Thus, by Millikan's definition (7) or Neander's definition (8), on the contrastive reading, there is no mindedness outside the GGG in w_2—all the earthly critters are functionless zombies. But, by principle (9), there must be instances of mindedness outside the GGG in w_2, because w_2 is an exact duplicate of w_1 outside of the GGG. Hence we have absurdity. This same result obtains in the case of the forward-looking definition: since every member of every population has a perfect propensity to survive and reproduce, no specific trait contributes causally to that propensity.

Suppose our evolutionary theorist of mind denies (9). Then we have the following absurdity: It is up to the aliens in the GGG to determine whether or not there are instances of teleology (including cases of mindedness) outside the GGG, by deciding whether to rescue the almost dead organisms that pop into the GGG. But how can beings in an impotent region bring about that there are, or are not, minds outside that region? That would be worse than magic (magic is presumably causal).

In the GGG story with post-transportation rescue, there is no natural selection, but surely there is mindedness. This shows that not only are Millikan-type stories insufficient for functionalist purposes, but *no* story on which the normativity of mental functioning is grounded in natural selection facts has a chance of succeeding.

4. Conclusions

Functionalism is the naturalist's best hope for a theory of mind. However, functionalist accounts of mind cannot merely make mind depend on the actual behavior of neural systems—they need to be based on the *normal* or *proper* behavior of neural systems. And only broadly Aristotelian theories are able to give an account of this normal behavior. The theory we specifically have offered makes use of the teleological concept of a power to E in C. We might also have considered a view focused on the disposition to E in C, where this disposition is irreducible, but powers have some additional metaphysical benefits.[4] We could also have opted for a theory that leaves normalcy un-analyzed.

The net result is that the only kind of naturalist theory of mind that is defensible is an Aristotelian naturalist theory of mind. Most contemporary naturalists do not consider Aristotelian naturalism to be a species of naturalism. But perhaps they will reassess this judgment if Aristotelian naturalism is the only hope for a naturalist theory of mind.

---

[4] For example, Pruss (2011) and other articles in this volume.

14

Power for the Mental as Such

David Robb

1. Introduction

The identity theory promises an elegant solution to the exclusion problem (Kim 1998; Kim 2005; Robb 2013). Mental properties face no threat of exclusion from, or preemption by, their physical 'base' properties, for every mental property *is* its physical base. Mental causation turns out to be just a kind of physical causation, perhaps empirically inscrutable, but philosophically no more problematic than any other sort of physical causation.

But in spite of its attractions, the identity theory faces a number of objections. These fall into two broad categories. In the first category are 'Leibniz's Law' arguments alleging that mental properties have some feature that no physical property does (or could) have. Candidates include privacy, subjectivity, qualitative feel, normativity, original intentionality, externality, and multiple realizability. As important as such objections are, I mention them only to set them aside, for in this chapter I'm concerned with an objection in the second category. Here there are arguments challenging, not so much the truth of the identity theory, but its ability to perform some crucial philosophical task. It may be said, for example, that identities are not appropriately explanatory, so that the identity theory will fail to explain psychophysical correlations, thus leaving the mind–body problem unresolved (Kim 2005, ch. 5). And there is the related objection—attributed to Max Black by Smart (1959)—that even if sensations are brain processes, qualitative feel will remain unreduced, for it will just reappear as a property of these brain processes. The objection I confront in this chapter belongs in the same broad category as these, though here the task for the identity theory is resolving the problem of mental causation. The worry is that even if the identity theory is true, it makes no significant progress on the exclusion problem, but merely relocates it.

In what follows, I'll argue that with the backing of a powers ontology, the identity theory can in fact deliver on its promise to solve the exclusion problem. I'll start by sketching the central worry—the as-such objection—and arguing that a version of it also threatens the identity theory's most prominent contemporary rival, non-reductive physicalism. I'll then present the basics of a powers ontology and argue that within its constraints, the as-such worry for the identity theory dissolves. It will not be as clear, however, that non-reductive physicalists can help themselves to the same solution. I'll end by considering an objection to this powers-based solution.

2. The as-such Objection

The identity theory, as I'll understand it, says that every mental property is physical. This entails that every mental *cause* is physical. It will be useful to begin with this weaker thesis, for it is here that, in recent history, the as-such objection has been most prominent.

Davidson (1980) says mental causes—events, on his view—are physical. This permits mental causation to be a kind of physical causation, apparently blocking exclusionary problems. But some critics (e.g. Honderich 1982) object that even if Davidson thereby secures the causal efficacy of mental events, he has not secured their efficacy *qua mental*. The mental is part of the causal order, but not, it seems, *as such*. There are at least two ways to make the point. First, by Davidson's own lights, psychophysical causal relations are grounded only in physical laws, for only such laws are strict. But then only the physical nature of a mental event, not its mental nature, is engaged in mental causation. Second, there are reasons to think that the physical nature of a mental event suffices for its behavioral effect, thereby preempting any would-be efficacy of its mental nature, whether or not there are psychophysical laws (strict or otherwise) in play.[1]

Formulating this objection requires an *ontological ascent* to natures, or properties, of causes: to ask whether the mental as such causes behavior is to ask about the causal efficacy of mental properties—or at least this is how Davidson's critics usually frame the problem, and in this I will follow them. The worry, then, is that even if mental events are physical, only their physical properties are efficacious in producing behavior. That is, when a mental event causes behavior, it is not as mental that it does so: the mental as such does no causal work.

One response to this problem—not to be attributed to Davidson—is to say about mental properties what Davidson said about mental events: mental properties are physical. In particular, mental properties are just those physical properties that are, Davidson's critics allow, causally efficacious with respect to behavior. This is what I'm here calling the identity theory. But now the as-such worry seems to arise again. For we can ask the same question about mental properties that we did about mental causes: granting that mental properties are, on the identity theory, causally efficacious, are they efficacious *qua* mental? After all, the reasoning goes, any mental property that's

---

[1] I am here compressing a large and complex set of issues, since I want to proceed quickly to my main topic. The first way is discussed in Sosa (1984), LePore and Loewer (1987), McLaughlin (1989), Antony (1991). The second is developed in Kim (1993, 1998, 2005) and addressed by a number of philosophers, some of whom are cited below. For an overview of both literatures, see Robb and Heil (2013).

also physical has a mental nature and a physical nature. And the same arguments used against Davidson apply here, for it looks as if only the physical nature of a mental property is engaged in mental causation. Psychophysical property identity seems not to help at all with the as-such objection, and indeed makes the ascent to properties look idle, a spinning of wheels.

Something has gone wrong, but what? I suspect that most philosophers writing in this area would say the mistake here is not in the ascent to properties, but in the thesis of psychophysical property identity. Often such philosophers, like Davidson, say that mental causes are physical. But they reject the identity theory in favor of *non-reductive physicalism*: mental properties cannot be reduced to physical properties, yet they nevertheless bear some close relation to them, a relation intimate enough to warrant the physicalist label.[2] The usual strategy is then to defend *compatibilism*, here the view that the causal efficacy of a mental property is compatible with (not preempted by) that of its distinct, physical base property. And while there are challenges for non-reductive physicalism and the compatibilist project, the as-such worry does not seem to be one of them. Since non-reductive physicalists reject the identity theory, mental properties on their view are *only mental*,[3] and so there is no dual nature in mental properties to give the as-such objection the traction it needs.

Nevertheless, it seems to me that non-reductive physicalism does in fact confront a version of the as-such problem. Non-reductive physicalists say that mental properties, while not physical, bear *some* intimate relation to their physical base properties; call it *realization* just to have a label. Even granting that the compatibilist project can secure the causal efficacy of mental properties, why think such properties are causally efficacious *qua mental*? Why not think instead that they enter the causal order only *qua physically realized*?

To make the point more concrete, consider a prominent version of non-reductive physicalism, the 'subset' account defended in Shoemaker 2003; Shoemaker 2007; Wilson 2009; Wilson 2011.[4] On this account, the (forward-looking) causal powers associated with a mental property on an occasion are included among the causal powers associated with its physical base property. (Since the inclusion is proper, the mental property is distinct from its base property, so there is no reduction, as desired.) Here then is a quick route to compatibilism: When a causal power of a mental property is manifested in behavior, this power will be among those associated with its physical base property. In that case, the causal efficacy of the physical property won't *exclude* the mental property's efficacy, but will rather *include* it, since the two properties share

---

[2] Sources of non-reductive physicalism in its contemporary form include Fodor (1974); Boyd (1980). For more recent developments, see, e.g., Antony and Levine (1997); Pereboom (2002); Wilson (2011).

[3] There is a sense in which no property can be *only* mental, as any mental property falls under a number of non-mental predicates, such as 'is a property' and 'is self-identical.' Here and below, when I say that a property is only mental, I mean just that it's mental and *not physical*.

[4] Shoemaker and Wilson credit the view to Michael Watkins.

the (token) manifested power. For the physical property to be efficacious in this case just is for the mental property to be efficacious.

Suppose that the subset account successfully secures the causal efficacy of mental properties. Still, has it secured the efficacy of mental properties *as such*? For all that's been said so far, it could turn out that the mental property is efficacious, not in virtue of being mental, but merely in virtue of sharing the manifested power with its physical base property. This is, if not the same problem I've raised for the identity theory, a very similar one, and equally worrisome.

Before I present a solution—one based on a powers ontology—a few remarks are in order about how I conceive of as-such questions. First, there is a reading of these questions on which they take on an explanatory-epistemic character. To ask whether a cause, or a causally efficacious property, is efficacious *qua F* is to ask whether conceiving of or describing it as *F* is appropriate or useful relative to, say, some explanatory scheme (Burge 1993), context of causal inquiry (Horgan 2001), or contrast class (Sinnott-Armstrong, unpublished). I do not deny the legitimacy and importance of these epistemic as-such questions. But here I'm looking at the metaphysics of mental causation, and so I am (temporarily) setting aside epistemic concerns. When I ask whether the mental as such is causally efficacious, I am wondering how the world is independently of any particular epistemic aims. In the memorable phrase of British emergentist C. Lloyd Morgan, there is something that is the "go of the world" that drives it forward (Seager 2012, 4). I want to understand how mental properties as such can provide the go of the world, and in particular, how they can drive human bodies forward. How this is related to our explanatory practices and the like is an important question, but it is not my focus here, which is on the metaphysics alone.[5]

Second, it may be thought that as-such questions, while appropriately asked of causes, are not appropriate, or receive trivial answers, when asked of properties. On one tradition, properties are individuated as finely as the predicates (or concepts) that pick them out. To ask, then, whether a mental property is this or that *qua mental* is odd, even nonsensical, as it suggests a mental property is anything other than what is revealed by its individuating mental predicate. But it will be clear below—if it is not already—that this is not how I am thinking of properties. Indeed, the identity theory would be a non-starter if properties were so finely individuated, for there is no hope of a semantic reduction of mental predicates to physical predicates. Since the identity theory is a substantive, live thesis, properties are not merely the "shadows cast by predicates."[6]

---

[5] See also Kim (1988), where metaphysics and epistemology are usefully disentangled. I should note that our explanatory purposes will play a supporting role in the final section, but only as a means of avoiding some apparent consequences of the view I'll defend. The epistemic will not secure the efficacy of the mental as such: this is a task for the powers ontology.

[6] The phrase is Armstrong's; for more discussion, see Heil and Robb (2003).

Third, in other work I have consistently rejected the legitimacy of (metaphysical) as-such questions when they are asked of properties (Robb 1997, 2001, 2013; Heil and Robb 2003). We can ask if an object or event causes something *qua* this or that, and an affirmative answer will assert the causal efficacy of some property. But I've held that we cannot then ask whether the property itself is efficacious *qua* this or that. I've rejected such a question as presupposing a mistaken ontology of properties, in particular, an ontology on which properties themselves have (second-order) properties. As will become clear below, I still think this ontology is mistaken. Indeed, that point will be central in what follows. And so I still think that *if* as-such questions, when applied to properties, presuppose second-order properties, these questions are illegitimate. Nevertheless, the present chapter is motivated by the thought that these questions can get some traction even within (what I take to be) the correct ontology of properties— get some traction and, I hope to show, receive some affirmative answers.[7]

3. Sketch of a Powers Ontology

I turn now to a powers ontology, for it can, I believe, deliver what the identity theorist needs in response to the as-such objection.

I take a powers ontology to be a version of a property ontology, according to which properties, and only properties, are ontologically basic, the "elements of being" (Williams 1966), the ultimate truthmakers. For example, bundled properties are truthmakers for truths about objects, so a property ontology can dispense with substance (Simons 1998; Robb 2005). Resembling properties are truthmakers for truths about types and kinds, so a property ontology can dispense with universals. Properties, then, I take to be particulars, also known as *tropes* or *modes* (Campbell 1990; Heil 2003). And internal relations among properties are truthmakers for relational predications, so a property ontology can dispense with irreducible relations (Mulligan 1998). A powers ontology is a property ontology plus the thesis that every property is a power. It's what a property ontology becomes when conjoined with the Eleatic Principle (Oddie 1982) that power is the mark of being.

On this ontology, what becomes of qualities, those properties that 'color' our world, that 'fill space'? Some philosophers have argued that a world without qualities is empty.[8] I find these arguments persuasive, and thus look for an ontology to accommodate, not eliminate, qualities. Accommodation in this case means identification: every quality is a power. I'll return to qualities—in particular, mental qualities— in a later section. For the moment I set them to one side.

---

[7] Another reason I now take as-such questions more seriously when applied to properties is that I'm more inclined to think that properties could be causes, and clearly as-such questions can legitimately be asked of causes. That said, I'm here neutral on whether properties are causes: see Crane (2008, 180–2) for some helpful remarks on the topic.

[8] Recently Blackburn (1990) (for categoricity), Heil (2003) (for qualities), and Unger (2006) (for 'qualitied' objects, though apparently not for qualities).

Since every property is a power, every property will have associated with it a causal profile specifying what manifestations result from partnering the property with other properties, themselves powers.[9] Consider, for example, the shape of my house key. This property is the power to cut open cardboard boxes, to open locks of a certain sort, to cause a certain kind of impression when the key is pressed into soft clay, to cause a distinctive visual experience in suitably placed perceivers, and so on. Here I've left out most of the power partners for each manifestation, but this at least starts to give a sense of the profile's 'multi-track' complexity (Heil 2003, 198–9; Williams 2011b). But in virtue of what does a property satisfy its profile? One could characterize the relation between property and profile as that of role-filler to role, but this merely postpones the metaphysical question, for what is it about the property that makes it a role-filler for this role?

It seems to me there are two answers a powers ontology cannot permit. One says the property satisfies its causal profile in virtue of the laws of nature, here construed as external relations among the property and its various power partners. This is the Humean answer, for example, though some non-Humeans, such as Armstrong (1983), can say this as well. But whatever the attractions of this picture, it entails that properties in themselves are inert, not powers. Moreover, it means that properties alone are no longer the ultimate truthmakers, for these external relations are needed as well. A powers ontologist can't accept either of these consequences. A second answer says a property satisfies its profile in virtue of having multiple, intrinsic, second-order properties,[10] each of which corresponds to a unique part of the profile. So, for example, my key's shape is the power to cut cardboard boxes, and this is in virtue of the shape's having a second-order property: call it C. Now if a property has second-order properties, the powers ontology requires that these too are powers, so C is a power. This immediately raises a red flag, for a regress threatens if a power's having a causal profile depends on its having a property with a causal profile. And there's another problem as well: what power is C exactly? Presumably it's the power to cut cardboard boxes, and *just* this power. But I don't think it's intelligible that C is the power to cut cardboard boxes but not the power to, say, make a certain sort of impression in soft clay. How could there be a property, second-order or otherwise, that's the power to cut cardboard boxes (when partnered with rigidity etc.) but *not* the power to make an impression of

---

[9] Compare the "conditional causal powers" in Shoemaker (1980) and the "reciprocal disposition partners" in Martin (2008), Heil (2003). Here a causal profile is a representation, say a description, concept, or proposition. A completed powers ontology must provide a nominalistically acceptable account of such representations, but I cannot take on that larger project here.

[10] 'Second-order property' can be read in either of two ways. Consider again my key and its shape, a first-order property. In the 'A-sense,' a second-order property is instantiated by *the key*, which has this second-order property by virtue of having some first-order property (here its shape) with a specified causal profile. In the 'B-sense,' a second-order property is instantiated by *the shape*; it's a property of a property. It seems clear that on the A-sense, one cannot explain the shape's causal powers in terms of a second-order property, for the latter simply consists in the shape's having the causal powers that need explaining. The proposal in the text, which uses the B-sense, at least has a chance of being explanatory, though I'll now argue that even it fails, at least within the constraints of a powers ontology.

a certain shape in soft clay (with those same partners)? It starts to look as if *C* really must have the causal profile of the *shape* of my key. But this is to collapse *C*, which was supposed to be a second-order property, back into the first-order property that is its bearer.

A powers ontologist should not find this result surprising. If powers are at the ground level, it looks like a mistake to explain their powerful natures in terms of further powers. On the ontology, a property doesn't *have* powers to do various things, it *is* the power to do those things (Marmodoro 2010a). Back to the question, then: What is it about a property that makes it fill the role specified by its causal profile? Nothing *about* the property, but just the property itself. The property, that is, is itself the truthmaker for its causal profile. The causal profile is complex, but its truthmaker is simple.

4. Power for the Mental as Such

Return then to the as-such problem confronting the identity theorist, now in the context of the powers ontology just sketched.

I assume for the moment, along broadly functionalist lines (Levin 2013), that what makes a mental property *mental* is its causal profile. Now if the identity theory is true, every mental property is physical, so the mental property will have a physical causal profile as well, most of which will include far more than what's required for the property to be mental. If these mental and physical components of the profile correspond to distinct natures—that is, distinct, intrinsic, second-order properties— of a mental property, the as-such worry is still with us. But the powers ontology blocks this: the mental and physical elements of the property's causal profile find their ontological correlate, or truthmaker, in just the property itself. Put another way, a mental property *is* its mental nature and its physical nature. But then for a mental property's physical nature to be causally engaged just is for its mental nature to be engaged, delivering a quick solution to the as-such problem.

The solution no doubt seems *too* quick, but I don't claim that it's easy, for it depends on the controversial details of the powers ontology sketched above, and there is at least one serious objection to the view, which I will consider in the last section. But setting these worries aside for the moment, I believe I can now pinpoint where the as-such objection goes wrong. After the ascent to properties, the critic assumes that if mental properties are physical, they aren't *wholly* mental, but rather partly mental, partly physical, thus raising as-such worries. Wanting a mental property that's wholly mental, the critic suggests non-reductive physicalism, on which mental properties are *only* (and so wholly) mental. As I argued earlier, however, it's not clear that moving to non-reductive physicalism helps with the as-such problem: even if mental properties are only mental, they may still not be efficacious *qua* mental. The lack of progress here suggests the critic was too quick in rejecting the identity theory. The mistake, in particular, was in thinking that a property that's both mental and physical must not be wholly mental. But a powers ontology permits it to be wholly mental *and* wholly physical. It's possible, that is, to be *wholly* mental without being *only* mental.

Before I look at some complications, it's worth pausing for a moment to consider whether non-reductive physicalists can help themselves to a similar solution. It seems to me they cannot, for they face a dilemma: either the causal powers associated with a mental property are included among those associated with its physical base property, or they are not. Suppose first that they are not. In that case, I don't see how non-reductive physicalists can avoid causal competition between the two properties, thereby blocking a compatibilist solution to the exclusion problem (Wilson 2011). Their view in that case would appear to be a version of emergentism. So suppose instead that the powers of the mental property are included among those of its physical base property, as on the Shoemaker–Wilson subset view. If, in response to the as-such problem, non-reductive physicalists were then to help themselves to a powers ontology, they could not avoid collapsing the mental property into its base property, resulting in the identity theory. On a powers ontology, a property *is* its 'associated' powers. If the shared power just *is* the mental property and also just *is* the physical property, then the mental property is the physical property. Here then, via the powers ontology, is another route to the frequent charge that non-reductive physicalism is unstable (Kim 1993, ch. 17; Crane 2001): it must abandon either physicalism for emergentism or non-reductivism for the identity theory.

5. Mental Qualities

I return now to the identity theory and the powers-based solution to the as-such problem. In the next section I'll consider an objection, but I first want to look briefly at mental qualities.

I take qualities to be properties, so on a powers ontology, all qualities are powers,[11] and this includes mental qualities, or *qualia* (Tye 2013). On the identity theory, any given quale will be some physical property that is unproblematically efficacious with respect to behavior. But when a mental quality is efficacious, is it efficacious *qua* mental? Suppose that what makes a mental quality *mental* is its qualitative feel. So when a quale is efficacious, is it moving the human body *as a quale*, in virtue of its qualitative feel? There are two strategies for answering this question.

One strategy ascends to second-order properties and says the qualitative nature of the quale is some intrinsic property of it: call it Q. The as-such question will then concern the efficacy of the quale as Q, that is, in virtue of having Q. But a powers ontology can't permit this. First, Q will, like all properties, have to be a power. But I argued in the last section that all of the powers a property 'has' are just the property

---

[11] I also believe, with Martin (2008) and Heil (2003), that all powers are qualities. I won't explore this thesis here, though it does mean that what I'm calling a powers ontology could equally be called a qualities ontology.

itself. Second, a less direct argument for the same conclusion asks how Q can account for the qualitative nature of the quale. It's hard to see how Q could do this unless Q itself had a qualitative nature. To block a regress, it seems we must not permit an even higher-order qualitative property for Q to have. Rather, Q just is its qualitative nature. But if we can say that about Q, why not say it about the original quale and be done with it? This leads to the second strategy, which is to say that the qualitative nature of a quale is just the quale itself. It won't be surprising that this is the option I favor: a quale doesn't *have* a phenomenal feel, it *is* a phenomenal feel. But then the as-such problem dissolves, since the causal efficacy of the quale just is its efficacy *qua* mental, as a quale.

6. Too Much Power?

I turn finally to a worry about the solution presented here: while it delivers power for the mental as such, it appears to deliver *too much* power.[12]

A non-mental example will illustrate what I have in mind. Consider again my house key. Its shape is a power, including the power to open a lock of a certain sort and the power to cut open cardboard boxes (as usual, I leave out most of the relevant power partners). Now on the view defended here, each of these elements of the causal profile is made true by the property itself. But this seems to have the absurd consequence that when my key opens a lock, the shape of my key is efficacious *as a box-cutter*. Indeed, *every* element of the shape's causal profile is 'activated' when the key opens my lock. And this looks like the wrong result.

The same worry applies when we turn to the mental. On the identity theory, a mental property's causal profile will include, not just what's distinctively mental, but elements that do not mention the property's manifestations in behavior. What these non-mental elements of the profile might be is an empirical issue, but for the sake of discussion, suppose the profile of a given mental property includes its ability to dissolve a certain chemical when suitable partners are present. So when this mental property is causally efficacious with respect to behavior, its mental causal profile is 'activated,' but so is the chemical part of its profile, each having its ontological correlate in the efficacious property itself. *Qua* mental, the property produces behavior, but also *qua* chemical dissolver. And again, this looks wrong.

I see no option here but to accept these results. When a property, mental or otherwise, is efficacious, every element of its causal profile is, in the relevant sense, active. This means that in the key example,

(S)   The shape of my key, when it's efficacious in opening my lock, is efficacious as a box-cutter.

---

[12] Versions of this problem, though in a different context, are in Pettit (1992, 256–8) and Yablo (1992, 259). What I say here is in the spirit of my reply to Yablo in Robb (1997).

But while I insist (S) is true, I think I can explain why it *seems* false, for it's tempting to infer the following from it:

(i) On this occasion, the power partners represented in the box-cutting part of the shape's causal profile are present.

(ii) On this occasion, the shape was involved in cutting a box.

(iii) Any property similar enough to this shape to cut a box would also be able to open my lock.

Each of (i)–(iii) is false in the example described. (iii) deserves some comment. Properties stand in internal similarity relations to one another, and these relations fall along various dimensions and come in degrees. The color sphere provides an example, where colors are arranged along three dimensions of similarity: hue, saturation, and brightness. What determines the color sphere are the properties themselves: a property does not 'have,' as second-order properties, a hue, saturation, and brightness. Nevertheless, we can speak of colors as similar along one dimension but not another. For example, two colors may be very close along the hue dimension, but one may be much brighter than another. Now imagine a *causal* sphere (or rather, hypersphere), where each of the many dimensions corresponds to a causal manifestation. The cutting open of a cardboard box would be one dimension, the opening of a lock another. It could turn out that two shapes are more similar along one dimension than another. For example, a 'sharp shape' and a 'dull shape' could be very close along the lock-opening dimension, but more distant along the box-cutting dimension. But when we say that the shape of my key, when it opens a lock, is efficacious as a box-cutter, this does seem to imply (iii). That is, (S) seems to imply that close similarity to the shape along the box-cutting dimension entails close similarity along the lock-opening dimension.

(To digress a bit further, I note that there are two ways to measure similarity along a causal dimension: (1) Measure it by similarity of manifestation, holding power partners fixed. So, for example, given the same partners, the dull shape cuts the box *roughly*, while the sharp shape cuts it *smoothly*. (2) Measure it by similarity of partners, holding the manifestation fixed. So, for example, the dull shape needs *much force* to cut the box, while the sharp shape needs *little force* to cut the same box. Note that either measure merely fixes the 'slots' along the dimension into which properties fall. It's still the properties themselves—and they alone—that determine *where* they fall along the dimension. In any case, the choice between (1) and (2) doesn't look crucial for present purposes.)

Returning to the main thread: I submit that (S) seems false because we notice (correctly) that (i)–(iii) are false, and, thinking that (S) entails them, we infer that it's false as well. But (S) doesn't entail any of (i)–(iii). At most, expressing (S) in a normal context *pragmatically* implies them. But expressing a truth can pragmatically imply a falsehood. I have no account to offer here of how expressing (S) pragmatically implies (i)–(iii), though I suspect it is because our purposes in expressing as-such propositions are often as much epistemic (in particular, explanatory) as metaphysical. But I've set aside these epistemic aims in this chapter: my concern is in securing the metaphysical efficacy of the mental as such.

Turn then to mentality. Here similar points apply, where the offending proposition is:

> **(M)**   When a mental property is efficacious with respect to behavior, it's efficacious *qua* chemical dissolver.

While I say that (M) is true, I claim that it seems false because it seems to entail the following:

> (i*)   On this occasion, the power partners represented in the chemical part of the mental property's causal profile are present.
>
> (ii*) On this occasion, the mental property was involved in dissolving a chemical.
>
> (iii*) Any property similar enough to the mental property to dissolve that same chemical would also be able to produce the same behavior.

But while each of (i*)–(iii*) is false, (M) doesn't entail them; expressing (M) merely pragmatically implies them.

Acknowledgments

For comments on a draft of this essay, I am grateful to Susan Schneider, an audience at Wake Forest University, and participants in the 2011 conference on Putting Powers to Work at St. Louis University.

Bibliography

Agar, Nicholas. 1993. "What Do Frogs Really Believe?" *Australasian Journal of Philosophy* 71 (1): 1–12.

Albert, David. 2000. *Time and Chance*. Cambridge, MA: Harvard University Press.

Anandan, Jeeva and Harvey Brown. 1995. "On the Reality of Spacetime Structure and the Wavefunction." *Foundations of Physics* 25 (2): 349–60.

Anscombe, G. E. M. 1971. *Causality and Determination: An Inaugural Lecture*. Cambridge: Cambridge University Press.

Antony, Louise. 1991. "The Causal Relevance of the Mental: More on the Mattering of Minds." *Mind and Language* 6 (4): 295–327.

Antony, Louise and Joseph Levine. 1997. "Reduction with Autonomy." *Philosophical Perspectives* 11 (s11): 83–105.

Aristotle. 1984. *The Complete Works of Aristotle: The Revised Oxford Translation*. Edited by Jonathan Barnes. Princeton, NJ: Princeton University Press.

Armstrong, D. M. 1968. *A Materialist Theory of Mind*. London: Routledge & Kegan Paul.

Armstrong, D. M. 1978. *Universals and Scientific Realism: A Theory of Universals*. Vol. 2. Cambridge: Cambridge University Press.

Armstrong, D. M. 1980. "Identity Through Time." In *Time and Cause: Essays Presented to Richard Taylor*, edited by Peter van Inwagen, 67–78. Dordrecht: D. Reidel Publishing.

Armstrong, D. M. 1983. *What is a Law of Nature?* Cambridge: Cambridge University Press.

Armstrong, D. M. 1997. *A World of States of Affairs*. Cambridge: Cambridge University Press.

Armstrong, D. M. 2000. "Difficult Cases in the Theory of Truthmaking." *The Monist* 83 (1): 150–60.

Armstrong, D. M. 2004. *Truth and Truthmakers*. Cambridge: Cambridge University Press.

Armstrong, D. M. 2007. "Truthmakers for Negative Truths and for Truths of Mere Possibility." In *Metaphysics and Truthmakers*, edited by Jean-Maurice Monnoyer, 99–104. Ontos Verlag.

Armstrong, D. M. 2010. *Sketch for a Systematic Metaphysics*. Oxford: Oxford University Press.

Armstrong, D. M., C. B. Martin, and U. T. Place. 1996. *Dispositions: A Debate*. Edited by Tim Crane. London: Routledge.

Arntzenius, Frank. 2000. "Are there Really Instantaneous Velocities?" *The Monist* 83 (2): 187–208.

Ashwell, Lauren. 2010. "Superficial Dispositionalism." *Australasian Journal of Philosophy* 88 (4): 635–53.

Baez, John. 2009. "What is a Background-Free Theory?" http://math.ucr.edu/home/baez/background.html.

Barnes, Winston H. F. 1945. "The Myth of Sense Data." *Proceedings of the Aristotelian Society* 45: 89–118.

Bauer, William A. 2011. "An Argument for the Extrinsic Grounding of Mass." *Erkenntnis* 74 (1): 81–99.

Bealer, George. 2010. "The Self-Consciousness Argument: Functionalism and the Corruption of Content." In *The Waning of Materialism: New Essays on the Mind–Body Problem*, edited by Robert C. Koons and George Bealer, 137–60. Oxford: Oxford University Press.

Beebee, Helen. 2000. "The Non-Governing Conception of Laws of Nature." *Philosophy and Phenomenological Research* 61 (3): 571–94.

Bennett, Karen. 2004. "Global Supervenience and Dependence." *Philosophy and Phenomenological Research* 68 (3): 501–29.

Bhaskar, Roy. 1978. *A Reaslist Theory of Science*. Hassocks, Sussex: Harvester Press.

Bigelow, John and Robert Pargetter. 1987. "Functions." *The Journal of Philosophy* 84 (4): 181–96.

Bird, Alexander. 1998. "Dispositions and Antidotes." *The Philosophical Quarterly* 48 (191): 227–34.

Bird, Alexander. 2007a. *Nature's Metaphysics: Laws and Properties*. Oxford: Oxford University Press.

Bird, Alexander. 2007b. "Regress of Pure Powers?" *The Philosophical Quarterly* 57 (229): 513–34.

Blackburn, Simon. 1990. "Filling in Space." *Analysis* 50 (2): 62–5.

Blanchard, Thomas and Jonathan Schaffer. Forthcoming. "Cause without Default." In *Making a Difference*, edited by H. Beebee, C. Hitchcock, and H. Price. Oxford: Oxford University Press.

Borghini, Andrea and Neil Edward Williams. 2008. "A Dispositional Theory of Possibility." *Dialectica* 62 (1): 21–41.

Boyd, Richard. 1980. "Materialism without Reductionism: What Physicalism Does Not Entail." In *Readings in Philosophy of Psychology*, edited by Ned Block, Vol. 1, 67–106. Cambridge, MA: Harvard University Press.

Braddon-Mitchell, David and Frank Jackson. 1996. *Philosophy of Mind and Cognition*. Cambridge, MA: Blackwell Publishing.

Broad, C. D. 1923. *Scientific Thought*. New York: Harcourt, Brace and Co.

Brower, Jeffrey E. 2005. "Aquinas's Metaphysics of Modality: A Reply to Leftow." *The Modern Schoolman* 82 (3): 201–12.

Burge, Tyler. 1993. "Mind–Body Causation and Explanatory Practice." In *Mental Causation*, edited by John Heil and Alfred Mele. Oxford: Clarendon Press.

Cameron, Ross P. 2008. "Truthmakers and Modality." *Synthese* 164 (2): 261–80.

Cameron, Ross P. 2010. "Truthmaking for Presentists." *Oxford Studies in Metaphysics* 6: 55–100.

Campbell, Keith. 1990. *Abstract Particulars*. Oxford: Basil Blackwell.

Carroll, John. 1994. *Laws of Nature*. Cambridge: Cambridge University Press.

Cartwright, Nancy. 1983. *How the Laws of Physics Lie*. Oxford: Clarendon Press.

Cartwright, Nancy. 1989. *Nature's Capacities and Their Measurement*. Oxford: Oxford University Press.

Cartwright, Nancy. 1999. *The Dappled World*. Cambridge: Cambridge University Press.

Cartwright, Nancy. 2009. "Causal Laws, Policy Predictions, and the Need for Genuine Powers." In *Dispositions and Causes*, edited by Toby Handfield, 127–57. Oxford: Clarendon Press.

Cartwright, Nancy and Jeremy Hardie. 2012. *Evidence-Based Policy: A Practical Guide to Doing it Better*. New York: Oxford University Press.

Chakravartty, Anjan. 2007. *A Metaphysics for Scientific Realism*. Cambridge: Cambridge University Press.

Choi, Sungho. 2005. "Do Categorical Ascriptions Entail Counterfactual Conditionals?" *The Philosophical Quarterly* 55 (20): 495–503.

Clark, Austin. 1993. *Sensory Qualities*. Oxford: Oxford University Press.

Clarke, Randolph. 1994. "Doing What One Wants Less: A Reappraisal of the Law of Desire." *Pacific Philosophical Quarterly* 75 (1): 1–11.

Clarke, Randolph. 2008. "Intrinsic Finks." *The Philosophical Quarterly* 58 (232): 512–18.

Clarke, Stephen. 2010. "Transcendental Realisms in the Philosophy of Science: on Bhaskar and Cartwright." *Synthese* 173 (3): 299–315.

Cohen, Daniel and Toby Handfield. 2007. "Finking Frankfurt." *Philosophical Studies* 135 (3): 363–74.

Cohen, Jonathan and Craig Callender. 2009. "A Better Best System Account of Lawhood." *Philosophical Studies* 145 (1): 1–34.

Cohen, Jonathan and Craig Callender. 2010. "Special Sciences, Conspiracy and the Better Best System Account of Lawhood." *Erkenntnis* 73 (3): 427–47.

Contessa, Gabriele. 2008. "Modal Truthmakers and Two Varieties of Actualism." *Synthese* 174 (3): 341–53.

Corry, Richard. 2009. "How is Scientific Analysis Possible?" In *Dispositions and Causes*, edited by Toby Handfield, 158–88. Oxford: Oxford University Press.

Crane, Tim. 2001. "The Significance of Emergence." In *Physicalism and its Discontents*, edited by Barry Loewer and Carl Gillet, 207–24. Cambridge: Cambridge University Press.

Crane, Tim. 2008. "Causation and Determinable Properties: On the Efficacy of Colour, Shape, and Size." In *Being Reduced: New Essays on Reduction, Explanation, and Causation*, edited by Jakob Hohwy and Jesper Kallestrup, 176–95. Oxford: Oxford University Press.

Davidson, Donald. 1980. "Mental Events." In *Essays on Actions and Events*. Oxford: Oxford University Press.

Des Chene, Dennis. 1996. *Physiologia: Natural Philosophy in Late Aristotelian and Cartesian Thought*. Ithaca, NY: Cornell University Press.

Divers, John. 2004. "Agnosticism about Other Worlds: A New Antirealist Programme in Modality." *Philosophy and Phenomenological Research* 69 (3): 660–85.

Dowe, Phil. 2000. *Physical Causation*. Cambridge: Cambridge University Press.

Dr. Seuss. 1961. *The Sneetches and Other Stories*. Random House.

Dretske, Fred. 1977. "Laws of Nature." *Philosophy of Science* 44 (2): 248–68.

Dretske, Fred. 1995. *Naturalizing the Mind*. Cambridge, MA: MIT Press.

Dummett, Michael. 1975. "Wang's Paradox." *Synthese* 30 (3–4): 301–24.

Eddon, M. and C. J. G. Meacham. 2015. "No Work for a Theory of Universals." In *A Companion to David Lewis*, edited by B. Loewer and J. Schaffer. Oxford: John Wiley & Sons.

Efird, David and Tom Stoneham. 2006. "Combinatorialism and the Possibility of Nothing." *Australasian Journal of Philosophy* 84 (2): 269–80.

Einstein, Albert. 1999. "On the Ether." In *The Philosophy of Vacuum*, edited by Simon Sanders and Harvey R. Brown, 13–20. Oxford: Oxford University Press.

Elga, Adam. 2004. "Infinitesimal Chances and the Laws of Nature." *Australasian Journal of Philosophy* 82 (1): 67–76.

Ellis, Brian. 2001. *Scientific Essentialism*. Cambridge: Cambridge University Press.

Ellis, Brian. 2002. *The Philosophy of Nature: A Guide to the New Essentialism*. Chesham: Acumen.

Ellis, Brian. 2009. *The Metaphysics of Scientific Realism*. Ithaca: McGill–Queen's University Press.

Ellis, Brian. 2010. "Causal Powers and Categorical Properties." In *The Metaphysics of Powers: Their Grounding and Their Manifestations*, edited by Anna Marmodoro. New York: Routledge.

Ellis, Brian and Caroline Lierse. 1994. "Dispositional Essentialism." *Australasian Journal of Philosophy* 72 (1): 27–45.

Fair, David. 1979. "Causation and the Flow of Energy." *Erkenntnis* 14 (3): 219–50.

Fara, Delia Graff. 2001. "Phenomenal Continua and the Sorites." *Mind* 110 (4): 905–35.

Fine, Kit. 1994. "Essence and Modality." *Philosophical Perspectives* 8: 1–16.

Fish, William. 2010. *Philosophy of Perception: A Contemporary Introduction*. New York: Routledge.

Fitch, G. W. 1996. "In Defence of Aristotelian Actualism." *Philosophical Perspectives* 10: 53–71.

Fodor, Jerry. 1974. "Special Sciences (Or: The Disunity of Science as a Working Hypothesis)." *Synthese* 28 (2): 97–115.

Frankfurt, Harry. 1969. "Alternate Possibilities and Moral Responsibility." *The Journal of Philosophy* 66 (23): 829–39.

Funkhouser, Eric. 2006. "The Determinable–Determinate Relation." *Noûs* 40 (3): 548–69.

Geach, Peter. 1969. *God and the Soul*. London: Routledge.

Goodman, Nelson. 1977. *The Structure of Appearance*. 3rd edn. Dordrecht: Reidel.

Grant, Edward, ed. 1974. *A Sourcebook in Medieval Science*. Cambridge, MA: Harvard University Press.

Grant, Edward. 1981. *Much Ado About Nothing: Theories of Space and Vacuum from the Middle Ages to the Scientific Revolution*. Cambridge: Cambridge University Press.

Green, Dan. 2003. "Vector Boson Fusion and Quartic Boson Couplings." *ArXiv High Energy Physics—Phenomenology e-prints* https://arxiv.org/pdf/hep-ph/0306160.pdf.

Hall, Ned. 2010. "Humean Reductionism about Laws of Nature." Wiley Online Library. doi: 10.1002/9781118398593. ch. 17.

Handfield, Toby. 2008. "Unfinkable Dispositions." *Synthese* 160 (2): 297–308.

Handfield, Toby, ed. 2009. *Dispositions and Causes*. Oxford: Clarendon Press.

Handfield, Toby and Alexander Bird. 2008. "Dispositions, Rules, and Finks." *Philosophical Studies* 140 (2): 285–98.

Hardin, C. L. 1988. "Phenomenal Colors and Sorites." *Noûs* 22 (2): 213–34.

Harré, Rom. 1970. *The Principles of Scientific Thinking*. London: Macmillan.

Harré, Rom and E. H. Madden. 1975. *Causal Powers: A Theory of Natural Necessity*. Oxford: Oxford University Press.

Hausman, Daniel. 1998. *Causal Asymmetries*. Cambridge: Cambridge University Press.

Hawley, Katherine. 2001. *How Things Persist*. Oxford: Oxford University Press.

Heil, John. 2003. *From an Ontological Point of View*. Oxford: Oxford University Press.

Heil, John. 2005. "Dispositions." *Synthese* 144 (3): 343–56.

Heil, John. 2012. *The Universe as We Find It*. Oxford: Clarendon Press.

Heil, John. 2013. "Contingency." In *The Puzzle of Existence: Why is there Something Rather than Nothing?*, edited by Tyron Goldschmidt, 167–81. London: Routledge.

Heil, John. 2016. "Causal Relations." In *The Metaphysics of Relations*, edited by Anna Marmardoro and David Yates. Oxford: Oxford University Press.

Heil, John and David Robb. 2003. "Mental Properties." *American Philosophical Quarterly* 40 (3): 175–96.

Heller, Mark. 1990. *The Ontology of Physical Objects—Four Dimensional Hunks of Matter*. Cambridge: Cambridge University Press.

Hellie, Benj. 2005. "Noise and Perceptual Indiscriminability." *Mind* 114 (455): 481–508.

Heumer, Michael and Ben Kovitz. 2003. "Causation as Simultaneous and Continuous." *The Philosophical Quarterly* 53 (213): 556–65.

Hirsch, Eli. 1982. *The Concept of Identity*. Oxford: Oxford University Press.

Holton, Richard. 1999. "Dispositions All the Way Around." *Analysis* 59 (1): 9–14.

Honderich, Ted. 1982. "The Argument from Anomalous Monism." *Analysis* 42 (1): 59–64.

Hoover, Kevin. 2001. *Causality in Macroeconomics*. Cambridge: Cambridge University Press.

Horgan, Terence. 2001. "Causal Compatibilism and the Exclusion Problem." *Theoria* 16 (1): 95–116.

Horwich, Paul. 1987. *Asymmetries in Time*. Cambridge, MA: MIT Press.

Hume, David. 1978. *A Treatise of Human Nature*. Edited by L. A. Selby-Bigge. Oxford: Clarendon Press.

Hüttemann, Andreas. 1998. "Laws and Dispositions." *Philosophy of Science* 65 (1): 121–35.

Ingthorsson, Rognvaldur. 2002. "Causal Production as Interaction." *Metaphysica* 3 (1): 87–119.

Jackson, F. C. and R. J. Pinkerton. 1973. "On an Argument Against Sensory Items." *Mind* 82 (326): 269–72.

Jacobs, Jonathan D. 2010. "A Powers Theory of Modality: Or, How I Learned to Stop Worrying and Reject Possible Worlds." *Philosophical Studies* 151 (2): 227–48.

Jacobs, Jonathan D. 2011. "Powerful Qualities, Not Pure Powers." *The Monist* 94 (1): 81–102.

Johnson, W. E. 1964. *Logic Part III: The Logical Foundations of Science*. New York: Dover.

Johnston, Mark. 1992. "How to Speak of Colors." *Philosophical Studies* 68 (3): 221–63.

Kant, Immanuel. 1921. *Critique of Pure Reason*. Edited by N. Kemp Smith. London: Macmillan.

Kim, Jaegwon. 1988. "Explanatory Realism, Causal Realism, and Explanatory Exclusion." *Midwest Studies in Philosophy* 12 (1): 225–39.

Kim, Jaegwon. 1993. *Supervenience and Mind*. Cambridge: Cambridge University Press.

Kim, Jaegwon. 1998. *Mind in a Physical World*. Cambridge, MA: MIT Press.

Kim, Jaegwon. 2005. *Physicalism, or Something Near Enough*. Princeton, NJ: Princeton University Press.

Kistler, Max. 2006. *Causation and Laws of Nature*. London: Routledge.

Kistler, Max. 2012. "Powerful Properties and the Causal Basis of Dispositions." In *Properties, Powers and Structures: Issues in the Metaphysics of Realism*, edited by Alexander Bird, Brian Ellis, and H. Sankey, 119–37. New York: Routledge.

Koslicki, Kathrin. 2012. "Varieties of Ontological Dependence." In *Metaphysical Grounding: Understanding the Structure of Reality*, edited by F. C. Benjamin Schneider. Cambridge: Cambridge University Press.

Lange, Marc. 2005. "How Can Instantaneous Velocity Fulfill Its Causal Role?" *The Philosophical Review* 114 (4): 433–68.

Lange, Marc. 2009. *Laws and Lawmakers: Science, Metaphysics, and the Laws of Nature*. Oxford: Oxford University Press.

Laudan, Larry. 2004. "The Epistemic, the Cognitive and the Social." In *Science, Values and Objectivity*, edited by Peter Machamer and Gereon Wolters, 14–23. Pittsburgh, PA: University of Pittsburgh Press.

Leftow, Brian. 2005a. "Aquinas on God and Modal Truth." *The Modern Schoolman* 82 (3): 171–200.

Leftow, Brian. 2005b. "Power, Possibilia and Non-Contradiction." *The Modern Schoolman* 82 (4): 231–43.

Leibniz, Gottfried Wilhelm and Samuel Clarke. 1965. *The Leibniz–Clarke Correspondence.* Edited by H. G. Alexander. Manchester: Manchester University Press.

LePore, Ernest and Barry Loewer. 1987. "Mind Matters." *The Journal of Philosophy* 84 (11): 630–42.

Levin, Janet. 2013. "Functionalism." In *The Stanford Encyclopedia of Philosophy*, Fall 2013 edn., edited by Edward N. Zalta. http://plato.stanford.edu/entries/functionalism/.

Lewis, David. 1979. "Counterfactual Dependence and Time's Arrow," *Noûs* 13: 455–76.

Lewis, David. 1983a. "New Work for a Theory of Universals." *Australasian Journal of Philosophy* 61 (4): 343–77.

Lewis, David. 1983b. "Survival and Identity." In *Philosophical Papers*, Vol. 1, 55–77. Oxford: Oxford University Press.

Lewis, David. 1986. *On the Plurality of Worlds*. Oxford: Basil Blackwell.

Lewis, David. 1994. "Humean Supervenience Dubugged." *Mind* 103 (412): 473–90.

Lewis, David. 1997. "Finkish Dispositions." *The Philosophical Quarterly* 47 (187): 143–58.

Lewis, David. 2009. "Ramseyan Humility." In *Conceptual Analysis and Philosophical Naturalism*, edited by David Braddon-Mitchell and Robert Nola, 203–22. Cambridge, MA: MIT Press.

Lewis, David K. 1969. *Convention: A Philosophical Study*. Cambridge, MA: Harvard University Press.

Locke, John. 1689 (1975). *An Essay Concerning Human Understanding*. Edited by Peter H. Nidditch. Oxford: Clarendon Press.

Loewer, Barry. 2007. "Laws and Natural Properties." *Philosophical Topics* 35 (1–2): 313–28.

Long, Joshua C., Hilton W. Chan, Allison B. Churnside, Eric A. Gulbis, Michael C. M. Varney, and John C. Price. 2003. "Upper Limits to Submillimetre-range Forces from Extra Space-time Dimensions." *Nature* 421: 922–5.

Longino, Helen. 1995. "Gender, Politics, and the Theoretical Virtues." *Synthese* 104 (3): 383–97.

Lotze, Hermann. 1884. *Metaphysics*. 2nd edn. Edited by Bernard Bosanquet. Vol. 1. Oxford: Clarendon Press.

Lowe, E. J. 2010. "On the Individuation of Powers." In *The Metaphysics of Powers: Their Grounding and their Manifestations*, edited by Anna Marmodoro, 8–26. New York: Routledge.

Lowe, E. J. 2011. "How *not* to Think of Powers: A Deconstruction of the 'Dispositions and Conditionals' Debate." *The Monist* 94 (1): 19–33.

Mackie, J. L. 1973. *Truth, Probability, and Paradox: Studies in Philosophical Logic*. Oxford: Clarendon Press.

McKitrick, Jennifer. 2003. "A Case for Extrinsic Dispositions." *Australasian Journal of Philosophy* 81 (2): 155–74.

McLaughlin, Brian P. 1989. "Type Epiphenomenalism, Type Dualism, and the Causal Priority of the Physical." *Philosophical Perspectives* 3 (1): 109–35.

McMichael, Alan. 1983. "A Problem For Actualism About Possible Worlds." *The Philosophical Review* 92: 49–66.

Manley, David and Ryan Wasserman. 2007. "A Gradable Approach to Dispositions." *The Philosophical Quarterly* 57 (226): 68–75.

Marmodoro, Anna. 2006. "It's a Colorful World." *American Philosophical Quarterly* 43 (1): 71–80.

Marmodoro, Anna. 2009. "Do Powers Need Powers to Make them Powerful? From Pandispositionalism to Aristotle." *History of Philosophy Quarterly* 26 (4): 337–52.

Marmodoro, Anna. 2010a. "Do Powers Need Powers to Make Them Powerful? From Pan-dispositionalism to Aristotle." In *The Metaphysics of Powers: Their Grounding and Their Manifestations*, 27–40. New York: Routledge.

Marmodoro, Anna, ed. 2010b. *The Metaphysics of Powers: Their Grounding and Their Manifestations*. London: Routledge.

Marmodoro, Anna. 2013. "Potentiality in Aristotle's Metaphysics." In *The Handbook of Potentiality*, edited by Kristina Engelhard and Michael Quante. Dordrecht: Springer.

Marmodoro, Anna. Unpublished. *Power Structuralism in Ancient Ontologies*.

Martin, C. B. 1984. "Anti-Realism and the World's Undoing." *Pacific Philosophical Quarterly* 65: 3–20.

Martin, C. B. 1993a. "The Need for Ontology: Some Choices." *Philosophy* 68: 502–22.

Martin, C. B. 1993b. "Power for Realists." In *Ontology, Causality and Mind: Essays in Honour of D. M. Armstrong*, edited by J. Bacon, K. Campbell, and L. Reinhardt, 175–94. Cambridge: Cambridge University Press.

Martin, C. B. 1994. "Dispositions and Conditionals." *The Philosophical Quarterly* 44 (174): 1–8.

Martin, C. B. 1997. "On the Need for Properties: The Road to Pythagoreanism and Back." *Synthese* 112 (2): 193–231.

Martin, C. B. 2008. *The Mind In Nature*. Oxford: Oxford University Press.

Martin, C. B. and John Heil. 1999. "The Ontological Turn." *Midwest Studies in Philosophy* 23 (1): 34–60.

Maudlin, Tim. 2007. *The Metaphysics Within Physics*. Oxford: Oxford University Press.

Mele, Alfred. 2003. *Motivation and Agency*. Oxford: Oxford University Press.

Mellor, D. H. 1974. "In Defence of Dispositions." *The Philosophical Review* 83 (2): 157–81.

Merricks, Trenton. 2009. *Truth and Ontology*. Oxford: Oxford University Press.

Millikan, Ruth Garrett. 1984. *Language, Thought, and Other Biological Categories*. Cambridge, MA: MIT Press.

Milton, John R. 1998. "Laws of Nature." In *The Cambridge History of Seventeenth-Century Philosophy*, edited by Daniel Garber and Michael Ayres, 680–701. Cambridge: Cambridge University Press.

Molnar, George. 2003. *Powers: A Study in Metaphysics*. Edited by Stephen Mumford. Oxford: Oxford University Press.

Moore, Michael S. 2003. *Causation and Responsibility*. Oxford: Oxford University Press.

Most, Steven B. 2010. "What is Inattentional about Inattentional Blindness." *Consciousness and Cognition* 19 (4): 1102–4.

Mulligan, Kevin. 1998. "Relations—Through Thick and Thin." *Erkenntnis* 48 (2-3): 325–53.

Mumford, Stephen. 1994. "Dispositions, Supervenience, and Reduction." *The Philosophical Quarterly* 44 (177): 419–38.

Mumford, Stephen. 1998. *Dispositions*. New York: Oxford University Press.

Mumford, Stephen. 2004. *Laws in Nature*. London: Routledge.

Mumford, Stephen. 2007. "Powers, Dispositions, Properties: *Or A Causal Realist Manifesto*." In *Revitalizing Causality: Realism About Causality in Philosophy and Social Theory*, edited by Ruth Groff, 139–51. London: Routledge.

Mumford, Stephen. 2009a. "Passing Powers Around." *The Monist* 92 (1): 94–111.

Mumford, Stephen. 2009b. "Powers and Persistence." In *Unity and Time in Metaphysics*, edited by Ludger Honnefelder, Edmund Runggaldier, and Benedikt Schick, 223–36. Berlin: Walter de Gruyter.

Mumford, Stephen and Rani Lill Anjum. 2011. *Getting Causes from Powers*. Oxford: Oxford University Press.

Mumford, Stephen and Rani Lill Anjum. Forthcoming. "Powers and Potentiality." In *Handbook of Potentiality*, edited by Michael Quante and Kristina Engelhard. Dordrecht: Springer.

Neander, Karen. 1991. "The Teleological Notion of 'Function.'" *Australasian Journal of Philosophy* 69 (4): 454–68.

Neander, Karen. 1995. "Misrepresenting and Malfunctioning." *Philosophical Studies* 79 (2): 109–41.

Nerlich, Graham. 1994. *What Spacetime Explains: Metaphysical Essays on Space and Time*. Cambridge: Cambridge University Press.

Oddie, Graham. 1982. "Armstrong on the Eleatic Principle and Abstract Entities." *Philosophical Studies* 41 (2): 285–95.

O'Neill, Eileen. 1993. "Influxus Physicus." In *Causation in Early Modern Philosophy: Cartesianism, Occasionalism, and Preestablished Harmony*, edited by Steven Nadline, 27–56. University Park, PA: Pennsylvania State University Press.

Papineau, David. 1993. *Philosophical Naturalism*. Oxford: Oxford University Press.

Pawl, Timothy. 2008. *A Thomistic Account of Truthmakers for Modal Truths*. Ph.D. thesis, Saint Louis University.

Pawl, Timothy. 2010. "The Possibility Principle and the Truthmakers for Modal Truths." *Australasian Journal of Philosophy* 88 (3): 417–28.

Pemberton, John. 2011. "Integrating Mechanist and Nomological Machine Ontologies to Make Sense of What-how-that Evidence." http://personal.lse.ac.uk/pemberto.

Pereboom, Derk. 2002. "Robust Nonreductive Materialism." *The Journal of Philosophy* 99 (10): 499–531.

Pettit, Philip. 1992. "The Nature of Naturalism." *Proceedings of the Aristotelian Society, Supp. Vol.* 66 (1): 245–66.

Pissarides, Christopher A. 2006. *Unemployment and Hours of Work: The North Atlantic Divide Revisited*. London: Centre for Economic Performance.

Plantinga, Alvin. 1974. *The Nature of Necessity*. Oxford: Clarendon Press.

Price, Huw. 1991. "Agency and Probabilistic Causality," *British Journal for the Philosophy of Science* 42: 157–76.

Proust, Joëlle. 2001. "A Plea for Mental Acts." *Synthese* 129 (1): 105–28.

Proust, Joëlle. 2010. "Mental Acts." In *A Companion to the Philosophy of Action*, edited by Timothy O'Connor and Constantine Sandis, 209–17. Oxford: Wiley-Blackwell.

Pruss, Alexander R. 2002. "The Actual and the Possible." In *Blackwell Guide to Metaphysics*, edited by Richard M. Gale, 313–33. Oxford: Blackwell Publishing.

Pruss, Alexander R. 2011. *Actuality, Possiblity and Worlds*. New York: Continuum.

Psillos, Stathis. 2006. "What Do Powers Do When They Are Not Manifested?" *Philosophy and Phenomenological Research* 72 (1): 137–56.

Raffman, Diana. 1994. "Vagueness without Paradox." *The Philosophical Review* 103 (1): 41–74.

Raffman, Diana. 2000. "Is Perceptual Indiscriminability Nontransitive?" *Philosophical Topics* 28 (1): 153–75.

Ramsey, F. P. 1929. "Theories." In *The Foundations of Mathematics and Other Logical Essays*, edited by Richard B. Braithwaite, 212–36. New Jersey: Littlefield and Adams.

Reichenbach, H. 1956. *The Direction of Time*. Berkeley, University of Los Angeles Press.

Robb, David. 1997. "The Properties of Mental Causation." *The Philosophical Quarterly* 47 (2): 178–94.

Robb, David. 2001. "Reply to Noordhof on Mental Causation." *The Philosophical Quarterly* 51 (1): 90–4.

Robb, David. 2005. "Qualitative Unity and the Bundle Theory." *The Monist* 88 (4): 466–92.

Robb, David. 2013. "The Identity Theory as a Solution to the Exclusion Problem." In *Mental Causation and Ontology*, edited by S. C. Gibb, E. J. Lowe, and R. D. Ingthorsson. Oxford: Oxford University Press.

Robb, David and John Heil. 2013. "Mental Causation." In *The Stanford Encyclopedia of Philosophy*, Spring 2013 edn, edited by Edward N. Zalta. http://plato.stanford.edu/entries/mental-causation/.

Roberts, John T. 2008. *The Law-Governed Universe*. Oxford: Oxford University Press.

Robinson, Howard. 1972. "Professor Armstrong on 'Non-physical Sensory Items'." *Mind* 81 (321): 84–6.

Rothschild, Lynn J. 2006. "The Role of Emergence in Biology." In *The Re-emergence of Emergence*, edited by Phillip Clayton and Paul Davies, 151–65. Oxford: Oxford University Press.

Rovelli, Carlo. 1997. "Halfway Through the Woods: Contemporary Research on Space and Time." In *The Cosmos of Science*, edited by John Earman and John Norton, 180–223. Pittsburgh, PA: University of Pittsburgh Press.

Ruby, Jane. 1986. "The Origins of Scientific 'Law'." *Journal of the History of Ideas* 47 (3): 341–59.

Russell, Bertrand. 1938. *Principles of Mathematics*. New York: W. W. Norton and Co.

Ryle, Gilbert. 1949. *The Concept of Mind*. London: Hutchinson.

Scaltsas, Theodore. 1989. "The Logic of the Dilemma of Participation and of the Third Man Argument." *Apeiron* 22 (4): 67–90.

Schaffer, Jonathan. 2008. "The Metaphysics of Causation." In *The Stanford Encyclopedia of Philosophy*, Fall 2008 edn, edited by Edward N. Zalta.

Schaffer, Jonathan. 2009. "On What Grounds What." In *Metametaphysics: New Essays on the Foundations of Ontology*, edited by David Chalmers, David Manley, and Ryan Wasserman, 347–83. Oxford: Oxford University Press.

Schrenk, Markus. 2008. "A Theory for Special Science Laws." In *Selected Papers Contributed to the Sections of GAP.6*, edited by E. A. S. Walter. 6th International Congress of the Society for Analytical Philosophy.

Schrenk, Markus. 2010. "The Powerlessness of Necessity." *Noûs* 44 (4): 725–39.

Schrenk, Markus. 2012. "Properties for and of Better Best Systems." Unpublished.

Schroeder, Timothy. 2004. *Three Faces of Desire*. Oxford: Oxford University Press.

Seager, William. 2012. *Natural Fabrications: Science, Emergence and Consciousness*. Berlin: Springer-Verlag.

Seddon, George. 1972. "Logical Possibility." *Mind* 81 (324): 481–94.

Shepard, Roger. 1962. "The Analysis of Proximities: Multidimensional Scaling with an Unknown Distance Function." *Psychometrika* 27 (2): 125–40.

Shepard, Roger. 1965. "Approximation to Uniform Gradients of Generalization by Monotone Transformations of Scale." In *Stimulus Generalization*, edited by David I. Mostofsky, 95–110. Stanford, CA: Stanford University Press.

Shoemaker, Sydney. 1979. "Identity, Properties and Causality." *Midwest Studies in Philosophy* 4 (1): 321–42.

Shoemaker, Sydney. 1980. "Causality and Properties." In *Time and Cause: Essays Presented to Richard Taylor*, edited by Peter van Inwagen, 109–36. Dordrecht: D. Reidel.

Shoemaker, Sydney. 1984. *Identity, Cause, and Mind: Philosophical Essays*. Cambridge: Cambridge University Press.

Shoemaker, Sydney. 1998. "Causal and Metaphysical Necessity." *Pacific Philosophical Quarterly* 79 (1): 59–77.

Shoemaker, Sydney. 2001. "Realization and Mental Causation." In *Physicalism and Its Discontents*, edited by Carl Ginet and Barry Loewer. Cambridge: Cambridge University Press.

Shoemaker, Sydney. 2003. "Causality and Properties." In *Identity, Cause, and Mind*, Expanded edn, 206–33. Oxford: Oxford University Press.

Shoemaker, Sydney. 2007. *Physical Realization*. Oxford: Oxford University Press.

Shoemaker, Sydney. 2011. "Realization, Powers, and Property Identity." *The Monist* 94 (1): 3–18.

Sider, Theodore. 2001. *Four Dimensionalism*. Oxford: Oxford University Press.

Simons, Peter. 1998. "Farewell to Substance: A Differentiated Leave-Taking." *Ratio* 11 (3): 235–52.

Simons, Peter and Joseph Melia. 2000. "Continuants and Occurrents: I—Peter Simons." *Proceedings of the Aristotelian Society, Supplementary Volume* 74: 59–75.

Sinnott-Armstrong, Walter. Unpublished. "Downward Mental Causation."

Smart, J. J. C. 1959. "Sensations and Brain Processes." *The Philosophical Review* 68 (2): 141–56.

Smith, Martin. 2007. "Ceteris Paribus Conditionals and Comparative Normalcy." *Journal of Philosophical Logic* 36 (1): 97–121.

Smith, Michael. 1994. *The Moral Problem*. Cambridge, MA: Blackwell Publishing.

Smolin, Lee. 1991. "Space and Time in the Quantum Universe." In *Conceptual Problems for Quantum Gravity*, edited by Abhay Ashtekar and John J. Stachel, 228–91. Boston, MA: Birkhauser.

Sosa, Ernest. 1984. "Mind–Body Interaction and Supervenient Causation." *Midwest Studies in Philosophy* 9 (1): 271–81.

Stalnaker, Robert. 1984. *Inquiry*. Cambridge, MA: MIT Press.

Sterelny, Kim. 1990. *The Representational Theory of Mind*. Oxford: Blackwell.

Swoyer, Chris. 1982. "The Nature of Natural Laws." *Australasian Journal of Philosophy* 60 (3): 203–23.

Thomson, Judith Jarvis. 1983. "Parthood and Identity Across Time." *The Journal of Philosophy* 80 (4): 201–20.

Tooley, Michael. 1977. "The Nature of Laws." *Canadian Journal of Philosophy* 7 (4): 667–98.

Tye, Michael. 2013. "Qualia." In *The Stanford Encyclopedia of Philosophy*, Fall 2013 edn, edited by Edward N. Zalta. https://plato.stanford.edu/archives/fall2013/entries/qualia/.

Unger, Peter. 2006. *All the Power in the World*. Oxford: Oxford University Press.

van Fraassen, Bas. 1989. *Laws and Symmetry*. Oxford: Clarendon Press.

van Inwagen, Peter. 1998. "Modal Epistemology." *Philosophical Studies* 92 (1–2): 67–84.

van Inwagen, Peter. 2001. "Two Concepts of Possible Worlds." In *Ontology, Identity, and Modality: Essays in Metaphysics*, 206–42. Cambridge: Cambridge University Press.

van Inwagen, Peter. 2010. "Ontological Arguments." In *A Companion to Philosophy of Religion*, 2nd edn. Chichester: Wiley Blackwell.

Wahlberg, Tobias Hansson. 2009. "4-D Objects and Disposition Ascriptions." *Philosophical Papers* 38 (1): 35–72.

Wiggins, David. 2001. *Sameness and Substance Renewed*. Cambridge: Cambridge University Press.

Williams, Donald C. 1966. "The Elements of Being." In *Principles of Empirical Realism*. Springfield, IL: Charles Thomas Publishing.

Williams, Neil E. 2005a. *The Power to Persist*. Ph.D. thesis, Columbia University.

Williams, Neil E. 2005b. "Static and Dynamic Dispositions." *Synthese* 146 (3): 303–24.

Williams, Neil E. 2011a. "Dispositions and the Argument from Science." *Australasian Journal of Philosophy* 89 (1): 71–90.

Williams, Neil E. 2011b. "Putting Powers Back on Multi-Track." *Philosophia* 39 (3): 581–95.

Wilson, Jessica. 2009. "Determination, Realization and Mental Causation." *Philosophical Studies* 145 (1): 149–69.

Wilson, Jessica M. 2010. "What is Hume's Dictum, and Why Believe It?" *Philosophy and Phenomenological Research* 80 (3): 595–637.

Wilson, Jessica. 2011. "Non-reductive Realization and the Powers-based Subset Strategy." *The Monist* 94 (1): 121–54.

Woodward, James. 2003. *A Theory of Explanation*. Oxford: Oxford University Press.

Wright, Crispin. 1975. "On the Coherence of Vague Predicates." *Synthese* 30 (3–4): 325–65.

Wright, Larry. 1973. "Functions." *The Philosophical Review* 82 (2): 139–68.

Yablo, Stephen. 1992. "Mental Causation." *The Philosophical Review* 101 (2): 245–80.

Zeimbekis, John. 2009. "Phenomenal and Objective Size." *Noûs* 43 (2): 346–62.

Zeimbekis, John. 2013. "Color and Cognitive Penetrability." *Philosophical Studies* 165: 167–75.

Zimmerman, Dean W. 1996. "Persistence and Presentism." *Philosophical Papers* 25 (2): 115–26.

Index